THE MEXICAN CHILE PEPPER COOKBOOK

Dave DeWitt & José C. Marmolejo

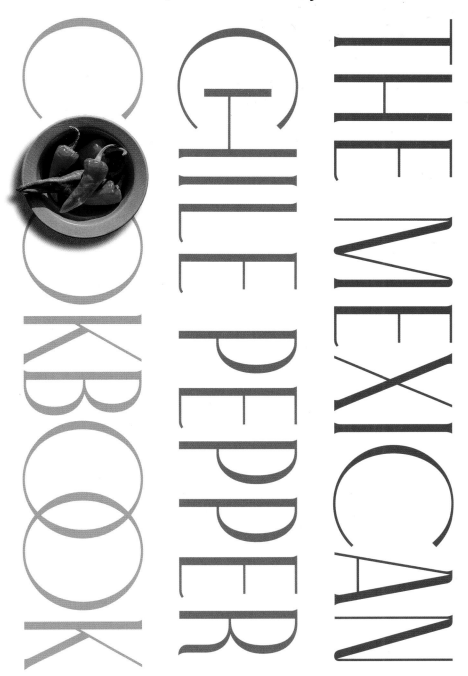

THE MEXICAN CHILE PEPPER COOKBOOK

University of New Mexico Press   Albuquerque

ISBN 978-0-8263-6351-0 (paper)
ISBN 978-0-8263-6352-7 (electronic)

Library of Congress Control Number:
2021948221

Founded in 1889, the University of New Mexico
sits on the traditional homelands of the
Pueblo of Sandia. The original peoples of New
Mexico—Pueblo, Navajo, and Apache—since
time immemorial have deep connections to the
land and have made significant contributions
to the broader community statewide. We honor
the land itself and those who remain stewards
of this land throughout the generations and
also acknowledge our committed relationship
to Indigenous peoples. We gratefully recognize
our history.

Cover illustration by Mindy Basinger Hill
Designed by Mindy Basinger Hill
Composed in Adobe Caslon Pro

DAVE dedicates this book to the memories of Marlin Bensinger and Jeffrey Gerlach.

JOSÉ dedicates this book to his children—Sofia, Natalia, Julieta, and Andres—who have enjoyed his cooking as well as his food anecdotes.

Chile, they say, is the king, the soul of the Mexicans—
a nutrient, a medicine, a comfort. For many Mexicans,
if it were not for the existence of chile, their national
identity would begin to disappear.

ARTURO LOMELí / *El Chile y Otros Picantes* (1986)

Contents

Acknowledgments

Special gratitude to Chuck Evans for the use of his extensive food library in Spanish and to Jeanette DeAnda for helping Dave learn the Spanish culinary language. Special thanks to Steve Hull and the rest of the University of New Mexico Press team for a great publishing effort. We would also like to thank the following people for their help on this project: Lula Bertrán, Cindy Castillo, Jesus Martín Cortez, Josefina Duran, Marta Figel, Lorenzo Fritz, Kathy Gallantine, Nancy and Jeff Gerlach, John Gray, Antonio Heras, Patrick Holian, Diana Kennedy, Jay Lewis, Leo Nuñez, Jim Peyton, Mark Preston, Maria Marcela Ramonet, Maria Lila Robles-Uscher, Robert Spiegel, Susana Trilling, and Robb Walsh.

Introduction

It has often been written that the only national cuisine of Mexico is the cuisine of chile peppers, and this book examines the ways chile peppers are used in Mexican cooking. First and foremost, in Mexican cuisine, more than in the cooking of any other country, chiles are utilized as a food as much as a spice. In massive quantities they are pureed into sauces, stuffed whole, chopped, roasted, powdered, pickled, and used as *rajas*, or "strips."

Our collection of Mexican recipes celebrates the chile's role as a primary vegetable in the national cuisine even though botanically they are berries and horticulturally they are fruits.

Important features of this book include:

- A wide selection of recipes in which chiles are the principal ingredient, including chiles rellenos, salsas, and pickled chiles.
- The most complete glossary of Mexican chile terminology ever published, along with a detailed glossary of other Mexican food terms and techniques.
- Regional hot and spicy recipes covering most of the thirty-two states of Mexico.
- Personal stories from the authors' exploration of Mexican cooking.

Readers and cooks should remember that this is a book focusing on chile-oriented Mexican dishes and is not intended to provide complete coverage of Mexican cuisine, which, in our opinion, is impossible to accomplish in a single volume.

José lives in Mexico City and has spent decades learning how his country cooks with chile peppers. Dave lives in Albuquerque, New Mexico, has visited Mexico more than fifty times, and is one of the foremost chile experts in the world, having authored or coauthored twenty-three books on chiles and spicy world cuisines. Hopefully, our love and appreciation of Mexico and its varied cooking styles comes across in this volume.

Fortunately, chiles and other Mexican ingredients are increasingly easy to find in the United States and Canada. Not only are they appearing in supermarkets and Latin markets, but they are also available from numerous online sources, including our favorite source, MexGrocer.com.

We continue to use the same heat scale that we devised for *Chile Pepper* magazine and many cookbooks: mild, medium, hot, and extremely hot. Each rating takes into consideration the types of chiles in the dish, the number of chiles used in the recipe, and the degree of dilution with the other ingredients. The relative heat of each recipe can be easily adjusted.

We hope you enjoy our hot and spicy trek south of the border.

PART ONE

THE PLANT

The Soul of the Mexicans
A Brief History of Chile Peppers in Mexico

Early Origins

In southern Mexico and the Yucatán Peninsula, chile peppers have been part of the human diet since about 7500 BC, and thus their usage predates the two great American civilizations, the Maya and the Aztec. From their original usage as a spice collected in the wild, chiles gained importance after their domestication, and they were a significant food when the Olmec culture was developing, around 1000 BC.

About 500 BC the Monte Albán culture, in the valley of Oaxaca, began exporting a new type of pottery vessel to nearby regions. These vessels resembled the handheld *molcajete* mortars of today and were called *suchilquitongo* bowls. Because molcajetes are used to crush chile pods and make salsas today, the suchilquitongo bowls are probably the first evidence we have for the creation of crushed chile and chile powders. Scientists speculate that chile powder was developed soon after the suchilquitongo bowls were invented, and both the tool and the product were then exported.

Using the same technology that proved the use of cacao at Chaco Canyon, New Mexico, researchers have analyzed the contents of the residue of pots from ancient Mexico and have discovered traces of chiles without cacao. This indicates that either chile sauces were being made, or that they were used to spice up other beverages, about a thousand years earlier than the Joya de Cerén archaeological site in El Salvador.

Terry Powis, associate professor of anthropology and his colleagues at Kennesaw State University in Georgia have chemically analyzed the residue in thirteen pottery vessels, including spouted jars, pots, and vases dating from 1,700 to 2,400 years ago that were found at an archaeological site in the state of Chiapas, which was at that time inhabited by the Mixe–Zoquean people.

"The best and most direct evidence for chile pepper use in Mesoamerica prior to our study is from Cerén," writes Powis in his article, "Prehispanic Use of Chili Peppers in Chiapas, Mexico." "So our work pushes back this date from circa AD 540 to circa 400 BC. To be honest, our study is the only one of its kind to show direct evidence of chile pepper use. In all of the other examples listed

Panoramic view of Monte Albán in Mexico taken from the North Platform. Photograph by Eke. Creative Commons Attribution-Share Alike 3.0, Wikimedia Commons.

The five vessels that tested positive for *Capsicum* from Chiapa de Corzo. Photograph by Roberto Lopez and Emiliano Gallaga Murrieta. Creative Commons Attribution 2.5 Generic license, Wikimedia Commons.

in the paper there is only indirect evidence—of chiles and pots found together. We actually linked the two together for the first time, and that is an important development. Therefore, we actually have the earliest known consumption of the peppers." Powis added, "During the mass spec analysis we were completely surprised by the fact that no cacao was present in any of the pots tested. In fact chile was present." The exact species of chile present was not identified, but Powis hopes to accomplish that in the future. The most logical species is the *Capsicum annuum*, which was domesticated in Mexico.

Because of the absence of cacao and the fact that the artifacts were found in places associated with high status individuals and rituals, the team speculated that chile peppers were possibly used to produce a spicy beverage or alternatively, a chile sauce that was stored in the spouted jars and subsequently poured as a dining condiment, possibly during ritual feasts.

Powis wondered, "Was the chile ground up to produce a paste or a salsa and subsequently used as a seasoning in foods that were offered to the Zoquean gods or chiefs? Or, were the peppers left whole in the pots? We assume that the presence of chile is in the form of a sauce or paste, and not whole given that no seeds or other macrofossils were identified in the interiors of the vessels."

If the residue is not from a chile paste, was it a spicy beverage other than hot cacao? "Why would there be evidence of chile peppers in a spouted jar?" Powis asked in his article. "It is commonly assumed that spouted jars were used for pouring a liquid into another container. Perhaps the peppers were not made into a sauce but a spicy beverage or alternatively a chile sauce that was stored in the spouted jars and subsequently poured as a dining condiment."

And if the chiles were used in a beverage other than hot cacao, what might it have been? Further analysis will be required, but two possibilities come to mind: *chicha*, the ancient corn beer, or pulque, the precursor to mescal, which is made from fermented agave sap. If the Mayans and other cultures loved their hot cacao spiced up with chiles, why not these other favorite beverages?

A carved glyph found in the ceremonial center of Monte Albán is further evidence of the early importance of chile peppers. It features a chile plant with three pendant pods on one end and the head of a man on the other. Some experts believe that the glyph is one of several "tablets of conquest" that marked the sites conquered by the Monte Albán culture.

The Spicy Legacy of the Mayas

When the Europeans arrived in the Western Hemisphere, people of Mayan ancestry lived in southern Mexico, the Yucatán Peninsula, Belize, Guatemala, and parts of Honduras and El Salvador. The Mayan civilization had long passed its height by that time, so there are no European observations about this classic culture. All that exists today are writings about their descendants; Mayan hieroglyphics, which are slowly being transliterated; ethnological observations of the present Mayan Indians, whose food habits have changed little in twenty centuries; and the archeological site of Cerén.

On an August evening in AD 595, the Loma Caldera vent in what is now El Salvador erupted, sending clouds of volcanic ash into the Mayan agricultural village of Cerén, burying it twenty feet deep and turning it into the New World equivalent of Pompeii. Miraculously, all the villagers escaped, but what they left behind gives us a good idea of the life they led, the food they ate, and the chile peppers they grew.

In 1976, while leveling ground for the erection of grain silos, a Salvadoran bulldozer operator noticed that he had plowed into an ancient building. He immediately notified the national museum, but a museum archaeologist thought that the building was of recent vintage and allowed the bulldozing to continue. Several buildings were destroyed. Two years later, Dr. Payson Sheets, an anthropologist from the University of Colorado, led a team of students on an archaeological survey of the Zapotitan Valley. He was taken to the site by local residents and quickly began a test excavation. Radiocarbon dating of artifacts proved that they were very ancient. He then received permission from the government to do a complete excavation of Cerén. The site was saved.

Ash from the Loma Caldera eruption also buried crops that were grown in the fields. The plants then rotted away, leaving perfect cavities, or molds, in the surrounding ash. Using techniques that were developed at Pompeii, the archaeologists poured liquid plaster into the cavities and then removed the ash. Afterward, the ancient crops were revealed, and the plants could be studied. Interestingly, the Native Americans of Cerén used row and furrow techniques similar to those still utilized today; corn was grown in elevated rows, and beans and squash were grown in the furrows in between. In a courtyard of a building, "We even found a series of four mature chile plants with stem diameters over

left Artist's rendering of the outdoor kitchen at Joya de Cerén. Artist unknown. Courtesy of the University of Colorado.

right The remains of the original structure at Joya de Cerén, buried by volcano eruption around AD 600 (El Salvador). Photograph by Mario Roberto Duran Ortiz. Creative Commons Attribution-Share Alike 3.0 Unported license, Wikimedia Commons.

5 centimeters (2 inches)," writes Dr. Sheets in his article, "Tropical Time Capsule." "They must have been many years old." Chile peppers are rarely found in archaeological sites in Mesoamerica, so imagine the surprise of the researchers when they discovered painted ceramic storage vessels that contained large quantities of chile seeds. "One vessel had cacao seeds in the bottom, and chiles above, separated by a layer of cotton gauze," Dr. Sheets revealed. "It is possible that they would have been prepared into a kind of *mole* sauce." Also found were corn kernels, beans, squash seeds, cotton seeds, and evidence of manioc plants and small agave plants, which were used for their fiber to make rope rather than being fermented for pulque, an alcoholic beverage, as was done in Mexico.

In addition to the vegetable crops of corn, chiles, beans, manioc, cacao, and squash, the archaeologists found evidence that the Cerén villagers also harvested wild avocados, palm fruits, and nuts and certain spices such as achiote, or annatto seeds. In fact, Dr. Sheets observed, "The villagers ate better and had a greater variety of foodstuffs than their descendants. Traditional families today eat mostly corn and beans, with some rice, squash, and chiles, but rarely any meat. Cerén's residents ate deer and dog meat." They also consumed peccary, mud turtle, duck, and rodents, but deer was their primary meat.

It is often a challenge for archaeologists to reconstruct ancient cuisines and cooking techniques. The Cerén villagers did not have metal utensils, but they did have fired ceramics that could be used to boil foods. They could grill over open flames and perhaps cook foods in ceramic pots using water or fruit juices. They did not fry their foods—the arriving Spaniards introduced that practice.

The cooks in Cerén had obsidian knives that could cut as cleanly as metal. They had metates for grinding corn into flour and molcajetes for grinding fruits, vegetables, chiles, and spices together into sauces.

By the time the Mayas reached the peak of their civilization in southern Mexico and the Yucatán Peninsula, around AD 500, they had a highly developed system of agriculture. Maize was their most important crop, followed closely by beans, squash, chiles, and cacao. Perhaps as many as thirty different varieties of chile were cultivated, and they were sometimes planted in plots by themselves but more often in fields already containing tomatoes and sweet potatoes.

Three species of chile were grown by the Mayas and their descendants in Mexico's Yucatán Peninsula and Guatemala, Belize, and parts of Honduras and El Salvador: *Capsicum annuum*, *Capsicum chinense*, and *Capsicum frutescens*—and they were all imports from other regions. *Capsicum annuum* probably originated in Mexico, while *Capsicum frutescens* came from Panama, and *Capsicum chinense* from the Amazon Basin via the Caribbean. The Mayas also cultivated cotton, papayas, vanilla beans, cacao, manioc, and agave.

MEXICAN CHILE DEFINED

"It is a product of acrid flavor, piquant and heat-generating, which from the earliest times the Indian made a part of his diet, approaching it with a kind of mystical and religious unction. Over the years it has come to set the tone, both in its general and special application, of the original Mexican cuisine."

AMANDO FARGA / *Eating in Mexico*, 1963

The importance of chiles is immediately seen in the most basic Mayan foods. According to food historian Sophie Coe, in her book *America's First Cuisines* (1994), "The beans . . . could be cooked in plain water or water in which toasted or untoasted chiles had been steeped. Such a chile 'stock' might be called the basis of the cuisine, so frequently does it turn up. It is in everything from the tortilla accompaniment of the very poorest peasant to the liquid for cooking the turkey for the greatest celebrations. There is even a reference to it in the *Popol Vuh*, the Mayan sacred text, where the grandmother grinds chiles and mixes them with broth, and the broth acts as a mirror in which the rat on the rafters is reflected for the hero twins to see."

Coe speculates that the first sauces were used for tortilla dipping. "The simplest sauce was ground dried chiles and water," she writes. "From this humble ancestor comes the line which terminates with trendy salsas beloved of a certain school of today's chefs." The ground or crushed chiles—sometimes in a thick sauce—were used to preserve and prolong the life of a piece of meat, fish, or other game. Since there was no refrigeration, fresh meat spoiled quickly, and by trial and error the earliest cooks realized that chiles were an antioxidant, preserving the meats to some degree.

"But even the original inventors of tortilla-dipping sauces varied them when they could," Coe added. "The ground toasted seeds of large and small squashes, always carefully differentiated by the Maya, could be added to the basic chile water, or you could mix epazote with the water and then add ground, toasted squash seeds to the flavored liquid." As more and more ingredients were added, a unique family of sauces was developed that led to the *pipians* and moles of today.

For breakfast the Mayas ate a gruel of ground maize spiced with chile peppers, which is usually called atole but is sometimes known as pozole. A modern equivalent would be cornmeal or masa mixed with water and ground red chiles to the consistency of a milkshake. A favorite drink was chocolate mixed with water, honey, and chile powder.

For the main, or evening, meal, stews of vegetables and meats heavily spiced with chiles were served. One of these was *chacmole*, which combined venison with chile, achiote, allspice, and tomato; it was an offering to the gods as well as a nourishing entrée. Various reports describe sauces made with chiles and black beans being wrapped in corn tortillas and covered with chile sauce, which may be the earliest references to enchiladas. As Coe noted, "The accepted wisdom was that tortillas and beans were boring; it took chile to make the saliva flow."

The Mayas seem to have invented tamales, too. Coe cites the Spanish chronicler Gonzalo Fernández de Oviedo who reported in 1526 in his work, *La Natural hystoria de las Indias*: "They brought certain well-made baskets, one with the *pasticci* [filled pies] of maize dough stuffed with chopped meat. . . . They ate it all, and praised that dish *pasticci*, which tasted as if it were spiced. It was reddish inside, with a good quantity of that pepper of the Indies which is called *asci* (the Antillean word for chile, modernized to *ají*)."

Mayan tamales were quite sophisticated, with many different fillings, including toasted squash seeds, deer hearts, quail, egg yolks, dove breasts, squash blossoms, and black beans. The Mayas kept domesticated turkeys, ducks, bees, and dogs, and their main game animals were deer, birds, iguana, and wild boar. Armadillos and manatees were considered delicacies. As with the Incas, meat dishes were reserved for Mayan royalty. Chiles are highly visible today in areas with a Mayan heritage. In the Yucatán Peninsula, descendants of the Mayans still grow habaneros, tomatoes, and onions in boxes or hollowed-out tree trunks that are raised up on four posts for protection against pigs and hens. These container gardens are usually in the backyard of the house, near the kitchen.

Aztec Chiles

In 1529, Bernardino de Sahagún, a Spanish Franciscan friar living in Nueva España (Mexico), noted that the Aztecs ate hot red or yellow chile peppers in their hot cacao and in nearly every dish they prepared! Fascinated by the

Aztec feast. Illustration from the *Florentine Codex*, late sixteenth century. Public domain, Wikimedia Commons.

Aztecs' constant use of a previously unknown spice, Sahagún documented this fiery cuisine in his classic study, *Historia General de las Cosas de la Nueva España* (1529), now known as the *Florentine Codex*. His work indicates that of all the pre-Columbian New World civilizations, it was the Aztecs who loved chile peppers the most. The marketplaces of ancient Mexico overflowed with chile peppers of all sizes and shapes. According to Sahagún, they included "hot green chiles, smoked chiles, water chiles, tree chiles, beetle chiles, and sharp-pointed red chiles." In addition to some twenty varieties of *chillis*, as the pungent pods were called in the Náhuatl language, vendors sold strings of red chiles (modern *ristras*), precooked chiles, and "fish chiles," which were the earliest known forms of ceviche, a method of preserving fish without cooking. This technique places the fish in a marinade of an acidic fruit juice and chile peppers.

Other seafood dishes were common as well in Aztec Mexico. "They would eat another kind of stew, with frogs and green chile," Sahagún recorded, "and a stew of those fish called *axolotl* with yellow chile. (It, of course, is not a fish but rather a critically endangered amphibian.) They also used to eat a lobster stew which is very delicious." The "lobster" may refer to freshwater crayfish. Apparently, the Aztecs utilized every possible source of protein. The friar noted such exotic variations as maguey worms with a sauce of small chiles, newt with yellow chiles, and tadpoles with *chiltecpitl*. Father Sahagún, one of the first behavioral scientists, also noted that chiles were revered as much as sex by the ancient Aztecs. While fasting to appease their rather bloodthirsty gods, the priests required two abstentions by the faithful: sexual relations and chile peppers.

Cacao and chiles were commonly combined in a drink called *chicahuatl*, which was usually reserved for the priests and the wealthy. Chicahuatl, a Náhuatl word that means "God's drink," is the origin of the Spanish word "chocolate." The

Aztec versions of tamales often used banana leaves as wrappers to steam combinations of masa dough, meat, and the chiles of choice. Sahagún wrote that there were two types of sauces called *chilemollis*: one with red chile and tomatoes and the other with yellow chile and tomatoes. These chilemollis eventually became the savory mole sauces for which Mexican cuisine is justly famous.

Aztec cookery is the basis for the Mexican food of today, and, in fact, many Aztec dishes have lasted through the centuries virtually unchanged. Since oil and fat were not generally used in cooking, the foods were usually roasted, boiled, or cooked in sauces. Like the Mayas, the Aztecs usually began the day with a cup of atole spiced with chile peppers.

The main meal was served at midday and usually consisted of tortillas with beans and a salsa made with chiles and tomatoes. The salsas were usually made by grinding the ingredients between two handheld stones, the precursors of molcajetes. Even today, the same technique is used in Indian villages throughout Mexico and Central America. A remarkable variety of tamales was also served for the midday meal. They were stuffed with fruits such as plums, pineapple, or guava; with game meat such as deer or turkey; or even with snails or frogs. Whole chile pods were included with the stuffing, and after steaming the tamales were often served with a cooked chile sauce.

It was this highly sophisticated chile cuisine that the Spanish encountered during their conquest of Mexico. Christopher Columbus "discovered" chile peppers in the West Indies on his first voyage to the New World. In his 1493 journal, he wrote, "Also there is much *ají*, which is their pepper, and the people won't eat without it, for they find it very wholesome. One could load fifty caravels a year with it in Hispaniola."

Dr. Diego Chanca, the fleet physician for Columbus on his second voyage, wrote in his journal that the Indians seasoned manioc and sweet potatoes with ají, and that it was one of their principal foods. Of course, both Columbus and his doctor believed that they had reached the Spice Islands, the East Indies.

Not only did Columbus misname the Indians, he also mistook chiles for black pepper, thus giving them the inaccurate name "pepper." But he did one thing right—he transported chile seeds back to Europe after his first voyage—which began the chile conquest of the rest of the world.

Explorers who followed Columbus to the New World soon learned that chiles were an integral part of the Indians' culinary, medical, and religious lives. In 1526, just thirty-four years after Columbus's first excursion, Captain Gonzalo Fernández de Oviedo noted that on the Spanish Main, "Indians everywhere grow it in gardens and farms with much diligence and attention because they eat it continuously with almost all their food."

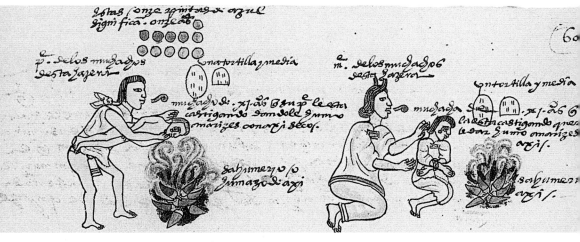

Chile punishment. *Codex Mendoza*, 1541.1542.
Public Domain, Wikimedia Commons.

Bernabé Cobo, a naturalist and historian who traveled throughout Central and South America in the early seventeenth century, estimated that there were at least forty different varieties. He wrote that there were "some as large as limes or large plums; others, as small as pine nuts or even grains of wheat, and between the two extremes are many different sizes. No less variety is found in color . . . and the same difference is found in form and shape."

The Aztec market in the capital, Tenochtitlán, contained a large number of chiles, and most of those had been collected as tribute, a form of taxation used by the Toltecs and Aztecs and later adopted by the Spanish. The payers of the tribute were the *macehuales* (serfs, or commoners); the collectors were Aztec officials or, later on, officials who worked for the Spanish. The tribute consisted of locally produced goods or crops that were commonly grown, and the tribute of each village was recorded in codices of drawn or painted pictographs.

According to many sources, chiles were one of the most common tribute items. The chiles were offered to the government in several different forms: as fresh or dried pods, as seed, in two one hundred-pound bundles, in willow baskets, and in Spanish bushels. After transport to the capital, the chiles were stored in warehouses where they were closely guarded and then sold. Chile peppers were considered to be the most valuable of the tributes.

One of the most famous tribute codices is the *Matrícula de Tributos*, which is part of the *Mendocino Codex*. This codex was compiled for the first viceroy of New Spain, Antonio de Mendoza, who ordered it made for Emperor Charles V to inform him of the wealth of what is now Mexico. Glyphs on the codex indicate the tribute paid to the Aztecs by conquered towns just before the Spanish conquest; the towns on one tribute list (in what is now San Luis Potosí) gave 1,600 loads of dry chiles to the imperial throne each year! The *Codex Mendoza*, or the *Mendocino Codex*, also reveals an early use of chile peppers as a form of punishment. One pictograph shows a father punishing his young son by forcing him to inhale smoke from burning chiles. The next image shows a mother threatening her daughter with the same punishment. Today, the Popolocán Indians who live near Oaxaca punish their children in a similar manner.

Wherever they traveled in the New World, Spanish explorers, particularly those that were nonmilitary, collected and transported chile seeds and thus further spread the different varieties. And not only did they adopt the chile as their own, but the Spanish also imported foods that they combined with chiles and other native ingredients to create even more complex chile cuisines.

Creating a Cuisine

The arrival of the Spanish in Mexico had a profound effect on the cuisine of the country, as the ingredients the explorers brought with them soon transformed the eating habits of the Indians. However, the Aztecs and their descendants did not give up their beloved staples such as chiles, corn, and cacao; they combined them with the new imports and thus created the basis for the Mexican cuisines of today.

People who want to rewrite history and blame Columbus solely for spreading diseases and importing old-world foods and livestock should understand that Columbus was merely the tip of the iceberg—the explorer who started the new-world fad. Many others who followed were strictly motivated by profit and the desire to find treasure in the New World, regardless of whether it was gold, silver, or crops that could be grown in the Americas and sold in Europe or to the new settlers. One of the first of these profit-hungry adventurers was Hernán Cortés.

William Dunmire, author of *Gardens of New Spain* (2004), maintains

Hernán Cortés. Engraving by William Holl; published by Charles Knight. Public Domain, Wikimedia Commons.

that "Cortés, too often identified solely as an infamous conqueror, was a man of multiple interests." And one of his main interests "was an ambition to oversee development of a Mexican economy based on integrating Old World Agriculture with what was then being practiced in the New." Cortés, now a major landowner, first planted sugarcane on his estates for refining into much-needed sugar, then directed his laborers to plant maize, beans, and chiles, and additionally, his favorite old-world crops. The result? "In no time, apple, peach, pear, plum, and citrus orchards had been established and were starting to bear fruit," Dunmire writes. And Mediterranean vegetables such as carrots, cauliflowers, turnips, horseradish, and lettuce "were not only grown on various estates, but as early as 1526, surplus produce was available and for sale in the markets of Mexico City."

But what the Spanish settlers of Mexico missed most of all was bread made from wheat, not native corn. "Fortunately," continues Dunmire, "cool, moist winters and warm summers of the Valley of Mexico, proved productive, if not ideal, for growing wheat, and Cortés had his Indian laborers planting it shortly after receiving his first shipment of seed grain. From then on, most Spaniards were able to enjoy fresh leavened bread, and wheat bread regained its accustomed culinary prominence as the colonial empire swelled." John Super, author of *Food, Conquest, and Colonization in Sixteenth-Century Spanish America* (1998), adds: "Despite the expense and obstacles, Spaniards planted wheat with an intensity lacking with other crops. Wheat was a cultural imperative, a driving

OLD-WORLD FOODS TRANSFERRED TO THE AMERICAS

grains / Barley, rice, wheat, rye

nuts / Almonds, pistachios

fruits / Apples, bananas, cherries, citrus fruits, eggplant, grapes, olives, melons, peaches, pears, plums, mangos

vegetables / Cabbage, capers, carrots, celery, cucumber, spinach, lettuce.

legumes / Soybeans, fava beans, peas

herbs / spices / flavorings / Basil, bay leaf, black pepper, cilantro, cinnamon, cumin, garlic, ginger, mint, mustard seed, nutmeg, parsley

roots / tubers / bulbs / Beets, onions, turnips

meats / Pigs, cattle, sheep, chicken, goats

A LUST FOR CHILES

Chile peppers were such a novelty to the Spanish explorers in Mexico that rumors were rampant about their medical properties. The Jesuit priest, poet, and historian José de Acosta wrote in his *Natural and Moral History of the Indies* (1590), "Taken moderately, chile helps and comforts the stomach for digestion." The priest undoubtedly had heard rumors about the reputed aphrodisiac qualities of chiles because he continued his description of chile with the following warning: "But if they take too much, it has bad effects, for of itself it is very hot, fuming, and pierces greatly, so the use thereof is prejudicial to the health of young folks, chiefly to the soul, for it provokes to lust." Despite the good father's suspicions, the only thing lustful about chiles was the desire everyone, including the Spanish, had to devour them.

force that shaped the social and physical landscape. Where wheat was planted and survived, Spanish society took root and grew."

The next Spanish food necessity was meat. Columbus is also blamed for importing old-world livestock to the New World and causing the environmental destruction wrought by pigs and cattle. It is true, as Alfred Crosby writes in *The Columbian Exchange* (1972), that "the first contingent of horses, dogs, pigs, cattle, chickens, sheep, and goats arrived with Columbus on the second voyage in 1493." But Columbus alone did not cause the enormous livestock population increases; all of the Spanish and Portuguese explorers were doing exactly the same thing. As early as 1514, Diego Velázquez de Cuéllar "wrote to the King that the pigs he had brought to Cuba had increased to 30,000." And four years later, Alonzo de Zuazo in Hispaniola wrote that if thirty or forty cattle strayed from the farm, they would grow to three or four hundred in three or four years, "breeding in the salubrious environment of the New World," as Crosby put it.

Pork was the first old-world meat to have a price set for it in Tenochtitlán, today Mexico City. In 1525, the price of fresh or salt pork was set at one real per pound. But the pigs bred faster than people could eat them, becoming a real nuisance in the city, and increased supplies of beef and mutton caused the price of pork to drop by three-quarters a year later. Livestock devastated native crops, causing friction between the Spanish settlers and the Indians, and the Spaniards ridiculously accused the Indians of deliberately planting their crops where they knew that they would be destroyed by pigs and cattle.

Throughout the centuries, an astonishing variety in Mexican cooking developed as a result of geography. From the Yucatán Peninsula, Mexico stretches more than two thousand miles to the deserts of the north, and so the length and size of Mexico, combined with the fact that mountain ranges separate the various regions, led to the development of isolated regional cuisines. This geographical variety is the reason that the cooking of tropical Yucatán differs significantly from that of the deserts of Chihuahua and Sonora. One common factor in Mexican cookery, though, is the prevalence of chile peppers. Unlike South America, where chiles are still mostly consumed by the Indian population, in Mexico everyone fell in love with the pungent pods. Chile peppers are Mexico's most important vegetable crop; they are grown all over the country, from the Pacific and Gulf coasts to mountainous regions with an elevation above eight thousand feet. Approximately 200,000 acres of cultivated land produce between 500,000 and 650,000 tons of fresh pods and 30,000 tons of dry pods, making Mexico number six among the chile-producing countries of the world. Although more than thirty different varieties are grown or collected in Mexico, the anchos/poblanos, serranos, *mirasols*, and jalapeños account for 75 percent of the crop. In 1988, Mexico exported 2,529 metric tons of fresh or dried chiles, worth $4.6 million, into the United States.

In 1985, each Mexican consumed about fourteen pounds of green chiles and nearly two pounds of dried chiles. The favorite chiles are about evenly divided between those harvested fresh and those utilized in dry form. The serranos and jalapeños are grown for processing and the fresh market, where they are the chiles of choice for salsas. Over 90 percent of the serrano crop is used fresh in homemade salsas. About 60 percent of the jalapeño crop is processed, either by canning or pickling, or is made into commercial salsas. Of the remainder, 20 percent is used fresh, and 20 percent is used in the production of chipotles, the smoke-dried form of the jalapeño.

How Many Moles?

Perhaps the most famous Mexican chile dishes are the moles. The word "mole," from the Náhuatl *molli*, means "mixture." Some sources say that the word is taken from the Spanish verb *moler*, meaning "to grind." Whatever its precise origin, the word used by itself embraces a vast number of sauces utilizing every imaginable combination of meats, vegetables, spices, and flavorings—sometimes up to three dozen different ingredients. Not only are there many ingredients, but there are also dozens of variations on mole—red moles, green moles, brown moles, fiery moles, and even mild moles. The earliest moles were simple compared with what was to come after the Spanish invasion.

Ana M. de Benítez, who reconstructed pre-Columbian dishes based on Sahagun's descriptions, used four different chiles (ancho, *mulato*, pasilla, and chipotle), plus tomatoes, garlic, pumpkins, tomatillos, and chayote, as the basis of her moles. The addition ingredients from the Eastern Hemisphere, such as almonds, raisins, garlic, cinnamon, and cloves, would eventually transform the basic mole of the Aztecs into a true delicacy.

Mole poblano, originally called *mole de olores* ("fragrant mole"), is the sauce traditionally served on special occasions (such as Sundays, birthdays, weddings, and religious celebrations) that combines chiles and cacao, a popular and revered food of the Aztecs, with sugar. Moctezuma's court consumed fifty jugs of chile-laced hot cacao a day, and warriors drank it to soothe their nerves before going into battle. However, the story of how chocolate was combined with chile sauces does not involve warriors but rather nuns. Legend holds that mole poblano was invented in the sixteenth century by the nuns of the Convent of Santa Rosa in the city of Puebla. It seems that the archbishop was coming to visit, and the nuns were worried because they had no food elegant enough to serve someone of his eminence. So, they prayed for guidance, and one of the nuns had a vision. She directed that everyone in the convent should begin chopping and grinding everything edible they could find in the kitchen. Into a pot went chiles, tomatoes, nuts, sugar, tortillas, bananas, raisins, garlic, avocados, and dozens of herbs and spices. The final ingredient was the magic one: chocolate. The chocolate, they reasoned, would smooth the flavor of the sauce by slightly cutting its heat. Then the nuns slaughtered their only turkey and served it with the mole sauce to the archbishop, who declared it the finest dish he had ever tasted.

This is a great legend, but a more likely scenario holds that the basic mole of the Aztecs was gradually transformed by a collision of cuisines. Regarding the use of cacao, since that delicacy was reserved for Aztec royalty, the military nobility, and religious officials, perhaps Aztec serving girls at the convent gave a royal recipe to the nuns so they could honor their royalty, the archbishop. At any rate, the recipe for mole poblano was rescued from oblivion and became a holiday favorite. De Benítez noted: "In the book on Puebla cooking, published in Puebla in 1877, we find recipes for making forty-four kinds of *moles*; there are also sixteen kinds of *manchamanteles* [tablecloth stainers] which are dishes with different kinds of chiles."

In Mexico today, cooks who specialize in moles are called *moleros*. In 1963, a group of moleros formed a mole cooperative of sixty partners who banded together for the good of their craft. They shared equipment such as pulverizers and mills and eventually organized a fair exclusively dedicated to mole: the Feria Nacional del Mole, or "National Mole Fair," held every year in October at the town of San Pedro Atocpan, just south of Mexico City.

One of the mole vendors at the Feria Nacional del Mole in San Pedro Atocpan, DF.
Photograph by Alejandro Linares Garcia. GNU Free Documentation License, Version 1.2,
Wikimedia Commons.

At the fair, thousands of people sample hundreds of different moles created by restaurateurs and mole wholesalers. This fair is the Mexican equivalent of chili con carne cookoffs in the United States; like chili cookoff chefs, the moleros take great pride in their fiery creations and consider each mole a work of art. Often the preparation of a family mole recipe takes as long as three days. Their recipes are family secrets not to be revealed to others under any circumstances; indeed, they are passed down from generation to generation.

"If one of my children wants to carry on my business as a molero and is serious about it," molero Villa Suárez told reporter William Stockton, "I will tell them all the secrets when the time comes." But he went on to indicate that if his children were not interested in becoming moleros, his secrets would die with him.

By 1982, the fair had grown so large that the committee moved the location and the date to accommodate all the visitors. The mole fair became a national event and was eventually placed on the secretary of tourism's calendar of fairs and festivals. Each year bigger and better events were presented. As a result, restaurants began featuring more mole specials, and tourists had more opportunities to experience the various moles. The National Mole Fair has certainly become one of the premier chile pepper events in the world.

The color of a particular mole depends mostly on the varieties of chile utilized. A green mole consists mostly of fresh herbs, pumpkin seeds, and serrano or poblano chiles, while a red mole could contain three or four different varieties of dried red chile, such as ancho, guajillo, and chipotle, among others. The brown and black moles owe their color to pasillas, mulatos, and *chilhuacles*, all of which are sometimes called *chile negro* because of their dark hues when dried. The dark color of *mole negro* is also the result of roasting the chiles, herbs, and spices until they are almost black, as is the custom in Oaxaca.

Other than chiles, there are literally dozens of other ingredients added to the various moles, including almonds, anise, bananas, plantains, chocolate, cinnamon, cilantro, cloves, coconut, garlic, onions, peanuts, peppercorns, pinons, pumpkin seeds, raisins, sesame seeds, toasted bread, tomatillos, tomatoes, fried tortillas, and walnuts. Undoubtedly, some moleros add coriander, cumin, epazote, oregano, thyme, and other spices to their moles.

But Puebla is not the only state in Mexico with a reputation for moles. Oaxaca, in the south, lays claim to seven unique moles—and dozens and dozens of variations. Susana Trilling, owner of the Seasons of My Heart cooking school located outside of Oaxaca city at Rancho Aurora, was our guide to the moles of Oaxaca. During a trip to her school, Dave was given lessons on preparing the famous mole negro oaxaqueño, while Susana described her experiences with the seven famous moles. She later wrote about the moles in a *Chile Pepper* magazine article titled "My Search for the Seventh *Mole*." Susana wondered about the number seven because there

Mole Negro. Photograph by José C. Marmolejo. Courtesy of Susana Trilling.

are seven regions in the state of Oaxaca, and, of course, seven days in the week. But then she read *Tradiciones Gastronómicas Oaxaqueñas* (1985), in which the author, Ana María Guzmán de Vázquez Colmenares, noted: "There must be something magical in the number seven, for the number of Oaxacan moles coincides with the wonders of the world, the theological virtues, the wise men of Athens—and for their wisdom which elected the number seven to represent justice."

"There may be seven *moles*," say the locals, "but thousands and thousands of cooks have their own private versions of all of the *moles*, so how many does that make?" One magazine writer suggested: "Oaxaca should be the land of 200 *moles*!"

For the record, the seven moles are as follows: mole negro, *mole coloradito*, *mole verde*, *mole amarillo*, *mole rojo*, manchamanteles, and *mole chichilo*. They are all descendants of *clemole*, believed to be the original mole of Oaxaca. Clemole was quite simple, composed of ancho and pasilla chiles, garlic, cloves, cinnamon, and coriander.

The Oaxacan *moles* are characterized by unusual chiles that are unique to the region. In a discussion with chile vendor Eliseo Ramírez, Dave learned that there are sixty varieties of chile grown only in the state of Oaxaca and nowhere else in Mexico. Of those sixty, he carried about ten. Some of these unusual chiles include *chiles de agua*, which grow erect and are pointed at the end. The chilhuacle are short and fat and come in three varieties: black, red, and yellow. The red variety is called "the saffron of the poor" because a small amount of ground *chilhuacle rojo* gives a similar coloring to foods. Other unique chiles are the red-orange *chiles onzas*, the yellow *costeño*, and the *pasilla oaxaqueño* or *pasilla de Oaxaca*. Pasilla de Oaxaca is a smoked chile from the Sierra Mixe, while *pasilla mexicano* is the regular pasilla, but in Oaxaca they call it "mexicano" to differentiate it from the smoked version.

In the market, Dave also learned an easy way to make moles. Instead of tediously grinding all of the ingredients on a metate, the cooks would go to the Benito Juárez market, buy all their chiles, nuts, and seeds, and have them custom ground in the special *molinos* (mills) in another section of the market. The result is a dark paste that is later converted into a mole sauce. Susana Trilling describes the more tedious process: "The chiles are toasted black, soaked and ground, and blended with fried tomatoes, tomatillos, and roasted garlic, and onions. Then come nuts and seeds—some toasted, some fried. Almonds, peanuts, pecans, chile seeds, and sesame seeds. There are almost always more sesame seeds than any other seed or nut. They have to be fried slowly and carefully, with lots of love and attention. Hence the affectionate Mexican *dicho* (saying): 'You are the sesame seed of my *mole*.'" But if you say, "You are the sesame seeds of all moles," it means the person is very popular or even nosy.

There are other special ingredients that characterize the different Oaxacan moles. Avocado leaves, today not so difficult to find in the United States and Canada, are used in mole negro. Fresh green herbs such as epazote and parsley are part of the source of the green color of mole verde, along with pumpkin seeds and green chiles. Pineapple and banana are added to manchamanteles, while string beans, chayote, and chiles costeños are ingredients in mole amarillo. Many different meats are added to moles, from chicken to beef to fish, but by far the most common meat served is turkey. In fact, turkey is so important in mole negro that Mexican writer Manuel Toussaint noted that the turkey in the mole was as important as the eagle in the Mexican flag, and another writer suggested that to refuse to eat mole negro was a crime of treason against the homeland!

Mexican chile peppers. Photograph by Timothy L. Brock on Unsplash.

Mexican Chile Basics

In our Glossary of Mexican Chiles, we define the enormous number of chile varieties we encountered in our research. Many of these chiles are unavailable except in local markets, so here we describe the chiles that are the most commonly used in Mexico and in the recipes in this book.

ANCHO/POBLANO

The ancho is the dried form of the poblano. The fresh pods range in length from three to six inches and in width from three to four inches. The fresh pods are roasted and peeled before they are used. Then they are stuffed for chiles rellenos, cut into strips, or chopped for use in vegetables. The reddish-brown anchos are usually toasted on a griddle and rehydrated before use. The anchos have a flavor that is often described as raisin-like and are sometimes ground into a powder. This variety is rather mild. Substitute: mulato.

CASCABEL

The spherical cascabel is about an inch and a half in diameter and is most often used in its dried form. When dry, the seeds rattle in the pod and account for the name, which roughly translates as "jingle bell." Cascabels are used in sauces and to spice up many other dishes, such as soups and stews. Cascabels have medium heat. Substitute: pasilla.

top Red and green poblanos.
Photograph by Harald Zoschke.
Used with permission.

middle left Chile ancho.
Photograph by José C. Marmolejo.

middle right Cascabel.
Photograph by Dave DeWitt.

left Chiltepín. Photograph
by Dave DeWitt.

CHILTEPÍN

Botanists believe that these wild chiles (*C. annuum var. aviculare*) are the closest surviving species to the earliest forms of chiles, which developed in Bolivia and southern Brazil long before mankind arrived in the New World. The small size of their fruits was perfect for dissemination by birds, and the wild chiles spread all over South and Central America and up to what is now the United States border millennia before the domesticated varieties arrived. It is possible that they have the widest distribution of any chile variety; they range from Peru north to the Caribbean, Florida, Louisiana, and Texas and west to New Mexico and Arizona.

There is a wide variation in pod shapes, from tiny ones the size and shape of BBs to elongated pods a half inch long. The chiltepínes are spherical *piquines* that measure about a quarter of an inch in diameter. By contrast, domesticated piquines have much longer pods, up to three inches. The chiltepínes most prized in Mexico are spherical and measure five to eight millimeters in diameter. They are among the hottest chiles on earth, measuring up to one hundred thousand Scoville Heat Units. Substitute: piquín.

CHIPOTLE

Literally, a chipotle is any smoked chile, but it generally refers to a smoked jalapeño. They are dark brown or red, about two inches long and an inch wide, and come in two forms: dried or canned in an adobo sauce. The dried chipotles are rehydrated before use and are sometimes ground into a powder. These chiles have medium heat. The related *morita* is a smoked-dried small jalapeño produced in Central Mexico. A versatile chile, it is used in salsas as well as in meat dishes. Pungent like other chipotles but more flavorful because of its light smoking process, which leaves its skin dark burgundy with wrinkles. It measures around an inch in length and half an inch in width. Substitute: none.

CHILE DE ÁRBOL

De árbol means "tree chile," an allusion to the appearance of the plant. The dried pods are about three inches long and three-eighths of an inch wide. They are used in cooked sauces of all kinds and are sometimes ground into a powder. The pods have medium heat. Substitute: *mirasol*.

top Chipotle Morita. Photograph by José C. Marmolejo.

bottom Chile de árbol. Photograph by José C. Marmolejo. Used with permission.

Chiles de árbol. Photograph by Harald Zoschke. Used with permission.

GUAJILLO

Similar in appearance to New Mexican varieties, the guajillo is mostly used in its dry form. It is four to six inches long and about an inch and a half wide. The pods are orange-red, medium-hot, and are mostly used in sauces. The fresh form is known as mirasol, which means "looking at the sun," an allusion to the erect pods. Substitute: dried red New Mexican chiles.

HABANERO

Grown in the Yucatán Peninsula, these lantern-shaped, orange chiles are one of the hottest peppers in the world. The pods are about an inch and a half long and an inch wide and have a distinctive aroma that is fruity and apricot-like. They are used primarily in their fresh form in Mexico but also appear dried in the United States and Canada. The fresh pods are used extensively in salsas and other Yucatecan dishes. There is no real substitute for the flavor of fresh habaneros; use the hottest fresh chiles you can find, such as cayenne or Thai. Substitute for dried habaneros: piquín.

JALAPEÑO

Perhaps the most common chile in Mexico, the familiar jalapeño is one to two inches long and about three quarters of an inch wide. Unless they are smoked to create chipotles, the jalapeños are used exclusively in their fresh form in a wide number of dishes. They have medium heat and are often found pickled in cans. Substitute: serrano.

NEW MEXICAN

New Mexico varieties are grown mostly in Chihuahua for export to the United States. Popular varieties are NuMex 6–4 Heritage and NuMex Big Jim Heritage. The pods range between six and eleven inches long, and they are used both in the fresh green and dried red forms. They are mild in heat, usually about eight hundred to one thousand Scoville Heat Units. Substitute: poblanos for fresh and *guajillos* for dried.

PASILLA

The fresh form of the pasilla is called *chilaca*, and it is used in a similar manner to New Mexican varieties or poblanos. In the dried form, the pods are five to six inches long and about an inch and a half wide. They are used in sauces

Habanero. Photograph by Harald Zoschke. Used with permission.

Green and red jalapeños. Photograph by Harald Zoschke. Used with permission.

Barker, a New Mexican variety. Photograph by Dave DeWitt.

Pasilla. Photograph
by Jeffrey Gerlach.
Used with permission.

and are sometimes stuffed. The pods are mild and are sometimes ground into powder. As the name "little raisin" implies, the pods have a raisin-like aroma and flavor. Substitute: ancho.

PIQUÍN

These small, erect pods are less than an inch long and a half-inch wide, and usually resemble miniature bullets. The pods of both are used in salsas, are added to soups and stews, or are ground into powder. They are hot to extremely hot. Substitute: chiltepín.

SERRANO

The serrano is mostly used their fresh green form and measures one to three inches long and a half-inch wide. It is the chile of choice in Mexico for fresh salsas and has medium heat. Red serranos can be found fresh and have a desirable sweet flavor. The name means "mountain chile" or "highland chile." These are often found pickled in cans. Substitute: jalapeño.

Piquín pods. Photograph by
Jeffrey Gerlach. Used with permission.

Red and green serranos.
Photograph by Dave DeWitt.

above Roasting chiles. Photograph by Harald Zoschke. Used with permission.

left Blistered chiles. Photograph by Sergio Salvador. Work for hire.

ROASTING AND PEELING CHILES

Poblanos and fresh New Mexican chiles are usually blistered and peeled before being used in recipes. Blistering or roasting the chile is the process of heating the fresh pods to the point that the tough, transparent skin is separated from the meat of the chile so it can be removed. To roast and peel chiles, first cut a small slit in the chile close to the stem end so that the steam can escape, and the pod won't explode. Our favorite roasting method, which involves relaxing with a Negra Modelo cerveza, is to place the pods on a charcoal grill about five to six inches from the coals. Blisters will soon indicate that the skin is separating, but be sure that the chiles are blistered all over or they will not peel properly. Although the chiles may burn slightly, take care that they do not blacken too much, or they will be difficult to peel. They can also be roasted by holding them in tongs over a gas flame or in a very hot iron skillet.

After they are blistered, immediately wrap the chiles in damp paper towels and place them in a plastic bag to steam for ten to fifteen minutes. The best way to avoid chile burns is to wear rubber or latex gloves during the peeling process. Remove the skin, stem, and seeds of each pod and process them any way you like: whole, in strips or rajas, or chop them coarsely. Place the chopped chiles in plastic ice cube trays and freeze them solid. Pop the cubes out and place them in Ziploc freezer bags and you'll have easy access to whatever amount of chile is needed for a recipe. The chiles will keep in your freezer for at least a year. About two cubes equal one chile.

TOASTING AND REHYDRATING CHILES

Many recipes call for toasting dried chiles and that is accomplished on a comal, or "griddle," or in a dry skillet over high heat. Use tongs to toast just long enough that the aroma is released but not enough to burn the pods. After toasting, the pods are usually rehydrated in hot water until they flesh out and soften.

Culinary Herbs for Mexican Cuisines

November 2, the Day of the Dead, used to be a fun day for José while growing up in northern Mexico. The whole family would get together and go to a small-town cemetery to clean the burial places of his grandparents, bring them fresh flowers, and say some prayers. The adults took care of all that while the kids impatiently waited for the action to start. After the cemetery duties were over, they would move to a neighboring hill and begin to set up a big tarp, build a fire, and start eating his mother's and aunt's delicacies. It was a de facto picnic and family reunion that he now misses. After a big lunch, all the cousins—around twenty of them—would go for what seemed like a long hike

Mexican oregano. Photograph by Leslie Seaton. Creative Commons Attribution 2.0 Generic license, Wikimedia Commons.

Hoja santa. Photograph by David Stang. Creative Commons Attribution-Share Alike 4.0 International license, Wikimedia Commons.

Cilantro. Photograph by Testmaskara. Creative Commons Attribution-Share Alike 4.0 International license, Wikimedia Commons.

in the surrounding desert-like hills. They would explore some abandoned mines, throw rocks at lizards, and pick dry orégano. The harvest was good, about what the family consumed in a year. Sprinkled in menudo or any stew, wild orégano was harvested by other families besides just José's, unbeknownst to him. Life and travels would show him later that oregano was available everywhere he went and that not all oreganos are the same.

In Mexican food, the orégano species *Lippia graveolens* is the preferred one. It is native to the Americas and grows almost everywhere in Mexico. It is used mainly in menudo and pozole and works wonders in dry chile sauces. The southern European species of oregano (*Origanum vulgare*), introduced in Mexico by the Spaniards and the same one found in Greece, Italy, France, Spain, and Portugal, and is the appropriate herb for Mediterranean recipes. Other European and Asian species exist, but while oreganos may seem to be all the same, their scientific names tell us that they are different plants belonging to different botanical families.

A native of Mexico, *hoja santa* (*Piper auritum*) also known as *acuyo*, *tlanepa*, or *momo*, was used by the Aztecs to aromatize cacao before the Europeans began to add sugar and create chocolate. It's in the same genus as black pepper, the flavor of this herb resembles that of anise, and it grows wild with its leaves measuring up to ten inches. Warm and humid climates are the best for its growth, but it definitely hates cold weather. While living in Austin, Texas, José had a hoja santa plant in his backyard, but as soon as the temperature went below seventy degrees, he lost it. A good wild fighter, it would come back in the spring—just wonderful! His favorite use of it is to fry it and place it in the middle of tortillas and eggs

Epazote. Photograph by Vegan
Feast Catering. Creative Commons
Attribution 2.0 Generic license,
Wikimedia Commons.

Pápalo. Photograph
by Marcia Stefani. Creative Commons
Attribution 2.0 Generic license,
Wikimedia Commons.

in his huevos rancheros. Cooks
in the southeast of Mexico use
it to wrap tamales and fish, add
it to moles and sauces for flavor complexity, and at times in
quesadillas. It is a pungent and
versatile ingredient.

José once met a French chef
living in California who couldn't stand cilantro. Being a Mexican, José couldn't
imagine that a culinary professional wouldn't like *pico de gallo* or guacamole,
where cilantro plays an important role in both flavor and looks. Left to flower
and set seed, cilantro (*Coriandrum sativum*) produces coriander seed, a spice
used to flavor vinegars and oils, and it is an important ingredient in curries. In
recent years, Mexico has more than doubled the export volume of fresh cilantro
to the United States, Canada, and Europe, reaching around sixty-five thousand
tons per year. It is eaten fresh on salsas and tacos, soups, and salads. Try it on
sandwiches—you'll love it!

Epazote (*Chenopodium ambrosioides*) is a wild herb used mainly in central
Mexico and the southeast. José's mother never liked it, so he didn't have it at
home. It wasn't until he moved south that he was exposed to this pungent plant
and developed a taste for it. It is native to the tropics of America, but Diana
Kennedy found a specimen in Central Park in New York City. Did someone
carry the seeds north? It needs to be boiled to extract the full flavor. Its name
comes from the Náhuatl word *epazotl* and means (are you ready?) . . . skunk
feces! In central Mexico you can find a purple variety, with the same flavor but

more exotic looks. Epazote can be found in street food like quesadillas, wild mushrooms, the sauce of chilaquiles, and tamales, and it is indispensable in beans!

Some people say that *pápalo*, or *pápalo quelite* (*Porophyllum ruderale*), has a taste like arugula mixed with pepper. José's opinion is that it tastes like mouthwash. There is a belief that this herb helps the digestion of fatty foods like greasy tacos, but José finds that it helps clean his mouth from onion flavor. Its name comes from the Náhuatl word *papalotl*, or "butterfly," due to its oval leaves, which can measure up to two inches. Pápalo quelite means "edible butterfly," and this pungent herb grows wild or can be cultivated. It is consumed fresh in tortillas, breads, and guacamole and gives any taco a different dimension. As in every vegetable eaten raw, it should be washed thoroughly.

Perejil, or "parsley" (*Petroselinum sativum*), has the same uses as cilantro and looks almost the same—both brought to America by the Spaniards. Even though José prefers the flavor of cilantro, while shopping in a hurry, both José and Dave have taken home Italian, or flat-leaf, parsley instead of cilantro more than once, so watch out! It is said that it is the most widely used herb in gastronomy around the world, and it is the herb of choice to crown *chiles en nogada*.

The avocado tree (*Persea americana*) is not technically an herb, but the use of its leaves in Mexican gastronomy is so extensive that most authors include it when writing about herbs. Mostly used in the southeast of Mexico and Michoacán, its popularity has been gaining fans in central and northern Mexico.

Italian parsley. Photograph by Tomasz Olszewski on Unsplash.

STALKING THE FLAMING CANARY

"The chile *canario*, which is found in limited quantities in the Oaxaca and Michoacán areas of Mexico, is the only member of the species *Capsicum pubescens* found in North America. At first glance, the pods look much like habanero chiles. They are found green, but more often they are bright yellow or orange, hence the name: canary peppers. There is no mistaking the *canario* for the habanero once you've cut one open because the seeds of the *canario*, like all members of the *pubescens* species, are always black. The plant itself is also impossible to mistake. *Capsicum pubescens* features purple flowers and dark purplish stalks that are covered with hairy fuzz. The chile *canario* is usually roasted, cut into strips and combined with lengthwise slices of raw onion and moistened with lime juice. This salsa is traditionally served with *totopos*, the Oaxaqueño version of tortilla chips. The chile *canario* is very thick-walled and has a rich, fruity flavor when roasted. Whether eaten raw or roasted, canarios are hot, but nowhere near as hot as habaneros. The mystery of the *canario* pepper is how this lone member of the South American *rocoto* family came to grow in North America. Does it represent the beginning of a northward spread of the species *Capsicum pubescens*? If so, why are the recipes for its use so well known among the Zapotec Indians of Oaxaca? Could the chile *canario* be the last vestige of an "endangered species," an old strain of Capsicum that is dying out in North America?

ROBB WALSH / *Chile Pepper*, 1992.

The first time José had it was in Oaxaca, added to refried beans, and it was a wonderful experience. Measuring up to four inches, the oval leaves are used as a flavoring for sauces, *moles*, barbacoa, stocks, as they impart a distinctive and complex anise-like flavor. They are used fresh, dried, ground, and chopped. They work wonders when mixed with chiles in moles, adobos, and cooking sauces.

There are many other herbs in Mexico used exclusively in regional cuisines, such as Oaxaca, Veracruz, and Michoacán but not in other regions. Among them are *chepiche*, *chipilín*, and *chaya* and many other herbs. It would take visiting every little town during the rainy season to discover them, but they are treasures of their ecosystems and local gastronomy. Much has been written on the role of herbs in cooking while ignoring the fact that an ecosystem's diversity is responsible for the variety of the species available. Mexico is considered a "megadiverse" country, since it contains 70 percent of the animal and vegetable species known to man, and it is home to more than five thousand different endemic plants . . . and there's still a lot of plants to be discovered!

Rajas con Crema

SLICED CHILES WITH CREAM

This is a rich accompaniment from Jalisco, an area famous for its food and traditions, and includes the famous city of Guadalajara, which is one of the most famous cities in Mexico. Dave's wife, Mary Jane, dined on this dish at a large restaurant there that specialized in cabrito (goat), and the waiters wore roller skates! Serve this classy dish over hot rice, and for the entree, serve a simple, spicy fish recipe from chapter 13.

8   poblano chiles, roasted, peeled, and seeds and stems removed

3   tablespoons butter

3   tablespoons vegetable oil

3   cups thinly sliced onion

½   teaspoon salt

¼   teaspoon freshly ground black or white pepper

2 to 2 ½ cups chicken broth

¾   cup cream

¼   pound grated *asadero* cheese or substitute *queso blanco* or Monterey Jack cheese

Slice the poblano chiles into strips and set aside.

Heat the butter and oil in a medium size sauté pan and add the onions. Sprinkle with the salt, pepper, and sauté for 3 minutes, or until they are just beginning to brown.

Stir in the reserved chile strips and toss the mixture over a low heat for 1 minute.

Add 2 cups of the chicken broth and the cream to the onion-chile sauté; bring the mixture to a light boil and reduce the heat immediately to a simmer. Stir the mixture frequently until it starts to thicken slightly, about 1 minute. If it thickens too much, too fast, add a few tablespoons of the chicken stock.

Sprinkle the cheese over the mixture and gently mix into the simmering mixture. Serve immediately over hot rice.

YIELD 4 to 5 servings   HEAT LEVEL Mild

Roasted poblano chiles for the *rajas*.
Photograph by José C. Marmolejo.

This recipe is an unusual fruity and slightly spicy dish from Guerrero. Mango and chile have a natural affinity with each other, as their flavors blend and meld to create a most delicious taste. Serve this dish with a chicken or fish entree from chapters 10 or 12.

7	guajillo chiles, toasted, seeds and stems removed or substitute dried red New Mexican chiles	3	cloves garlic
		½	teaspoon salt
		3	tablespoons butter
		6	ripe mangos, peeled and cut into small cubes

Cubed mango for the Mango Chile. Photograph by insjoy on iStock.

Place the toasted chiles in a small bowl, cover with hot water, and soak them for 15 minutes.

Drain the chiles and reserve the soaking water; place the chiles in a blender with the garlic and the salt and puree, adding a few tablespoons of the reserved soaking water if the chile mixture gets too thick in the blender.

Heat the butter in a small sauté pan and add the pureed chile mixture and simmer for 10 minutes.

Remove the puree from the heat and allow it to cool.

When the mixture has cooled to room temperature, stir in the cubed mangos and serve.

YIELD 4 servings   HEAT LEVEL Medium

Chiles Pasilla Tlaxcaltecas

Here's a dessert dish from Tlaxcala that norteamericanos will find very unusual! Piloncillo is unrefined brown sugar, and dark brown sugar makes a good substitute. It is delicious, especially if you serve it after a spicy seafood dish from chapter 9; the sweet taste will complement the hot and spicy flavoring of the seafood.

5   tablespoons olive oil

1   tablespoon butter

3   cups thinly sliced onion

5   cloves garlic, minced

2   cups water

2   cups piloncillo or substitute
    dark brown sugar

12 pasilla chiles, seeds and stems
    removed, soaked in water to
    soften them

½   pound *manchego* cheese
    or substitute Parmesan,
    cut into 12 thick strips

Heat the oil and the butter in a large sauté pan and sauté the onions for 1 minute. Add the garlic and sauté for 2 minutes more.

Add the water and the piloncillo, bring the mixture to a boil, reduce the heat, and simmer the mixture until it thickens to the consistency of honey.

Stuff each chile with a piece of the cheese, taking care not to break the chile.

Place the stuffed chiles in the simmering skillet and sauté over a low heat until the cheese starts to soften.

Place two chiles on a plate and drizzle some sauce over them.

YIELD 6 servings   HEAT LEVEL Mild

Pasilla pod before softening.
Photograph by Harald Zoschke.
Used with permission.

Chiltepín country: Sierra Madre Mountains, Sonora. Photograph by Dave DeWitt.

2 } The Chiltepín Harvest and Chile Sauces and Condiments

Dave describes his visit to the Sonoran chiltepín harvest.

My amigo Antonio Heras swears that the motto of the Sonoran bus lines is "Better Dead Than Late," and I believe him. The smoke-belching buses were flying by us on curves marked by shrines commemorating the unfortunate drivers whose journeys through life had abruptly ended on that mountain road. We waved the buses on and cruised along at a safer speed to enjoy the spectacular vistas on the way to the valley of the *chiltepíneros*.

It was November 1990, the time of the Sonoran chiltepín harvest, yet the temperature was in the upper eighties. My wife, Mary Jane, and I had accepted the invitation of Antonio to visit the home of his mother, Josefina Duran, the "Chile Queen," who lives in the town of Cumpas. From there, we journeyed through the spectacular foothills of the Sierra Madre—chiltepín country. Our destination was the Rio Sonora Valley and the villages of La Aurora and Mazocahui.

As we drove along, Antonio and I reminisced about our fascination with the wild chile pepper.

A Fiery Flashback

During the early days of the *Chile Pepper* magazine, Antonio and I had attended a symposium on wild chiles that was held in October 1988 at the Desert Botanical Garden in Phoenix. The leader of the conference was the ecologist Dr. Gary Nabhan, author of *Gathering the Desert* (1985), then director of Native Seeds/SEARCH, and an expert on chiltepines. Other chile experts attending included Dr. W. Hardy Eshbaugh, a botanist from Miami University of Ohio; Dr. Jean Andrews, author of *Peppers: The Domesticated Capsicums* (1984); and Cindy Baker of the Chicago Botanical Garden.

As the conference progressed, I was amazed by the amount of information presented on chiltepines. Botanists believe that these wild chiles are the closest surviving species to the earliest forms of chiles, which developed in Bolivia and southern Brazil long before mankind arrived in the New World. The small size of their fruits made them perfect for dissemination by birds, and the wild chiles spread all over South and Central America and up to what is now the United States border millennia before the domesticated varieties arrived. In fact, Dr. Eshbaugh believes they have the widest distribution of any chile variety; they range from Peru north to the Caribbean, Florida, and Louisiana and west to Arizona.

There is a wide variation in pod shapes, from tiny ones the size and shape of BBs to elongated pods a half inch long. By contrast, domesticated piquines have much longer pods, up to three inches. The chiltepines most prized in Mexico are spherical and measure five to eight millimeters in diameter. They are among the hottest chiles on earth, measuring up to one hundred thousand Scoville Heat Units.

The word "chiltepín" is believed to be derived from the Aztec language (Náhuatl) that combines the word *chilli* with *tecpintl*, meaning "flea chile," an allusion its sharp bite. That word was altered to *chiltecpin*, then to the Spanish chiltepín, and finally Anglicized to *chilipiquin*, as the plant is known in Texas. Its botanical name is *Capsicum annuum var. gabrisculum*.

In Sonora and southern Arizona, chiltepines grow in microhabitats in the transition zone between mountain and desert, which receives as little as ten inches of rain per year. They grow beneath "nurse" trees such as mesquite, oak, and palmetto, which provide shelter from direct sunlight, heat, and frost. In the summer, there is higher humidity beneath the nurse trees, and legumes such as mesquite fix nitrogen in the soil—a perfect fertilizer for the chiltepines. They also protect the plant from grazing by cattle, sheep, goats, and deer. Chiltepines planted in the open, without nurse trees, usually die from the effects of direct solar radiation.

Although the chiltepín plant's average height is about four feet, there are reports of individual bushes growing ten feet tall, living twenty-five to thirty years, and having stems as big around as a man's wrist. Chiltepines are resistant to frost but lose their leaves in cold winter weather. New growth will sprout from the base of the plant if it dies back.

There is quite a bit of legend and lore associated with the fiery little pods. In earlier times, the Papago Indians of Arizona traditionally made annual pilgrimages into the Sierra Madre range of Mexico to gather chiltepines. Dr. Gary Nabhan discovered in the mid-1970s that the Tarahumara Indians of Chihuahua value the chiltepines so much that they build stone walls around the bushes to protect them from goats. Besides spicing up food, Indians use chiltepín powder on their nipples to suppress lactation, which helps nursing mothers wean their babies. When inhaled, chiltepín powder also causes sneezing, which promotes contractions that aid in childbirth. And, of course, the hot chiles induce gustatory sweating, which cools off the body during hot weather.

In 1794, Padre Ignaz Pfefferkorn, a German Jesuit living in Sonora, described the wild chile pepper: "A kind of wild pepper which the inhabitants call chiltipin is found on many hills. It is placed unpulverized on the table in a salt cellar and each fancier takes as much of it as he believes he can eat. He pulverizes it with his fingers and mixes it with his food. The chiltipin is the best spice for soup, boiled peas, lentils, beans and the like. The Americans swear that it is exceedingly healthful and very good as an aid to the digestion." In fact, even today, chiltepínes are used—amazingly enough—as a treatment for acid indigestion.

Padre Pfefferkorn realized that chiltepínes were one of the few crops in the world harvested in the wild rather than cultivated. (The same is true today. Others are piñon nuts, Brazil nuts, and some varieties of wild rice.) This fact has led to concern for the preservation of the chiltepín bushes because the harvesters often pull up entire plants or break off branches. Dr. Nabhan believes that the

Green chiltepínes.
Photograph by Dave DeWitt.

Chiltepín cluster.
Photograph by Chiltepinster. Creative Commons Attribution-Share Alike 3.0 Unported license, Wikimedia Commons.

chiltepín population is diminishing because of overharvesting and overgrazing. In Arizona, a chiltepín reserve has been established near Tumacacori at Rock Corral Canyon in the Coronado National Forest. The Native Seeds/SEARCH organization has been granted a special use permit from the National Forest Service to initiate permanent marking and mapping of plants, ecological studies, and a management plan proposal.

The symposium on wild chiles was fascinating, and we even got to taste some chiltepín ice cream. But it was even more interesting to see the chiltepíneros in action two years later.

In the Village of the Dawn

The only way to drive to the "Village of the Dawn" (La Aurora) is to ford the Rio Sonora, which was no problem for Antonio's Jeep. The first thing we noticed about the village was that nearly every house had thousands of brilliant red chiltepínes drying on white linen cloths in their front yards. We stopped at the modest house of veteran chiltepínero Pedro Osuna and were immediately greeted warmly and were offered liquid refreshment. As Pedro measured out the chiltepínes he had collected for Antonio and Josefina, we asked him about the methods of the chiltepíneros.

> **MEXICAN CHILE PROVERBS**
>
> "The chile is the same as the needle: equal sharpness."
>
> "Don't be afraid of the chile, even though it's so red."
>
> "We eat this food because our ancestors came from Hell."

He said that the Durans advanced him money so he could hire pickers and pay for expenses such as gasoline. Then he would drive the pickers to ranches where the bushes were numerous. He dropped the pickers off alongside the road, and they wandered through the rough cattle country handpicking the tiny pods. In a single day, a good picker could collect only six quarts of chiltepínes. At sunset, the pickers returned to the road, where Pedro met them. The ranchers who owned the land would later be compensated with a liter or so of pods.

Usually, the pods would be dried in the sun for about ten days, but because that technique is lengthy and often results in the pods collecting dust, Antonio had built a solar dryer behind Pedro's house. Antonio's dryer sends air heated by a solar collector through a chimney lined with racks that support screens holding the fresh chiltepínes—a much more efficient method than sun drying. Modern technology, based upon ancient, solar-passive principles, had arrived at the Village of the Dawn.

Chiltepínes drying on linen. Photograph by Dave DeWitt.

I asked Pedro how the harvest was going, and he said it was the best in more than a decade because the better-than-average rainfall had caused the bushes to set a great many fruits. Antonio added that during the drought of 1988, chiltepínes were so rare that there was no export crop. According to Pedro, factors other than rainfall also had an influence on the harvest—specifically, birds and insects. Mockingbirds, Pyrrhuloxia (Mexican cardinals), and other species readily ate the pods as they turned red, but the most significant damage to the plant was caused by grasshoppers.

The total harvest in Sonora is difficult to estimate, but at least twenty tons of dried pods are collected and sold in an average year. Some chiltepíneros have suggested that in a wet year like 1990, fifty tons might be a better estimate. The total export to the United States is estimated at more than six tons a year, and the Durans account for much of that. As I watched Antonio and his mother weigh huge sacks of chiltepínes on the small scale in front of the market, I asked Antonio about prices.

He declined to tell me what he paid the chiltepíneros, but he offered a wealth of information about other pricing information. Between 1968 and 1990, the wholesale price of chiltepínes had multiplied nearly ten-fold. Between 1987 and 1990, the price had nearly tripled, mostly because of the 1988 drought. Currently, chiltepínes are being sold in South Tucson in one-quarter ounce packages for $2, which equates to a phenomenal $128 per pound. Thus, chiltepínes are the second most expensive spice in the world, after saffron.

Why do people in the United States lust after these tiny pods? Dr. Nabhan suggests that chiltepínes remind immigrants of their northern Mexico homeland and help them reinforce their Sonoran identity. Also, they have traditional uses in Sonoran cuisine, as evidenced by the recipes we collected. In addition to spicing up Sonoran foods, they are an antioxidant, and thus help preserve *carne seca*, the dried meat we call jerky. No wonder the Chile Queen and her son work hard to import many hundreds of pounds of pods.

After the sacks of chiltepínes were loaded into the Jeep, we were joined by *Arizona Republic* reporter Keith Rosenblum, who was writing a story on the chiltepíneros. We went for lunch in the nearby village of Mazocahui, passing signs reading "Se vende chiltepín" (Chiltepínes for sale). At the rustic restaurant, which was really the living room of someone's

Chiltepín vendor, Cumpas, Sonora.
Photograph by Dave DeWitt.

house, we sat down for a fiery feast. Bowls of chiltepínes were on the table, and the extremely hot salsa casera was served with carne adobada, carne machaca, beans, and the superb, extremely thin Sonoran flour tortillas.

The Future of Chiltepínes

On the drive back to Cumpas, Antonio spoke of his dreams and the problems inherent in achieving them. He wanted to create a chiltepín plantation where all the bushes were centrally located and irrigated, thus eliminating wasted time and money with pickers wandering for miles through rough country.

I reminded him of the problems with previously cultivated chiltepín crops that we had learned about at the symposium. In those experiments, growers had planted the chiltepínes in rows under artificial shade and had irrigated them as if they were growing jalapeños. The cultivated chiltepínes had the tendency to produce pods 50 percent larger than the wild variety, which did not seem authentic and thus were rejected by consumers. Several reasons for the occur-

Dried chiltepínes ready for bagging.
Photograph by Dave DeWitt.

rence of the larger pods had been advanced. There was the natural tendency of growers to select larger pods for their seed stock for the following year, which is how chiles developed from BB-sized to the large pods we have today. Also, increased water and fertilizer could enlarge the pods.

The wild plants, when cultivated, were susceptible to chile wilt, the fungal disease aggravated by too much water. In one test planting near the Rio Montezuma, the chiltepín plants were wiped out by moth caterpillars, yet a wild population just two miles away was unaffected. One possible explanation had been offered: during times of drought, chiltepínes went dormant, as did their nurse plants. However, during the drought, chiles that were cultivated in rows and irrigated stuck out like sore thumbs and attracted pests.

But Antonio had a plan to eliminate those problems. He would mimic nature, he told me, and improve on it only slightly. He envisioned a "natural plantation," one near Cumpas where he would plant thousands of chiltepín plants under mesquite nurse trees and use drip irrigation. There were plenty of friends and relatives—especially kids—to scare off birds, to spread netting to defeat grass-

> **DIFFERING VIEWS ON THE HEAT SCALE**
>
> The Mexican says: "It's not hot."
>
> The foreigner understands: "It's hot."
>
> The Mexican says: "It's just a little hot."
>
> The foreigner understands: "It's very hot."
>
> The Mexican says: "It's mostly hot."
>
> The foreigner understands: "Don't get near it. It's dangerous."
>
> The Mexican says: "It's very hot."
>
> The foreigner understands: "It burns like hell."
>
> The Mexican says: "It's very, very hot."
>
> The foreigner understands: "Abandon the establishment."
>
> MEXICAN PROVERB

hoppers, and to pick the crop. Dogs would guard the crop from unauthorized harvesters, and Antonio's solar dryers would provide a clean, perfect crop. It seemed eminently logical to me, and I wished him luck.

Back in the town of Cumpas, loud salsa music enlivened the streets as if a fiesta were in progress. Josefina and her assistant, Evalia, prepared a wonderful, chiltepín-spiced meal. We drank some *bacanora*, an agave distillate from Sonora, the magical Mexican moonshine, and dined on an elegant—and highly spiced—menu of Sonoran specialties.

NOTE *Antonio never achieved his chiltepín dreams; the project had way too many variables. We still are in contact with each other, and he now sells heavy machinery manufactured in the United States to companies in Mexico. I checked on chiltepín prices online in 2021 and found eight ounces for $46.00, or $5.75 per ounce.*

This diabolically hot sauce is also called chiltepín pasta *(paste). It is used in soups and stews and to fire up machaca, eggs, tacos, tostadas, and beans. This is the exact recipe prepared in the home of Josefina Duran in Cumpas, Sonora. After I returned to Albuquerque, I made this sauce and it sat in my refrigerator for years, and because it was so hot, I never came close to finishing the jar of it.*

2	cups chiltepínes		1	teaspoon coriander seed
8 to 10	cloves garlic		1	cup water
1	teaspoon salt		1	cup cider vinegar
1	teaspoon Mexican oregano			

Chiltepín House Sauce. Photograph by Phương Huy. Public Domain, Wikimedia Commons.

Combine all ingredients in a blender and puree on high speed for 3 to 4 minutes.

Refrigerate for 1 day to blend the flavors. It keeps indefinitely in the refrigerator.

YIELD 2 cups　HEAT LEVEL Extremely hot

FIGURE 2.8 Pickled Chiltepínes.
Photographer unknown. Sunbelt Archives.

Chiltepínes en Escabeche

PICKLED CHILTEPÍNES

In the states of Sonora and Sinaloa, fresh green and red chiltepínes are preserved in vinegar and salt. They are used as a condiment or are popped into the mouth when eating any food—except, perhaps, oatmeal. Since fresh chiltepínes are not available in the United States, adventurous cooks and gardeners must grow their own. The tiny chiles are preserved in three layers in a 1-pint, sterilized jar.

Fresh red and/or green chiltepínes (about 2 cups)

3   cloves garlic, peeled

3   teaspoons salt

3   tablespoons cider vinegar

Water

Fill the jar ⅓ full of chiltepínes.

Add 1 clove garlic, 1 teaspoon salt, and 1 tablespoon cider vinegar.

Repeat this process twice more and fill the jar to within ½ inch of the top with water.

Seal the jar and allow to sit for 15 to 30 days.

YIELD 1 pint   HEAT LEVEL Hot

CHILE SAUCES AND CONDIMENTS

Mexico, which grows more varieties of chiles than any other country, also has the greatest number of different kinds of hot sauces, and they are so important to the cuisine that an entire book could be written on the subject. We are presenting a mere sampling of Mexican chile sauces and condiments in this chapter—additional sauces are found within other recipes in this book. In the Mexico of yesterday, most of the grinding of sauces was done in a molcajete, a stone mortar. As in many modern Mexican homes, we have substituted a food processor or blender, although some traditional cooks may prefer the old-fashioned method. Cooked sauces are generally fried in lard; we have offered vegetable oil as a substitute in deference to health-conscious eaters.

Since many common Mexican sauces such as pico de gallo and guacamole are repeated again and again in cookbooks, we have decided to focus our attention on the sauces that are not so well known outside of Mexico.

Salsa Chile de Árbol   CHILE DE ÁRBOL SAUCE

This is the sauce that commonly is bottled in liquor bottles and sold in the mercados and at roadside stands in central and northern Mexico. It is sprinkled over nearly any snack food, from tacos to tostadas.

30	chiles de àrbol, seeds and stems removed	1	tablespoon sesame seeds
	Water for soaking	3	cloves garlic
¼	teaspoon ground cumin	1	tablespoon pepitas (pumpkin seeds)
¼	teaspoon ground allspice	1	cup cider vinegar
½	teaspoon ground cloves	¾	cup water

Chiltepínes salsa. Photographer unknown. Sunbelt Archives.

Soak the chiles in the water until softened, about 1/2 hour.

Toast the sesame seeds and pumpkin seeds in a skillet until they pop and are brown.

Combine the seeds with the drained chiles and the remaining ingredients in a blender and puree for about 3 minutes.

Strain the mixture through a sieve and bottle.

It will keep for months in the refrigerator.

YIELD 2 CUPS   HEAT LEVEL Hot

Chipotles Adobados   CHIPOTLE CHILES IN ADOBO SAUCE

Here's a pickled chile recipe from Tlaxcala. These smoky, sweet-hot pickled chiles can form the basis of a dipping sauce for tostadas if they're further pureed, or they can be served as a condiment with enchiladas or grilled or roasted meats.

8	ounces dried chipotle chiles, stems removed	1	cup piloncillo, or ½ cup packed brown sugar
	Water for soaking	6	black peppercorns
1	quart vinegar	3	bay leaves
1	head garlic, peeled and crushed	1	teaspoon ground cumin
			Salt to taste

Soak the chipotles in water until they rehydrate (at least 1 hour), then drain.

In a saucepan, add half of the vinegar, half of the garlic, and all of the piloncillo.

Cook this mixture for about 20 minutes, then add the chipotle and remaining garlic, peppercorns, bay leaves, cumin, remaining vinegar, and salt to taste.

Cook for about 30 minutes, covered, over medium heat.

Add the chipotle chile mixture, stir well, and store in sterilized jars.

YIELD About 1 ½ quarts   HEAT LEVEL Hot

Chipotle Chiles in Adobo Sauce. Photograph by Bursera Linanoeg Huy, Creative Commons Attribution-Share Alike 4.0 International license, Wikimedia Commons.

Yucatecan Radish Relish. Photograph by El Gran Dee. Creative Commons Attribution 2.0 Generic license, Wikimedia Commons.

Salpicón

YUCATECAN RADISH RELISH

Nancy and Jeff Gerlach wrote in Chile Pepper *magazine about collecting this salsa in their favorite region in Mexico, the Yucatán Peninsula: "The first time we were served this salsa of 'little pieces' we were surprised by the use of radishes, which added not only flavor, but an interesting texture to the salsa. For variety, add some diced tomatoes or avocados." Serve this relish over seafood.*

2   habanero chiles, stems and seeds removed, diced, or substitute 4 jalapeño or 4 serrano chiles

1   large red onion, diced

8 to 10 radishes, thickly sliced

3   tablespoons lime juice, fresh preferred

3   tablespoons chopped fresh cilantro

Combine all of the ingredients, except the cilantro, in a bowl and allow to sit for an hour to blend the flavors. Toss with the cilantro and serve.

YIELD ⅔ cup   HEAT LEVEL Medium

Xnipec

This classic Yucatecan salsa is definitely wild. Xnipec, pronounced "SCHNEE-peck," is Mayan for "dog's nose." Serve it—carefully—with grilled poultry or fish.

	Juice of 4 limes
1	onion, red or purple preferred, diced
4	habanero chiles, seeds and stems removed, diced
1	tomato, diced
2	tablespoons cilantro, minced

Soak the diced onion in the lime juice for at least 30 minutes. Add all of the other ingredients and mix, salt to taste, and add a little water if desired.

YIELD 1½ cup   HEAT LEVEL Extremely hot

Salsa Xcatic

This sauce was collected for us by Marta and Alan Figel, owners of On the Verandah restaurant in Highlands, North Carolina, where they have a large hot sauce collection. Marta was on assignment for Chile Pepper *magazine at the time, and she described the principal chile in this salsa designed for use on seafood: "The Yucatán peninsula is identified with its native fiery chile, the habanero, and the lesser known chile xcatic (pronounced sch-KA-tik). It is pale green to bright yellow, much hotter, and resembles the New Mexican chile in shape and size."*

9	xcatic chiles, seeds and stems removed, finely chopped; or substitute four yellow wax hot chiles
1	medium white onion, finely chopped
¼	cup vegetable oil
½	teaspoon salt
2	tablespoons white vinegar
	Freshly ground black pepper to taste

Sauté the chiles and onion in the oil for 20 minutes at low heat. Place in a blender with the remaining ingredients and puree until smooth.

YIELD 1 cup   HEAT LEVEL Medium

Ingredients for a fresh habanero
salsa. Photograph by Chel
Beeson. Work for hire.
Sunbelt Archives.

Xcatic chiles. Photograph by Pachuli Yo.
Creative Commons Attribution-Share
Alike 4.0 International license, Wikimedia
Commons.

This simple, all-purpose sauce calls for roasting the vegetables, a process that is typical of Yucatán and imparts a distinctive flavor. Don't worry about removing all the skins from the habaneros and tomatoes—some charred bits will give the sauce extra flavor. This sauce is wonderful over tacos of all kinds, as well as enchiladas, chiles rellenos, and tamales.

2	habanero chiles, roasted, seeds and stems removed, chopped
4	medium tomatoes, roasted, peeled, and chopped
1	small onion, roasted, peeled, and chopped
¼	teaspoon Mexican oregano
2	tablespoons vegetable oil
¼	teaspoon salt

To roast the vegetables, preheat a dry skillet until very hot.

Place the unpeeled vegetables on the skillet and roast for 10 to 15 minutes, turning frequently.

If you have a stovetop grill, roast the vegetables over the flame until the skins are blackened, about 5 minutes. The vegetables can also be roasted under a broiler. After roasting, remove the larger pieces of the skins.

Place the tomatoes, chopped vegetables, and oregano in a blender or food processor and puree

until smooth.

Heat the oil in a skillet and sauté the sauce for about 5 minutes. Add the ¼ teaspoon salt (or more to taste).

YIELD 2 CUPS   HEAT LEVEL Hot

Roasted Habanero-Tomato Sauce. Photograph by Dave DeWitt.

Here is a classic Yucatán seasoning paste from Jeff and Nancy Gerlach, who commented in Chile Pepper *magazine: "This is the most popular of all the different* recados *and is very typical of Yucatán. It is used to add both flavor and color to foods, and is most commonly used for* pibiles *or stewed pork dishes. The red color comes from the annatto seeds, which also add a unique flavor to this tasty paste. Available commercially as achiote paste,* recado rojo *is far better when prepared at home." Many cooks add red chile powder to this recipe.*

4	tablespoons ground annatto seeds (see note)
1	tablespoon dry oregano, Mexican preferred
10	whole black peppercorns
½	teaspoon salt
4	whole cloves
2	whole allspice berries
½	teaspoon cumin seeds
	Red chile powder if desired
3	cloves garlic, chopped
3	tablespoons distilled white vinegar

Ingredients for Achiote Paste. Photograph by Paul Goyette, Creative Commons Attribution-Share Alike 2.0 Generic license, Wikimedia Commons.

Place all the dry ingredients in a spice grinder and process to a fine powder.

Transfer the powder to a blender, add the remaining ingredients and grind to a thick paste, adding a little water if the mixture is too thick.

Allow to sit for an hour or overnight to blend the flavors.

NOTE *Annatto is available in Latin markets or online, through mail-order.*

YIELD ½ cup   HEAT LEVEL Varies

The chiles, tomatoes, and squash seeds make this a very New World dish, as squash has been a Mexican staple for millennia. Typically, cooked chicken or turkey is added to this sauce from southern Mexico.

1 ½	cups ripe tomatoes, chopped
½	cup tomatillos
2	pasilla chiles, seeds and stems removed
2	guajillo chiles, seeds and stems removed, or substitute New Mexican red chiles
¾	cup water
¼	cup lime juice
½	cup sesame seeds
1	tablespoon squash or pumpkin seeds (pepitas)
1	cinnamon stick, 1-inch long, broken up
2	teaspoons crushed hot New Mexican red chile
½	cup French bread, cubed and moistened with chicken broth
¼	teaspoon achiote (annatto seed)
2	cups chicken broth
1	tablespoon flour

Combine the tomatoes, tomatillos, and chiles in ¾ cup water and ¼ cup lime juice in a saucepan and cook over medium heat for 10 minutes.

Toast the sesame seeds, squash (or pumpkin) seeds, cinnamon stick, and crushed chile in a dry skillet over low heat for about 10 minutes.

In a food processor or blender, process the toasted ingredients, and then add the cooked tomato mixture, stirring into a smooth paste. Add the bread, achiote, 2 cups of chicken broth, and flour and process everything until smooth.

Return the sauce to the stove and heat through.

YIELD About 4 cups   HEAT LEVEL Medium

Commercial jar of Pipián Rojo.
Photograph by José C. Marmolejo.

Bullfighter-Style Chiles. Photograph by José C. Marmolejo.

Chiles Toreados

BULLFIGHTER-STYLE CHILES

José says that these chile snacks have been "fought" or turned around in oil in a skillet or comal and are therefore spicier. He suggests that diners hold one of the serranos by the stem and chew it to their liking. Many restaurants in Mexico will offer chiles toreados *free of charge at your request.*

6	serrano chiles or more	Sea salt to taste
	Vegetable oil as needed	Soy sauce to taste (optional)
½	lime's worth of lime juice	

Sauté the serranos in oil in a small skillet until they're dark. They will blister. Keep them whole—with seeds and veins—and do not remove the burnt skin.

Place them in a small bowl that contains the rest of the ingredients. Once cold they will shrink and wrinkle.

YIELD 6 or more servings   HEAT SCALE Hot

Milpa showing corn, squash, and beans. Photograph by Feria de Productores.
Creative Commons Attribution 2.0 Generic license, Wikimedia Commons.

3 〉〉 The Milpa and the Mostly Meatless Origin of Mexican Cuisine

Modern agriculture relies on industrial farming practices, such as the use of chemical pesticides, to keep humanity fed against all catastrophic predictions of overpopulation, diseases, and pests. Traditionally, however, agriculture relied on the beneficial relationships between plants—what we refer to as permaculture today. Science has confirmed that legumes, for example, through an association with the right kind of bacteria, are able to fix nitrogen from the air into the soil for later absorption by other plants. Other species benefit from this phenomenon, including corn.

The Mexicas, a.k.a. the Aztecs, knew that planting beans and corn together was more beneficial than planting them apart. In this agricultural method, known as milpa, beans also benefited from corn by using it as a support for their vines. A win-win situation, as we say these days. Squash, also commonly grown in a milpa, grows wide leaves and covers the soil from the sun, thus preserving moisture and preventing weed growth. Milpa agriculture is a method of food production in which several plant species (principally beans, corn, and squash) coexist in the same space, contributing to each other's development. Also present in the milpa are quelites—wild edible plants (now cultivated)—like purslane, chard, kale, and another 350-plus species that continue to be harvested wild in Mexico. Culinary and medicinal herbs are a must around the milpa. We also find our beloved chiles forming a barrier against pests. Defining the borders of milpas, we find nopales and magueyes, or cacti and agaves, respectively, that enrich the Mexican diet. Any bees? You bet!

In 2010, UNESCO recognized traditional Mexican cuisine as a "comprehensive cultural model comprising farming, ritual practices, age-old skills, culinary techniques and ancestral community customs and manners." The study of milpa agriculture made possible its understanding as well as its diffusion, and Mexican cuisine was designated as an "Intangible Cultural Heritage of Humanity." This distinction is shared by French and Japanese cuisines as well as the Mediterranean diet. This recognition gave way to declaring November 16 Mexican Gastronomy Day. Another Mexican fiesta day? Sure, why not?

Chiles, along with corn, beans, and squash, comprise the trilogy that complemented corn and became the foundation of traditional Mexican food. These four ingredients have been present daily in all homes from pre-Columbian times to this day in a wide array of preparations and combinations in addition to whatever meat was served. Thus, the ancient agricultural production model of these staples, the milpa, was here to stay.

While the tortilla continues to be used as a plate when you add something on top (rolled or not), or as an edible spoon when you cut it in half and use both hands to scoop up your meal, or as a meal by itself when you just add salt and/or salsa, beans remain on center stage, waiting to be seasoned in multiple ways (and chiles reign as Mexicans' spice of choice) and to be served on a dish or spread on a tortilla or tostada. Squash, another staple of the milpa, has an infinite number of uses. It can be eaten raw in a salad, grilled, boiled, baked, sautéed, stuffed, used in soups and stocks, and is very easy and quick to prepare. It marries well with cheese, chiles, and other vegetables, as well as corn, rice, and even pasta. And we haven't gotten to the blossoms yet! Those beautiful flowers can be used as decoration, become the stuffing of quesadillas, or be stuffed themselves.

Growing beans on corn. Photograph by Feria de Productores. Creative Commons Attribution 2.0 Generic license, Wikimedia Commons.

As you can see, the Mexican milpa is abundant, nutritious, and best of all—sustainable. Still found in the Sierra Tarahumara and central and southern Mexico, the milpa method remains as a source of food, spice, and health to small peasants, an ecosystem for organic vegetables to grow, and a cultural treasure to Mexico. Perhaps we should all grow a milpa.

How to Make a Milpa

Many of us have idyllic dreams of being self-reliant, living in contact with nature, producing natural, organic foods, and living free from an office setting—boss

IN THE AZTEC MARKET

When the Spanish forces under Cortés arrived in Tenochtitlán (now Mexico City) in 1519, they were astounded by the size and complexity of the market at the great plaza of Tlatelolco. According to descriptions by Bernal Díaz del Castillo, it resembled a modern flea market, with thousands of vendors hawking every conceivable foodstuff and other products. The noise of the market could be heard three miles away, and some of the soldiers who had traveled to such places as Rome and Constantinople said it was the largest market they had ever seen. Every product had its own section of the market, and chiles were no exception; they were sold in the second aisle to the right. Sometimes chiles were used as a form of money to buy drinks or other small items.

included. The milpa could bring us closer to those dreams, and that's why we prepared a simple "how to" method—adapted to the United States and Canada—for making a milpa at home.

Traditionally, the milpa has been the "backyard garden" of common folk and marginal or small farmers in Mexico and some parts of Latin America and has been for centuries the basis of their sustenance and a source of food for the whole year. As every year is different climate-wise, some years milpa growers had shortages and others, surpluses. This natural phenomenon gave way to the barter method, which is still used to bolster resources in small communities.

For the suburban citizen, however, milpa agriculture is a remedy for sedentary living, stress, or too much social networking and streaming TV. If outdoor space is limited, we have good news: milpa agriculture is a space-saving practice because several plant varieties share the same space, and it can be done in rows or beds. The size and variety of species in our milpa will depend on land, water, and labor available. Climate will be determinant, however.

To get started, we need corn, beans, and squash, the necessary basics. Preferably using heirloom seeds, we plant squash in a greenhouse, cold frame, or indoors under lights about a month before we plant the corn outside in the spring. Using rows or beds, we will need to plant two grains of corn together in a straight line at a distance between six and eight inches from each other. The distance between corn rows should be around thirty inches. When the corn plants are between six and eight inches high, we plant the beans. We need three or four bean seeds around each corn plant. They will grow looking for support for their vines, but we may need to guide them to start their climb. Once corn

Sometimes gardeners expand their milpas into separate plots, like this chile pepper section with newspaper mulch. Photograph by Dave DeWitt.

and beans are in place, we will bring the squash plants out and place them in the middle of the corn rows roughly six feet from each other. Our milpa is started.

Instead of planting pinto beans, you may substitute chickpeas, peas, or fava beans. Instead of squash, you can plant cucumbers, watermelons, or cantaloupes; they all cover the ground, producing the same effect as mulch. After you finish this, you have our basic milpa that you can enhance with still more plant species.

Chiles are an excellent choice to complement our basic milpa crops. Plant your favorite varieties of chiles in rows alternating with the cornrows. Also, rows of tomatoes, onions, and garlic in between the corn rows are not only a good idea, they are also highly recommended. Don't we want to be able to make a salsa or *pico de gallo* from scratch at harvest time? Fine herbs and medicinal herbs can be planted along the perimeter, while perennial herbs can go into pots for the winter, and we can move them indoors to a sunny window.

Something important we need to keep in mind is that in the following years, the gardener should rotate the corn and beans around the milpa to allow the beans to work the nitrogen fixation miracle in the whole area. Additionally, don't overlook your seed supplier's instructions as they are key to successful germination and growth. And finally, please use compost. It's good for the environment and especially for your milpa.

One year of growing a milpa will give you much knowledge and experience. You will develop the instincts to know what your plants need in order to thrive. This will be your milpa; your sustainable garden that will provide food and pleasure; a space that bees will love to visit; and one you will be proud to show off to your guests. And all thanks to the Aztecs!

THE EPITOME OF MEXICAN CUISINE

"During this epoch Mexico attained a high degree of grandeur in its cuisine. This was the result of the crops of the Indian; the innumerable contributions from Spain; the spices, fruits and rice which poured in with every arrival at Acapulco of the historic *Nao de la China*, the Manila Galleon, which arrived from the distant Philippine archipelago. This splendor also derived from the use of slaves; the visits by pirates who made frequent incursions along the Mexican coasts; the French invaders; immigrants from all parts of the world; bringing about a veritable gastronomic revolution of major proportions, unequalled by most countries of the world."

AMANDO FARGA / *Eating in Mexico*, 1963

These vegetarian milpa recipes call for cooked summer squash of a variety that suits your taste. They need to be baked, boiled, or grilled whole to avoid losing their interior moisture and sweet flavor. They can be the main dish or a side to meat dishes.

Poblanos Rellenos de Calabacitas y Setas
SQUASH STUFFED WITH OYSTER MUSHROOMS AND POBLANOS

Here's a simple recipe that yields a complex flavor. If desired, you may devein the poblanos or enjoy the flavor plus a little less pungency.

4	squash, such as zucchini, cooked
4	poblano chiles, roasted, peeled, deseeded, and sliced. Deveining is optional.
4	ounces oyster mushrooms, sliced
1	medium onion, chopped
2	cloves garlic, minced
	Vegetable oil or butter
	Salt to taste

Cut the squash in half (lengthwise), remove the seeds, and keep them warm in the oven. Sauté the poblanos, mushrooms, onions, garlic, and squash seeds for 3 to 5 minutes and add the salt. Stuff the squash halves and enjoy!

YIELD 4 servings   HEAT LEVEL Medium

Squash Stuffed with Oyster
Mushrooms and Poblanos.
Photograph by José C. Marmolejo.

Chickpeas and Squash with Serranos. Photograph by José C. Marmolejo.

Garbanzos con Calabacitas y Chiles Serranos
CHICKPEAS AND SQUASH WITH SERRANOS

This dish can be eaten alone or used as a side to a meat dish or be the stuffing of quesadillas. It's perfect for lunch or for a light dinner.

1   pound cooked chickpeas

4   squash cooked and cut into chunks

2 to 4 serrano chiles, deseeded and
     sliced. Deveining is optional

1   onion, chopped

2   cloves garlic, minced

     Vegetable oil

     Salt to taste

In a saucepan, sauté the chickpeas, squash, serranos, onions, and garlic together for between 3 and 5 minutes, and add the salt. It is ready to enjoy! Quick and easy!

YIELD   4 Servings   HEAT LEVEL   Medium to Hot

Chilacayote Stuffed with Corn,
Epazote, and Chile de Árbol.
Photograph by José C. Marmolejo.

Chilacayotes Rellenos de Granos de Maíz con Epazote y Chile de Árbol
CHILACAYOTES STUFFED WITH CORN, EPAZOTE, AND CHILE DE ÁRBOL

Chilacayotes *are a spherical wild variety of squash. They are best harvested when their diameter is between 3 and 5 inches for our purposes.*

4	chilacayotes or any spherical tender squash, cooked
1	pound sweet corn, cooked
4	chiles de árbol, destemmed and crushed
1	onion chopped
	Juice of two lemons
	A sprig of epazote or substitute cilantro
	Cooking oil
	Salt to taste

Cut about an inch in the top of the chilacayote on the side of the stem and remove the seeds.

In a saucepan, sauté the corn, chiles, and onions for about 5 minutes.

Add the lemon juice, epazote, and salt, and sauté for another 3 minutes.

Stuff the squash with the sautéed mix and serve! Buen provecho!

YIELD 4 Servings   HEAT LEVEL Hot

Relleno de Verduras de la Milpa GRILLED MILPA VEGETABLES STUFFING

This dish was created as a stuffing, but it can be served as a side dish or a main vegetarian course. Here are three suggestions for using it as stuffing. Your creativity is the limit. Enjoy a flavorful, nutritious, and healthy meal!

2	ears of corn grilled with leaves on and the kernels cut off of them
6	chiles poblanos grilled, peeled, and deseeded. Deveining is optional.
8	squash grilled whole
1	tomato, chopped
½	onion, chopped
2	cloves garlic, minced

1 to 2 serrano chiles, chopped (optional)

Salt to taste

Vegetable oil

Cut the poblanos into strips. Sauté them with the corn kernels in a pan.

Add the tomato, onion, garlic, chiles, and the salt. Reserve the squash.

Grilled Milpa Vegetables Stuffing. Photograph by José C. Marmolejo.

Grilling the milpa harvest. Photograph by José C. Marmolejo.

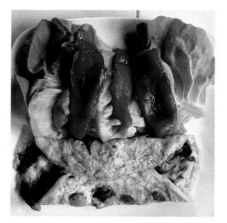

Grilled Milpa Vegetables Omelet.
Photograph by José C. Marmolejo.

Grilled Calabacitas Stuffed with Corn
and Poblano Strips. Photograph by José C.
Marmolejo.

Calabacitas Asadas Rellenas de Granos de Maíz y Rajas de Poblano
GRILLED CALABACITAS STUFFED WITH CORN AND POBLANO STRIPS

You may add two slices of Monterey Jack cheese if so desired.

Cut the 4 squash into halves, remove the seeds, and fill with the stuffing.

Add cheese (optional), heat and serve. Reserve the leftovers.

YIELD 2 Servings   HEAT LEVEL Hot

Tacos Vegetarianos
SOFT VEGETARIAN TACOS

You will need 6 corn or flour tortillas.

Chop the remaining four squash and mix with the stuffing leftovers.

On heated tortillas, add the stuffing hot and serve folded or rolled.

These tacos will be good at any time of day or night. After making the tacos you still will have enough stuffing for an omelet!

YIELD 2 Servings   HEAT LEVEL Hot

Omelet de Verduras Asadas
GRILLED VEGETABLE OMELET

You will need 4 beaten eggs and butter. Salt to taste. Two slices of Monterey Jack cheese (optional).

Put the eggs on a buttered pan and add a layer of the stuffing leftovers.

After flipping the omelet add the cheese. Once the cheese is melted, roll or fold and serve. Enjoy!

YIELD 2 Servings   HEAT LEVEL Hot

PART TWO

RECIPES

4 }} Small Bites

Appetizers are a Mexican tradition. In fact, eating between meals is not only allowed, it's encouraged. Some of the best foods we have ever eaten in Mexico have been appetizers that are essentially street foods. In no other place in the world have we ever seen such luscious tropical fruits, tangy popsicles, savory empanadas, or fresh fish tacos than in Mexico's little street stands, all manned by friendly cooks. In Mexico and Spain there are at least four terms in Spanish for appetizers and snacks, so to understand their differences, why not ask a Mexican? According to José, they are:

Antojitos mexicanos literally means "little Mexican whims" and refers to a variety of small dishes that are not considered main dishes: *taquitos, gorditas, empanaditas*, etc. They could be a mid-morning snack, a side dish, or a light dinner. Unfortunately, today it seems like people love to stuff themselves with these foods, replacing real meals with low-cost, high-carb, high-fat (but spicy) street food.

Entremeses are finger foods from the Spanish tradition, like olives, prosciutto, sardines, *jamón serrano*, etc. served before lunch or dinner. This is not Mexican food, nor a Mexican food term, but some Mexican restaurants use this term on their menus.

Aperitivos are alcoholic drinks served before lunch and dinner that are supposed to stimulate the appetite.

Botanas are snacks from peanuts to chips and salsa to small pieces of cheese, ham, etc. They go along with an alcoholic drink before lunch or dinner.

Diana Kennedy expressed amazement at the variety of Mexican appetizers. In *The Cuisines of Mexico* (1972), she writes: "Without doubt the Mexicans are the most persistent noshers in the world; who wouldn't be, with such an endless variety of things to nibble on along the streets and in the marketplace. A whole book could be devoted to that alone. Even if you think you are not hungry you will be enticed, by the smell, the artistry with which the food is displayed, or just because it is something new to try, for Mexican cooks are among the most creative anywhere."

Mexican small bites. Photograph by Plateresca on iStock.

Most Mexican snack foods don't have recipes, let alone names, like slices of mango or pineapple that are sprinkled with red chile powder. Some are already prepared for you, like *chapulines* (fried grasshoppers). José explains: "If raising or cooking chapulines does not appeal to you, they can be found already cooked in Mexican markets and in some baseball stadiums in the United States as snacks. They come in different sizes and with different condiments: fried in olive oil with garlic; just with salt; with chile powder and lemon; or *au naturel*. The large ones can be added to an omelet; the small ones are best added to rice or pasta after the rice or pasta has been cooked; the ones salted with lime and pepper are the best companions to a double shot of mescal (with beer recommended as a chaser); and my favorite presentation: garlic and olive oil grasshoppers added to a guacamole taco." And then the snack becomes the appetizer.

After all, appetizers are, first and foremost, party foods and finger foods. We've assembled an impressive collection of both in this chapter; they are sure to give you a taste for taquitos or a craving for quesadillas. Sit back and enjoy this journey through the "little whims" of Mexico. We're certain you'll be up and cooking in no time!

Aros de Jalapeño con Queso de Chorizo
JALAPEÑO RINGS WITH CHORIZO CREAM CHEESE

Our friend Lula Bertrán, from Mexico City, credits the invention of this recipe to her husband, Alberto. "He likes onion rings," she told us. "One day while eating them he said, 'Why don't you do this with chiles?'" You can make these using poblano chiles, but you'll at least have to double the amounts for the batter and the cream cheese mixture. They will be much larger and much milder. Dave wrote this down as Lula prepared it in her kitchen for a sequence in the three-part chile documentary series that Dave and José worked on, Heat Up Your Life. The three-part series is available on YouTube.

2	cups water	½	teaspoon baking powder
4	large jalapeños, roasted, peeled, seeds and stems removed, cut into 1/4-inch rings	½	teaspoon salt
		½	cup milk
			Vegetable oil for deep frying
3	tablespoons vinegar	½	cup fried chorizo sausage
½	cup flour	½	cup cream cheese

Preheat the oven to 200 degrees F.

Place the water in a large saucepan. Heat the water on high until it boils.

Reduce the heat to a simmer, add the jalapeño rings and vinegar, and cook for 5 minutes. Remove from heat and cool. Drain the rings and pat dry.

Combine the flour, baking powder, salt, and milk in a bowl to make a batter.

Dip the rings into the batter and fry in hot oil until they are crisp and brown. Drain on paper towels.

Combine the chorizo with the cheese to make a paste. Fill the rings with the paste, warm in the oven, and serve hot.

Jalapeño Rings with Chorizo Cream Cheese. Photograph by Wes Naman. Work for hire. Sunbelt Archives.

NOTE *Use fresh red jalapeños in this dish for an eye-catching and sweeter finish.*

YIELD 4 servings   HEAT LEVEL Medium

This recipe for a dangerous dip features chipotle—the designer chile of the '90s beloved by today's chileheads worldwide.

Chipotle Chiles Cordobesa-Style.
Photograph by Polina Tankilevitch on Pexels.

4	cups water
4	dried chipotle chiles, seeds and stems removed
1	cup packed brown sugar
	Salt to taste
2	cups white wine vinegar
⅓	cup olive oil
4	pounds onion, chopped
1	head garlic, sectioned
½	teaspoon salt
¼	teaspoon thyme
¼	teaspoon oregano
1	bay leaf
1	cup sour cream
1	cup mayonnaise
1	tablespoon lemon juice
1	bag carrots (about 8) peeled and cut into sticks
1	stalk celery, cut into sticks

Place the water, chiles, brown sugar, and salt in a saucepan and heat on low until the chiles rehydrate and the skins are easily loosened.

Once the skins are removed, add the vinegar. Remove the pan from the heat and add the olive oil, onion, garlic, salt, thyme, oregano, and bay leaf.

Puree the onions/chiles mixture in a blender in batches.

In a small bowl, mix the pureed onions/chiles, sour cream, mayonnaise, and lemon juice together.

Serve with the carrot and celery sticks.

YIELD 10 to 12 servings   HEAT LEVEL Medium

Envueltos de Chiles Poblanos con Flores de Calabaza
POBLANO CHILE AND SQUASH BLOSSOM BURRITOS

These vegetarian burritos feature one of the most popular Mexican chiles, the poblano. Not surprisingly, the very best poblano chiles are grown in central Mexico. The heat level for this pungent pod ranges from mild to medium, depending on the growing conditions before it is picked. Choose the darkest colored poblanos, as they offer the best flavor.

8	poblano chiles, roasted and peeled, seeds and stems removed, cut into strips	18	small flour tortillas
3	large tomatoes, grilled	3	tablespoons chopped onion,
3	cloves garlic, peeled and chopped	½	cup shredded Monterey Jack cheese
8	squash blossoms, cleaned	1	avocado, pitted, halved, and chopped
1	tablespoon water	1	poblano chile, seeds and stem removed, grilled, and sliced lengthwise
⅓	cup vegetable oil		

In a skillet, add the chiles, tomatoes, garlic, and water, then sauté in the oil.

When the ingredients are cooked, stir in the squash blossoms, then remove the mixture from the stove and set aside.

In a separate skillet, heat the oil to hot and using tongs, quickly dip each tortilla into it for 3 seconds a side.

Remove the tortillas and drain them on paper towels.

Fill the tortillas with equal amounts of the blossom mixture and onion, then roll each one up and place on a platter.

Top the tortillas with your favorite salsa from chapter 2, garnished with cheese, avocados, and chile strips, and serve.

YIELD 18 rolls   HEAT LEVEL Medium

Poblano Chile and Squash Blossom Burritos.
Photograph by Tatyana Consaul on iStock.

Sonoran-Style Chile with Cheese.
Photograph by bhofack2 on iStock.

Chile con Queso Estilo Sonora   SONORAN-STYLE CHILE WITH CHEESE

Who could ask for a more perfect combination of chile and cheese? This recipe is a specialty of the state of Sonora, which has millions of acres of agricultural land developed along the coastal plains.

¼	stick butter
3	jalapeño chiles, seeds and stems removed, minced
5	poblano chiles, roasted, peeled, seeds and stems removed, chopped
1	medium onion, chopped
2	tomatoes, chopped
4	cloves garlic, finely chopped
¾	cup milk
	Salt and pepper to taste
1	cup grated Chihuahua cheese, or substitute mild cheddar
2	tablespoons cilantro, chopped

Melt the butter in a skillet and sauté the chiles, onion, tomatoes, and garlic until the onions are soft.

Next, add the milk, salt, and pepper. Let this mixture cook for a few minutes so that the flavors blend, then add the cheese, stirring well.

Remove the mixture from the heat and place it in a glass bowl.

Garnish with the cilantro. Serve with baked tortilla strips or tostadas for dipping.

YIELD 4 to 6 servings   HEAT LEVEL Medium

Flautas con Crema

This recipe was collected from Guanajuato, which was founded by the Spaniards more than four hundred years ago. This dish is also known as "disappearing tacos" since they vanish quickly when served at a party!

1	tablespoon chopped cilantro	¾	cup vegetable oil
1	large tomato, chopped	30	corn tortillas
½	onion, chopped	1 ¾	pounds beef or pork, grilled and shredded
6	serrano chiles, stems and seeds removed, chopped	1	cup sour cream
2	medium avocados, peeled, pitted, and mashed		Cream to taste
1	tablespoon lemon juice	1	small head lettuce, chopped

In a medium-sized mixing bowl, combine the cilantro, tomato, onion, chiles, avocados, and lemon juice and mix well.

In a heavy skillet, heat the oil and fry the tortillas for 3 seconds per side, then drain on paper towels.

Stuff the tortillas with the meat and roll.

Next, return the rolls to the skillet and fry until crisp.

In a small bowl, mix the sour cream and cream together until blended, then serve over the flautas, along with the tomato/chile mixture.

Top with chopped lettuce.

YIELD 30 flautas HEAT LEVEL Medium

Rolled Tacos with Cream Sauce. Photograph by Lloyd Blunk on Unsplash.

Quesadillas de Flor de Calabaza · SQUASH BLOSSOM QUESADILLAS

This recipe from Tlaxcala requires the use of a comal, which is a round, flat griddle on which tortillas are cooked. Traditional comales in Mexico are made of unglazed earthenware and used over an open fire. If you do not have a comal, an electric skillet will also work.

2 ⅓ cups cornmeal

Water as necessary

3 tablespoons vegetable oil

1 onion, chopped

2 cloves garlic, peeled and chopped

2 serrano chiles, seeds and stems removed, sliced

12 squash blossoms, cleaned

Epazote leaves to taste, chopped

Salt to taste

In a bowl, moisten the cornmeal with the water and 1 tablespoon of the oil until it reaches a thick, pasty consistency. Set aside.

In a skillet, heat the remaining oil and sauté the onion, garlic, chiles, squash blossoms, epazote, and salt, and set aside.

Using a tortilla press, form the masa into tortillas, and heat them on a comal; cook until done (about 3 minutes).

When all of the tortillas are cooked (you should have about eight), spread an equal portion of the squash blossom mixture over each tortilla.

Slice the tortillas into quarters and serve.

YIELD 32 slices   HEAT LEVEL Medium

Squash Blossom Quesadillas. Photograph by bonchan on iStock.

Nuevo León's Green Quesadillas. Photograph by allakranı on iStock.

Quesadillas Verdes de Nuevo León NUEVO LEÓN'S GREEN QUESADILLAS

These quesadillas earned their name from the poblanos that are cooked with the masa. This recipe is a favorite in the state of Nuevo León.

1	onion, finely chopped
2	tablespoons vegetable oil
2	pounds pork ribs, baked, and meat cut off the bones
3	tomatoes, grilled and peeled
5	small poblano chiles, stems and seeds removed, grilled, and peeled
½	cup cream
1 ⅓	cups corn masa
½	teaspoon baking powder
1	cup wheat flour
1	teaspoon salt
	Salt and pepper to taste
	Vegetable oil for frying

In a large skillet, fry the onions in 2 tablespoons oil until soft.

Add the rib meat and tomatoes, and cook over medium heat until the tomatoes liquefy.

Season with salt and pepper and set aside.

In a medium bowl, mix the chiles with the cream. Add the masa, baking powder, flour, and salt. Mix well.

Break the masa into eight small sections and roll out each on a floured surface.

Place a small amount of the pork mixture in each one, then fold over to form the semicircular quesadillas and fry in oil in an electric skillet until done.

YIELD 8 quesadillas HEAT LEVEL Mild

Chilaquiles Caprichosos, a la Cerveza WHIMSICAL BEER CASSEROLE

This recipe from Michoacán is perfect for just about any party, as it incorporates beer, one of the best-known party beverages on earth. Although Negra Modelo is our favorite, there are more than twenty varieties of beer brewed in Mexico, all of which are the perfect accompaniment to any of the hot and spicy foods in this book.

⅓	cup vegetable oil		1	cup chopped tomato
12	tortillas		12	ounces Mexican dark beer
1	chicken breast, cooked, boned, and shredded		3	eggs
			1	cup heavy cream
3	serrano chiles, seeds and stems, chopped			Salt and pepper to taste
			1	cup grated mild cheddar cheese

Preheat the oven to 350 degrees F.

Heat the oil in a skillet and using tongs, fry the tortillas for 3 seconds per side, and drain them on paper towels. Place them in a 9-by-13-inch baking dish.

Cover the tortillas with the shredded chicken and set aside.

In a large bowl, mix the chiles with the tomato, beer, eggs, cream, salt, and pepper.

Pour this mixture over the tortillas and bake for 30 minutes or until done.

Sprinkle with grated cheddar cheese and serve.

YIELD 6 to 8 servings   HEAT LEVEL Medium

Whimsical Beer Casserole.
Photograph by Robi_J on iStock.

Avocado Salad. Photograph by Nikodem Nijaki. Creative Commons
Attribution-Share Alike 3.0 Unported license on Wikimedia Commons.

Ensalada de Guacamole

AVOCADO SALAD

*A native of the tropics, the avocado flourishes in the balmy weather of Mexico.
Although avocados have earned a reputation for being high in fat, a half of one
avocado has only 138 calories and is chock-full of vitamin C. Also, more than 75
percent of the fat in avocados is unsaturated, which means it's good fat.*

½ small onion, finely chopped

2 serrano chiles, seeds and stems removed, minced

1 teaspoon minced cilantro

¼ teaspoon salt

2 medium avocados

1 large tomato, chopped

1 tablespoon cilantro, chopped

2 teaspoons lemon juice

Using a mortar and pestle, grind together the onions, serranos, cilantro, and salt until it resembles a paste, then set aside.

Next, cut the avocados in half, remove the pits, and scoop out the flesh into a separate bowl.

Add the paste to the avocado and mash together with a fork. Add the tomato, cilantro, and lemon juice, mixing to a thick, smooth consistency.

Serve immediately in small bowls with tostadas.

YIELD 4 servings HEAT LEVEL Medium

White and Black Taquitos. Photograph by FakirNL. Creative Commons Attribution-Share Alike 4.0 International license, Wikimedia Commons.

Taquitos Blancos y Negros WHITE AND BLACK TAQUITOS

This recipe from the coastal city of Veracruz is often served with a variety of dipping sauces. Why not serve yours with some of the scintillating sauces from chapter 2?

¼	cup butter
2	ears corn, shucked, cleaned, and kernels removed
½	onion, chopped
2	jalapeño chiles, seeds and stems removed, chopped

1	pound black beans, cooked and mashed
½	cup vegetable oil
20	corn tortillas
2	cups grated mild Cheddar cheese
2	cups cream

In a large saucepan, heat the butter and fry the corn until done.

Add the onion, jalapeños, and beans, and cook until the moisture is almost gone. Set aside.

Heat the oil in a skillet and fry the tortillas for 3 seconds per side. Drain on paper towels.

Stuff the tortillas with the corn and bean mixture, then place them in a baking dish.

Add the grated cheese and cream, cover, and bake at 300 degrees F for 10 minutes, or until the cheese has melted.

YIELD 8 to 10 servings   HEAT LEVEL Mild

~~~~~~

Chiles Rellenos

The chile that is most commonly stuffed in Mexican cuisine is the poblano, shown here in a statue honoring the pod at the Exposición Artística on Avenida Paseo de la Reforma in Mexico City.

Few food ingredients are as versatile as chiles, and few dishes are as versatile as chiles rellenos. José grew up loving roasted, cheese-stuffed poblanos; the kind that are rolled on wheat flour, dipped in a beaten eggs mix, fried in vegetable oil, and covered with *caldillo*—a light tomato sauce. It was always a treat with the implicit risk of a spicy sting as heat level was often inconsistent even in the same pepper variety due to genetic variability.

One of the most creative forms of Mexican cooking is stuffing chiles. The immense variety of chiles in Mexico, and the vast choice of meats, cheeses, vegetables, and mushrooms available, makes this cooking option a heaven for cooks and chileheads alike.

Notwithstanding the fact that the most popular chiles rellenos in Mexico are poblanos stuffed with ground beef or cheese—and *chiles en nogada*, a September specialty—a regional map of chiles rellenos could be easily created.

Chiles güeros rellenos de camarón are popular in Jalisco. The northern states use New Mexican and poblano varieties. In the lower central part of Mexico—the Bajío region—*chiles de chorro*, a variety between the poblano and the Anaheim, are stuffed with ground beef, cheese, or beans, battered, fried, and covered with caldillo. In Oaxaca *chiles de agua* and pasillas oaxaqueños—a smoked variety found only there—are the norm. Both very hot but flavorful; they are often stuffed with vegetables aside from beef and *quesillo*—a typical Oaxacan cheese. In the Isthmus of Tehuantepec chipotles are stuffed with plantain, potatoes, pineapple, raisins, and nuts. They are a real treat. In the fall Puebla offers the famous *chiles en nogada*, but year-round ancho and pasilla chiles are stuffed with ground or shredded beef or cheese.

In central Mexico anchos are stuffed with a mixture of vegetables—corn kernels, squash, carrots, and squash blossoms among other vegetables. Mexico City offers everything; however, anchos stuffed with shrimp or a mix of sea-

Statue honoring the poblano chile at the Exposición Artística on Avenida Paseo de la Reforma, Mexico City. Photograph by Juan Carlos Fonseca Mata. Creative Commons Attribution-Share Alike 4.0 International license, Wikimedia Commons.

food are popular and served cold. Xalapa, Veracruz, home of the jalapeños, has in its markets special piles of big ones selected for stuffing. Big chipotles are also selected in Xalapa for this noble purpose. In the Yucatán Peninsula, xcatics are very popular stuffed with Gouda cheese or fried baby shark covered with "kool" sauce—a white sauce that reminds one of a bechamel, made of poultry stock, flour, whole olives, and capers, and epazote—the only American ingredient. This is a sauce originally used for *queso relleno*, a Yucatecan specialty.

As you can tell, traveling in Mexico can be a rich chile adventure. Always ask for their typical regional dishes and if you wish, state that you are interested in the local chiles rellenos specialty. There is always something to be discovered, and you will not be disappointed.

José's friend Ricardo Muñoz-Zurita's style of traditional Mexican cuisine is reflected in the following two recipes for stuffed chiles that appear in his book, *Los Chiles Rellenos en México* (2009). He was nice enough to give them to José. The remaining recipes in this chapter are ones that we collected during our travels in Mexico.

DENIAL OF CHILE

"Chiles were as significant when they were absent as when they were present. The concepts, familiar to Europeans, of fasting and penance were widespread in Mesoamerica, and without exception the basic penance was to deny oneself salt and chile."

SOPHIE COE / *America's First Cuisines*, 1994

Chiles Anchos Capones Rellenos, Número Uno
STUFFED SEEDLESS ANCHO CHILES

The word capón *translates as "castrated," but in this case merely means seedless. Yes, dried chiles such as anchos and pasillas can be stuffed, but they must be softened in hot water first. They have an entirely different flavor than their greener, more vegetable-like fresh versions.*

10	ancho chiles		3	cups small green onions, without the green ends
1	quart hot water		1	cup pork lard or substitute vegetable oil
2	pounds *queso añejo* or Romano cheese, grated		¼	cup flour
8	cups chicken stock			Salt to taste

Stuffed Seedless Ancho Chiles.
Photograph by Dave DeWitt.

In a dry skillet, lightly toast the ancho chiles without burning them.

Soak the chiles for 5 minutes in hot water to soften them, then drain and dry them.

With a knife, make a slit in the side of each pod and deseed them. Stuff the chiles with the cheese and set aside. You can tie them to keep the stuffing from falling out if you wish.

Heat the chicken stock and boil the green onions for 3 minutes. Remove the onions from the stock and set both aside.

Heat the lard until lightly smoking. Fry the chiles on both sides, starting on the open side.

Remove the chiles from the oil and drain on paper towels.

Fry the green onions in the lard. Remove and set aside.

Add the flour to the lard and stir until completely mixed without letting the mixture turn brown. Pour the chicken stock in the pan and stir until no more lumps are seen.

Simmer the sauce to thicken for 5 minutes while stirring. Add the chiles and let simmer 2 more minutes. The sauce should be smooth, but not too thick. Add stock if necessary.

Serve the chiles immediately with some green onions on the side.

YIELD 8 to 10 servings   HEAT LEVEL Mild

Chipotles Rellenos de Plátano Macho
CHIPOTLE CHILES STUFFED WITH PLANTAIN

The final result of this stuffed chile botana is the pleasantly contrasting flavors of the sweet stuffing, the smoky chiles, and the tangy vinaigrette. Piloncillo is unrefined, dark brown sugar that is sold in Mexico in cone shapes, and you can purchase it in Latin American markets or online.

1	quart water
¼	cup piloncillo substitute brown sugar
30	large dried chiles chipotles (morita-type recommended)
1	tablespoon sugar
1	teaspoon salt
¼	cup cider vinegar
¾	cup olive oil
½	teaspoon freshly ground black pepper
¼	cup corn oil
1	cup finely chopped onion

1	teaspoon finely chopped garlic
1	cup peeled, seeded, and chopped tomato
2	cups cubed plantain (¼-inch cubes)
¼	cup of grated piloncillo or brown sugar
5	ounces fresh goat cheese
2	cups of flour
½	teaspoon salt
7	eggs, whites and yolks separated
2	cups corn oil
	Mixed lettuce

In a pot, combine the water with the piloncillo or brown sugar and bring to a boil until the sugar is completely dissolved. Turn off the flame, add the chiles, and soak for 20 minutes until soft.

Make a small slit in the chiles, remove the seeds and veins carefully, and let the chiles drain. Set them aside.

To make the vinaigrette, combine the sugar, salt, vinegar, olive oil, and pepper in a jar and shake well. Set aside.

Heat the corn oil in a skillet and sauté the onion and garlic. Add the tomatoes and simmer for 15 minutes.

Stir in the plantains and the piloncillo or brown sugar and simmer until the plantains are completely cooked.

Simmer, stirring well, until a soft paste of all the ingredients has been obtained.

Remove from the stove, mix with the cheese, and stuff the chiles chipotles.

Roll the stuffed chiles in the flour and salt, then shake off the excess flour.

Beat the egg whites until stiff, add yolks, and beat until a batter forms.

Heat the 2 cups corn oil in a heavy pot, dip the chiles in the batter, then fry them quickly until they are a light golden brown.

Serve one or two chiles on a bed of mixed lettuce with the vinaigrette over the top.

YIELD 15 servings as a salad or appetizer.

HEAT LEVEL Medium

Close-up of the *morita*-type of chipotle. Photograph by Armando Olivo Martín del Campo. Creative Commons Attribution-Share Alike 4.0 International license, Wikimedia Commons.

Bean and Cheese Chiles Anchos Rellenos. Photograph by Alejandro Linares Garcia. Creative Commons Attribution-Share Alike 4.0 International license, Wikimedia Commons.

Chiles Anchos Rellenos de Frijoles con Queso, Número Dos
BEAN AND CHEESE CHILES ANCHOS RELLENOS

Here is another variation on stuffed anchos. Since anchos are so mild, we've added some serranos to spice up this particular dish.

6	large ancho chile peppers
	Boiling water
1 ½	cups refried beans
½	onion finely chopped
2	cloves garlic finely chopped

2	serrano chiles, seeds and stems removed, minced
1	tablespoon vegetable oil for frying
12	ounces Monterey Jack or cream cheese
	Salt to taste

Carefully make a side cut on the anchos and remove the seeds and veins, then rinse them.

Dip the chiles in boiling water for 1 minute. Remove them, drain, and reserve them.

In a pan, splash about a tablespoon of vegetable oil and sauté the onion, garlic, and serrano.

Add the beans and salt. Refry for 3 minutes, then stuff the mixture into the chiles, and add the cheese. Heat the stuffed peppers in the oven and serve with your favorite sauce from chapter 2.

YIELD 6 servings   HEAT LEVEL Medium

Poblanos Rellenos de Cordero con Caldillo

LAMB-STUFFED POBLANOS RELLENOS WITH CALDILLO

This C. rellenos recipe is unusual because it has no cheese in it, and the meat used is lamb, not beef chicken, or goat. Lamb is more commonly used in barbacoa or birria from Jalisco, rather than in chiles rellenos, but this recipe is very tasty no matter what meat is used.

FOR THE CALDILLO

3   medium tomatoes

½   onion

1   clove garlic

1   serrano chile, seeds and stem removed

1   pinch fine herbs

     Vegetable oil

     Salt to taste

FOR THE RELLENOS

6   poblano chiles

1   pound ground lamb

     Vegetable oil

½   onion finely chopped

1   clove garlic finely chopped

1   ounce raisins

1   ounce almonds, chopped

     Salt to taste

To make the caldillo, place all ingredients in a skillet and roast over high heat, taking care not to burn them.

Transfer the roasted ingredients to a blender and process to a thick sauce.

Cook the sauce in a pan with little oil for 5 minutes, then set aside.

To make the rellenos: using tongs, roast the poblanos directly over coals or an open flame until they blister.

Immediately place them in a plastic bag and wait until they cool off.

Open them carefully with a sharp knife and rinse the peppers while removing the burnt skin, seeds, and veins. Drain and reserve them.

Brown the lamb in a pan with a little oil, then add the onion, garlic, and salt, and sauté for 3 minutes.

Lamb-Stuffed Poblanos Rellenos with Caldillo. Photograph by José C. Marmolejo.

Next, add the raisins and almonds. Keep the heat low for another 5 minutes.

Stuff the chiles and place them on plates.

Cover them with the caldillo and serve.

YIELD 6 servings   HEAT LEVEL Medium

Cheese-Stuffed
Manzano Chiles.
Photograph by
José C. Marmolejo.

Chiles Manzano Rellenos de Queso
CHEESE-STUFFED MANZANO CHILES

The red rocoto *chiles resemble miniature apples, so they are nicknamed* manzano.
The yellow rocotos are nicknamed canario, *or "canary." They are* Capsicum
pubescens—*the only species of chile with black seeds. Also, they are very hot.*

12	manzano chiles
	Boiling water
8	ounces cream cheese
8	ounces ricotta cheese
1	sprig chopped fresh cilantro leaves

Rinse the manzanos and using tongs, dip them in boiling water for 1 minute.

After they cool off, cut the crowns off the chiles and remove the seeds and veins. In a bowl, mix the cheeses with the cilantro. Add the salt.

Stuff the chiles with the cheese mix and place them in the refrigerator for one hour.

They can be served cold or oven warm.

YIELD 6 servings   HEAT LEVEL Hot

The use of chipotle chiles in this recipe from Sinaloa adds a smoky dimension to the taste of the crab. We recommend the meat from freshly cooked crab legs, but if it is unavailable, good-quality canned crab meat can be substituted. But nothing beats fresh crab!

4	tomatoes, roasted, peeled, and chopped		2	cups cooked, shredded crab meat
1	cup chopped onion		½	cup minced onion
½	cup chicken broth		1	teaspoon dried Mexican oregano; or 2 teaspoons fresh, minced
½	cup water		2	tomatoes, peeled, deseeded, and chopped
3	chipotle chiles in adobo sauce (available in cans), diced			2 to 3 tablespoons chicken broth
½	teaspoon salt		½	cup flour
¼	teaspoon freshly ground black pepper		3	egg whites, stiffly beaten
8	green chiles (poblanos or New Mexican), roasted, peeled, and seeds removed		1 ½	cups corn oil

To make the salsa, put the tomatoes, chopped onion, chicken broth, water, chipotle chiles, salt, and pepper in a small saucepan.

Bring the mixture to a boil, then lower the heat and allow the mixture to simmer while you stuff the chiles.

In a small bowl, mix together the crab, onion, oregano, and tomatoes. If the mixture seems dry, add 1 tablespoon of the chicken stock at a time.

Stuff the chiles with this mixture. Dredge the stuffed chiles in the flour, dip them into the egg whites, and then deep fry them in the oil for 2 minutes per side, or until golden brown.

Drain them on paper towels.

Arrange the rellenos on a warm dinner plate and top with the warm salsa.

YIELD 4 servings   HEAT LEVEL Medium

Chiles Anchos Rellenos, Número Tres

STUFFED ANCHO CHILES, THIRD VERSION

Ancho chiles are stuffed again, this time topped with a tomatillo salsa. However, be careful to choose anchos that are fairly fresh. Look for pods that are still bendable and whose aroma can be detected through their packaging.

FOR THE SALSA

¼ cup vegetable oil

4 tomatillos, finely chopped

½ cup water

2 onions, finely chopped

¼ teaspoon dried Mexican oregano

2 tablespoons chopped cilantro

FOR THE STUFFED CHILES

4 cups water

6 large ancho chiles, stems and seeds removed

13 ounces of aged cheese, such as Romano, sliced into 6 equal pieces

5 tablespoons butter

½ cup vegetable oil

6 tortillas

6 eggs, scrambled

1 head lettuce, shredded or chopped

1 avocado, peeled, pitted, and sliced

7 ounces cheddar cheese, grated

To prepare the salsa, heat the oil in a saucepan and fry the onion. Then add the tomatillos, water, oregano, and cilantro. Let the mixture cook on high heat until the tomatillos are fully cooked, then set aside.

To prepare the chiles, pour the water into a large saucepan and bring to a boil. Place the chiles in the boiling water for 2 minutes to rehydrate them. Drain the chiles and carefully pat them dry on paper towels.

Fill each chile with a slice of cheese and set aside. In a large skillet, melt the butter over medium heat, then add the oil, and turn the heat on high. Brown the chiles in the butter-oil mixture. Once they are browned, remove them from the oil, drain them on a paper towel, and place them on a platter.

Briefly dip the tortillas in the hot oil and place them on a separate plate. Place one chile on top of each tortilla, then top each with a spoonful of salsa and egg.

Decorate the plates with the lettuce, avocado slices, and grated cheese.

YIELD 4 to 6 servings   HEAT LEVEL Medium

Stuffed Ancho Chiles, Third Version.
Photograph by José C. Marmolejo.

Shrimp-Stuffed Chiles. Photograph by Dave DeWitt.

Chiles Rellenos con Camarones

SHRIMP-STUFFED CHILES

This rellenos recipe from Veracruz makes a very sophisticated presentation. The unique combination of ingredients, from slightly salty to herbal to spicy, transforms the flavor of the shrimp. Serve this with a rice dish from chapter 10.

FOR THE RELLENOS

2	pounds fresh shrimp, peeled and cleaned
	Water to cover
1 ¼	cups chopped onion
3	cloves garlic, minced
2	tablespoons olive oil
⅓	cup chopped green olives
2	serrano chiles, stems and seeds removed, minced
½	cup minced parsley

3	tablespoons capers
½	teaspoon oregano
8	New Mexican green chiles, roasted, peeled, and seeds removed

FOR THE SALSA

2	tablespoons olive oil
1	pound peeled, deseeded, chopped tomatoes (about 4 1/2 cups)
1	clove garlic, minced
½	cup chopped onion
1	tablespoon tequila

Place the shrimp in a saucepan, cover with water, add a cup of the chopped onion, one-third of the minced garlic, and bring the mixture to a boil. Turn down the heat and simmer for 2 minutes.

Remove the shrimp and chop them coarsely. Reserve 1 cup of the shrimp broth.

Heat the olive oil in a large skillet and sauté the remaining onion and garlic for 1 minute. Add the green olives, serrano chiles, parsley, capers, oregano, and reserved shrimp, and sauté for 30 seconds.

Stuff the poblano chiles with this mixture, place in an oiled baking dish, and set aside.

To make the salsa, heat the olive oil in a large saucepan, add the tomatoes, garlic, and onion, and sauté for 2 minutes, adding enough of the reserved shrimp broth to give the salsa a heavy pouring consistency.

Stir in the tequila and sauté for 30 seconds.

Pour the sauce over the stuffed chiles, cover the mixture with foil, and bake at 325 degrees F for 15 minutes, or until the rellenos are hot.

YIELD 4 servings   HEAT LEVEL Medium

Chiles Rellenos de Aguacate   AVOCADO-STUFFED CHILES

These tasty rellenos from Zacatecas can be served at room temperature or slightly chilled. Try serving them at a buffet; the entree could be a spicy meat or chicken entree from chapter 7 or 8.

3	large, ripe avocados, peeled and pitted	¾	cup grated queso blanco cheese, or substitute Monterey Jack
2	teaspoons fresh lemon juice	3	tablespoons olive oil
1	teaspoon fresh lime juice	6	poblano chiles, roasted, peeled, seeds and stems removed, left whole
½	teaspoon salt		
¼	teaspoon freshly ground black whole pepper		
¼	cup minced onion	6	tablespoons sour cream

In a ceramic or Pyrex bowl, coarsely chop the avocados; next, add the citrus juices, salt, pepper, onion, cheese, and olive oil and mix well with the avocados. Stuff the avocado mixture into the chiles; arrange the stuffed chiles on a platter and cover each chile with the sour cream. Serve at room temperature.

YIELD 6 servings   HEAT LEVEL Mild

Preparing the avocado. Photograph by Louis Hansel on Unsplash.

Squash blossom. Photograph by AllieKF.
Creative Commons Attribution 2.0
Generic license, Wikimedia Commons.

Chiles Rellenos de Verduras

VEGETABLE RELLENOS

Squash blossoms are a common ingredient in many Mexican recipes. Check with a Latin American market in your area; if it doesn't carry them, you can probably special order them. The flavor of the blossoms is exquisite. The heat of this recipe is mild, so serve it with one of the spicier fish or meat entrees.

2	tablespoons butter
2	tablespoons vegetable oil
1	cup coarsely chopped carrots
1	cup chopped onion
3	cups chopped chayote squash, or substitute zucchini
½	cup fresh corn kernels
1	cup chopped squash blossoms
½	teaspoon salt
¼	teaspoon freshly ground black pepper
1	cup milk
½	cup grated queso blanco cheese, or substitute Monterey Jack
10	poblano chiles, roasted, peeled, seeds and stems removed
⅔	cup cream

Heat the butter and oil in a saucepan and add the carrots, onion, squash, and corn and sauté for 2 minutes.

Add the squash blossoms, salt, and black pepper and sauté until the pan is almost dry.

Add the milk, bring the mixture to a boil, reduce the heat to a simmer, and simmer until the mixture has thickened, about 4 to 5 minutes.

Stir in the cheese and remove the pan from the heat.

Using a teaspoon, stuff the chiles with the cooked squash mixture.

Arrange the stuffed chiles on a warmed serving platter and drizzle 1 tablespoon of cream over each chile. Serve warm.

YIELD 5 to 10 servings   HEAT Level Mild

Chiles Rellenos de Mariscos

SEAFOOD-STUFFED POBLANO CHILES

The state of Quintana Roo has become popular, along with the rest of the Yucatán Peninsula, for both its Mayan ruins and delicious seafood. The use of habanero chiles in this recipe is also very typical of the area. The suggested seafood is a combination of fish, crab, and shrimp. To make the white sauce, melt 2 tablespoons butter in a small saucepan, mix in 2 tablespoons flour and one cup milk. Heat and reduce the sauce, stirring constantly.

3	tablespoons corn oil		1	whole egg and 1 egg white, beaten
1	pound mixed seafood, cleaned and chopped		¾	cup flour
2	cloves garlic, finely chopped			Vegetable oil for frying
½	teaspoon salt		2	tablespoons vegetable oil
¼	teaspoon freshly ground black pepper		1	cup chopped onion
½	teaspoon dried Mexican oregano		1	habanero chile, seeds and stems removed, minced
3	tablespoons finely chopped cilantro		1	xcatic chile, seeds and stems removed, minced; or substitute yellow wax hot
3	tablespoons white sauce			
6	poblano chiles, roasted and peeled, seeds removed		4	cups peeled, deseeded, chopped tomatoes

In a pan, heat the oil and sauté the seafood; add the garlic, salt, black pepper, oregano, and cilantro and simmer until the seafood is cooked, about 2 minutes.

Remove the skillet from the heat and stir in the white sauce to bind the ingredients. Add more white sauce, if necessary. Using a small spoon, stuff the seafood mixture into the chiles.

Dredge the chiles in the flour, dip them into the beaten egg mixture, and fry in the hot oil for 2 minutes on each side.

Drain them on paper towels and place them on a heated platter.

Heat the 2 tablespoons of oil in a medium skillet and sauté the onion, habanero, and xcatic chiles for 1 minute.

Add the tomatoes and cook the sauce for 2 minutes over a low heat.

Spoon the sauce over the rellenos and serve.

YIELD 3 servings   HEAT LEVEL Hot

Ripe poblano pod ready for stuffing. Photograph by Harald Zoschke. Used with permission.

Classic chicken stock ingredients. Photograph by Wes Naman.
Work for hire. Sunbelt Archives.

5 }} Seasoned Soups and Stews

Today, soups in Mexico come in a variety of colors, consistencies, and combinations, and if you are Mexican or a resident of Mexico, it is unthinkable not to have at least one bowl a day. However, soup is not even mentioned by the early Spanish historians and chroniclers; the closest mention is of the thick stews (*guisados*) that the Indians cooked in their large, clay ollas. Food historians believe that the soup course was introduced by the French or other European influences.

The traditional *comida* starts with a *sopa* (soup) course, followed by a *sopa seca* (dry soup)—a starchy dish containing rice, macaroni, noodles, or tortillas and served between the starter soup and the entrée. There is an unbelievable variety of soups—from delicious clear broths (consommés) to soups thick with vegetables to hearty meat soups and stews that are literally a meal in themselves. The herbs and chiles, used judiciously and creatively, work together to really get one's taste buds working overtime.

Even though our first soup recipes call for vegetables and chiles—no meat—the basis for these (and others to follow) is a good chicken stock (*caldo de pollo*). So, get out your stockpot and make a few gallons of rich chicken stock, freeze it, and you will be well on your way to creating excellent Mexican soups.

Thanks to W. C. Longacre for sharing this recipe with us. He perfected it when he owned W. C.'s Mountain Road Café in Albuquerque, and it became the basis for many of his superb soups.

There are no chiles in this stock, as the cook will be adding them while making the soup. However, you could add some red chile sauce to this stock and create a spicy consommé.

1	(4-to-5-pound) roasting hen, free-range if possible	4	cloves garlic
		1	bunch parsley, washed
1	gallon water	1½	teaspoons peppercorns
½	tablespoon salt	1	large carrot, cut in half
4	whole bay leaves	1	celery stalk, including leaves
1	medium onion, cut in half		

To prepare the chicken, set it on a cutting board. With the flat side of a cleaver, press down on the breast until you hear the bone break. Turn on its side and with the dull side of the cleaver, hit the drumstick at the midpoint one time with enough force to crack the bone. Do the same to the wing. Turn the hen on the other side and repeat.

Turn the hen with the breast down and strike the backbone perpendicularly twice, each about a third of the way in from each side, to crack the back. (Breaking the chicken bones releases marrow into the stock, which adds more flavor.)

In a large stockpot, combine the water, salt, bay leaves, onion, garlic, parsley, peppercorns, carrot, and celery and bring to a boil. Add the chicken and boil, uncovered, for 1 to 1 ¼ hours, adding more water to keep the chicken covered. Skim off any foam that rises.

To test the chicken for doneness, pull on one of the legs. It should separate without force at the joint and there should not be any visible blood. Do not overcook the chicken.

Remove the chicken and save for other recipes in this book. Strain the stock and reserve. For a clearer stock, line the strainer with cheesecloth. Chill the stock in the freezer until the fat congeals, then remove it with a spoon.

YIELD About 1 gallon

Aguachile stored in a bottle. Photograph by Sergio Salvador.
Work for hire. Sunbelt Archives.

Aguachile

CHILE WATER

This recipe comes from our friend and guide to the north of Mexico, Antonio Heras, who says it is one of the most basic chiltepín dishes known and is prepared only in the state of Sinaloa, where the chiltepines produce fruit all year long. This simple soup is served in mountain villages, and everyone makes his or her own in a soup bowl. Alternately, the aguachile *can be stored in a bottle for a week to increase its pungency and then put into a bowl with the other ingredients.*

6	chiltepínes (or more to taste), crushed
	Pinch of Mexican oregano
	Pinch of salt
1	garlic clove, peeled and chopped
¼	ripe tomato, diced
	Boiling water

Add all of the ingredients, except the water, to a large soup bowl and mix together.

Next, add the boiling water to the mixture until the desired consistency has been reached, and mash everything together with a large spoon.

An alternate method calls for storing water with chiltepínes in a bottle for a week to increase the heat level of the aguachile, then it is boiled and transferred to a bowl with the other ingredients.

YIELD 1 serving or more   HEAT LEVEL Medium

Chile Strips Soup.
Photograph by Aneta Pawlik
on Unsplash.

Consommé de Rajas

CHILE STRIPS SOUP

This soup from Michoacán is spicy and clean to the palate and is good to serve at a dinner party when richer foods will follow the soup course.

2	tablespoons vegetable oil		1	teaspoon salt
1	cup chopped onion		2	quarts chicken broth
2	cloves garlic, peeled and minced		2	teaspoons flour
1	cup chopped tomatillos		½	cup warm water
6	poblano chiles, roasted and peeled, seeds and stems removed, cut into strips			

Heat the oil in a large saucepan; add the onion and sauté for 1 minute.

Next, add the garlic and tomatillos and sauté for 3 minutes.

Add the chile strips and salt and continue to sauté for 2 more minutes.

Pour in the broth and bring the mixture to a boil, reduce the heat, and simmer for 5 minutes.

With a fork, mix the flour into the ½ cup warm water. Pour this through a fine sieve into the simmering soup and stir until the ingredients are blended.

Simmer for 5 minutes. Serve hot, garnished with an Italian parsley leaf.

YIELD 4–6 servings   HEAT LEVEL Mild

Sopa de Chiles Poblanos

This chile soup from Veracruz has a kind of smooth, easy heat, and the addition of the evaporated milk adds a touch of richness. Serve the soup with a salad from chapter 10 for a light lunch or dinner.

6	poblano chiles, roasted, peeled, seeds and stems removed
¼	onion
3	cloves garlic, peeled
1 ½	cups water

1	can evaporated milk
2	beef bouillon cubes
1	cup water
1	tablespoon sweet (unsalted) butter
4	croutons

Puree the chiles, onion, and garlic in a blender with ½ cup of the water.

Pour this mixture into a small saucepan, add the milk, and heat slowly.

Dissolve the bouillon cubes in 1 cup of boiling water and add to the chile-milk mixture.

Stir in the butter and simmer for 5 minutes, taking care that it does not boil.

Heat the oil in a small saucepan and fry the tortillas until they are crisp and then drain, or you can substitute tortilla chips.

Ladle the soup into warmed bowls and top with the croutons.

YIELD 4 servings   HEAT LEVEL Mild

Poblano Chile Soup.
Photograph by Zai Aragon
on iStock.

Since this soup from Veracruz is light, serve it as a first course for a large dinner. The combination of squash and corn is very common in Mexican cuisine as well as in parts of the American Southwest. Any summer squash will work in this soup.

2	tablespoons butter
2	tablespoons vegetable oil
1	pound zucchini squash, cubed
1	cup chopped onion
3	poblano chiles, roasted, peeled, seeds and stems removed, diced
1	cup chopped tomato
1	cup whole corn kernels
½	teaspoon salt
1	quart chicken stock
½	pound crumbled queso fresco, or substitute feta cheese (see note)

Zucchinis for Summer Squash Soup.
Photograph by Angele on Pexels.

Heat the butter and the oil in a casserole pot; add the squash and the onion and sauté for 2 minutes, stirring often.

Add the chiles, tomatoes, corn, salt, and chicken stock and bring to a boil.

Reduce the heat to a simmer, cover, and cook for 30 minutes, or until the squash is tender.

Stir in the cheese and serve.

NOTE *Look for Cacique brand cheese in the grocery store; it is a US company that manufactures Mexican-style cheeses.*

YIELD 5 servings   HEAT LEVEL Mild

Sopa Simple de Aguacate Estilo Querétaro
EASY AVOCADO SOUP, QUERÉTARO STYLE

Since the avocado tree is native to tropical America, it is only fitting that we include a recipe that showcases its delicate taste. The preferred variety for this soup is the criollo, which is mashed with its skin on to impart a slight anise flavor.

3	criollo avocados	1	teaspoon salt
1 ½	quarts rich homemade chicken broth	1	cup half-and-half
2	serrano chiles, seeds and stems removed		*Garnish*: Splashes of sour cream

If you are using criollo avocados, do not peel them. Simply wash them, cut them in half, and remove the pits.

Place the avocados in a blender along with 2 cups of the chicken broth, the chiles, and salt, and puree.

(If you are using rough-skinned avocados, peel and split them, discard the pits, put them in a blender with 3 whole anise seeds and 2 cups of the chicken stock, the chiles, and salt, and puree.)

Pour the remaining broth into a medium-sized saucepan, heat just to the boiling point, add the pureed avocado mixture, the cream, and heat through. Serve in warm soup bowls and garnish with the sour cream.

YIELD 5 servings   HEAT LEVEL Medium

Easy Avocado Soup, Querétaro Style. Photograph by Sedaeva on iStock.

Chickpea Soup with Chipotles. Photograph by Zeleno on iStock.

Crema de Garbanzo con Chiles Chipotles
CHICKPEA SOUP WITH CHIPOTLES

Chickpeas, also known as garbanzo beans, have a mild, nutty flavor that is enhanced by the addition of chiles, chicken broth, and cream in this creamed soup from Sinaloa.

2 ½	cups cooked chickpeas (garbanzos)	¾	cup minced onion
4	cups chicken stock	1	teaspoon salt
2	chipotle chiles in adobo sauce	1	cup half-and-half
1	tomato, roasted and peeled	*Garnish*: ½ cup reserved whole
2	tablespoons vegetable oil		chickpeas, divided

Reserve ½ cup of the chickpeas. Place the remaining chickpeas in a blender with 2 cups of the chicken stock, the chiles, and the tomato and chop for 10 seconds.

Heat the oil in a small saucepan and sauté the onion for 2 minutes.

Add the chickpea mixture from the blender, the reserved ½ cup of coarsely chopped chickpeas, the salt and pepper, and the remaining 2 cups of chicken stock.

Bring the mixture to a low boil, reduce the heat, add the half-and-half cream, and heat for 5 minutes. Do not let it boil.

Serve hot, and garnish each serving with some of the whole chickpeas.

YIELD 4 servings   HEAT LEVEL Medium

Xonequi SPINACH AND BLACK BEAN SOUP GARNISHED WITH AVOCADO

*This soup from Veracruz is spicy and substantial and can be a meal in itself.
The spinach, beans, chiles, and avocado add a unique flavor and texture.*

5	dry chipotle chiles, seeds and stems removed	2	pounds fresh spinach, cleaned and coarsely chopped
2	ancho chiles, seeds and stems removed	2	cups rich homemade chicken stock
1	onion, cut into eighths	2	cups cooked and drained black beans
2	cloves garlic, peeled	1	teaspoon salt
2	cups water	¾	cup chopped cilantro
2	tablespoons vegetable oil		*Garnish*: Chopped avocado.
6	tablespoons butter		

Lightly toast the chiles in a skillet for 2 to 3 minutes, but do not let them burn.

Place the chiles in a blender with the onion, garlic, and 1 cup of water; chop coarsely and reserve.

Heat the oil and 2 tablespoons of the butter in a large casserole pot and pour in the chile mixture. Sauté this mixture for 10 minutes over low heat.

Bring the remaining cup of water to a boil in a saucepan, add the spinach, and cook for 1 minute.

Pour the spinach and the cooking water into the simmering chile mixture. Add the chicken stock and beans, and salt to taste; bring this mixture to a low boil, then reduce to a simmer.

Mix the remaining butter into the masa, add the salt, and the chopped cilantro.

Serve the soup hot and garnish with the chopped avocado and a little cilantro.

YIELD 6 servings   HEAT LEVEL Hot

Spinach and Black Bean Soup Garnished with Avocado. Photograph by Bhofack2 on iStock.

Sopa de Tortilla con Chiles Pasilla
TORTILLA SOUP WITH PASILLA CHILES

The only constant in this basic recipe from Chihuahua is the broth; all of the other ingredients—and there are many—may vary, depending on what's available and the cook's mood. The garnishes vary, too; it's all part of the fun of making and eating this soup!

4	pasilla chiles, seeds and stems removed
	Water as needed
4	quarts rich homemade chicken broth
3	large tomatoes, peeled
2	onions, quartered
2	cloves garlic, peeled
1	teaspoon salt
¼	cup fresh cilantro
2	tablespoons vegetable oil
½	cup cream
3	dozen corn tortillas, cut into ¼-inch strips, fried and drained, or substitute 4 cups broken tortilla chips

Tear the four pasilla chiles into strips, cover with hot water, and rehydrate for 15 minutes.

Heat the chicken broth in a large casserole almost to the boiling point; reduce the heat to a simmer while you prepare the rest of the ingredients.

Put the rehydrated chiles in a blender, add the tomatoes, onions, garlic, salt, and cilantro and puree for 10 seconds.

Heat the oil in a small skillet, add the blended chile mixture, and sauté for 5 minutes.

Stir this mixture into the simmering chicken broth, add cream, cover, and simmer for 30 minutes.

Cut the tortillas into strips. Fry the strips and distribute them to eight bowls.

Tortilla Soup with Pasilla Chiles.
Photograph by Enio DePaz on iStock.

Ladle the simmering chicken-chile stock over the strips.

YIELD 8 servings   HEAT LEVEL Medium

Caldo Puchero

POT OF VEGETABLE STEW WITH CHILTEPÍNES

Like most stews, this one takes a while to cook, about 4 hours. It is interesting because it contains a number of pre-Columbian ingredients, namely chiltepínes, corn, squash, potatoes, and beans. The spicy heat can be adjusted by adding or subtracting chiltepínes.

15	chiltepínes, or more or fewer to taste
1	beef soup bone with marrow
1	cup dried garbanzo beans
4	cloves garlic, peeled and 3 stalks celery, cut into 1-inch chopped pieces
	Water as needed
1	acorn or butternut squash, peeled, seeds removed, and cut into 1-inch cubes
3	ears corn, cut into 2-inch rounds
4	carrots, cut into 1-inch rounds

1	head cabbage, quartered
3	green New Mexican chiles, roasted, peeled, seeds and stems removed, chopped
2	large potatoes or sweet potatoes, cut into 1-inch cubes
3	zucchini squash, cut into 1-inch cubes
1	onion, quartered
2	cups fresh string beans, cut into 1-inch pieces

Garnish: Small bunch of parsley

In a large soup kettle combine the chiltepínes, soup bone, beans, garlic, and twice as much water as needed to cover. Bring to a boil, reduce the heat, and simmer for 1 hour.

Pot of Vegetable Stew with Chiltepínes. Photograph by KabVisio on iStock.

Add the acorn or butternut squash, the corn, and more water to cover 1 inch above vegetables and simmer for 30 minutes.

Add the carrots and cabbage and simmer for 15 minutes.

Add the green chiles, celery, and potatoes and cook for 30 minutes.

Add the zucchini, onion, and string beans and simmer for 30 to 45 minutes, until everything is tender.

When ready to serve, remove the kettle from the heat, remove the soup bone, and add the cilantro.

YIELD 8 servings   HEAT LEVEL Hot

Some cooks make this soup with mashed beans and a garnish of crumbled chiles; however, in this recipe eggs are added, and chile is both in the soup and crumbled on top as a garnish.

3	ancho chiles, seeds and stem removed
2	guajillo chiles, seeds and stems removed, or substitute New Mexican
1	pound tomatoes, peeled and deseeded
1	teaspoon Mexican oregano
1	large onion, quartered
2	large cloves garlic, peeled

10	corn tortillas, cut into 1/4-inch strips, fried, and drained
4	eggs, beaten
2	quarts chicken broth

Garnishes:

¼	cup minced onion
½	cup grated Cotija cheese, or substitute Parmesan

Cut the chiles in half; put half of them in a blender and set the other half aside.

Coarsely crush the chiles in the blender, pour into a bowl, and reserve.

Add the remaining chiles to the blender along with the tomatoes, oregano, onion, and garlic and puree the mixture and reserve.

Put the fried tortilla strips in a large bowl, cover with the beaten eggs, and toss.

Add the pureed chile tomato mixture and lightly toss with the tortillas.

Pour the broth into a large saucepan and bring to a boil. Reduce the heat to a simmer, and after 1 minute add the egg-coated tortilla-chile mixture. Simmer for 3 minutes.

Serve in soup bowls and garnish with the chopped chiles, minced onion, and grated cheese.

YIELD 8 servings HEAT LEVEL Medium

Tarascan Soup.
Photograph by
Warren Price
on iStock.

Sonoran Cheese Soup.
Photograph by Bhofack2
on iStock.

Caldo de Queso Estilo Sonora

SONORAN CHEESE SOUP

Simple ingredients are combined to make this quick recipe from northern Mexico. Sonoran Cheese Soup is a flavorful soup, as well as being attractive to serve, with its flecks of red and green. Mexican cheeses are increasingly available in supermarkets, especially in the western parts of the United States.

2	tablespoons vegetable oil
1	tablespoon butter
4	cups cubed potatoes
1	large onion, sliced
2	scallions, sliced
1	cup peeled, chopped tomatoes
1	teaspoon salt
4	poblano chiles, roasted, peeled, seeds and stems removed, diced
1	quart milk at room temperature
2	cups warm water
3	cups grated Chihuahua cheese, or substitute mild cheddar
	Warm tortillas

Heat the oil and butter in a large skillet and sauté the potatoes for 7 minutes, until they start to brown. Add more oil if they start to stick. Add the onion and scallions and sauté for 1 minute.

Transfer the sautéed mixture to a medium-sized saucepan, stir in the tomatoes, salt, chiles, and milk and bring the mixture to a low boil; add the water and stir.

When the mixture is hot, but not boiling, turn off the heat and stir in the cheese.

Serve immediately with warm tortillas.

YIELD 6 servings   HEAT LEVEL Mild

Rancho Aurora Garlic
Soup. Photograph by
ALLEKO on iStock.

Sopa de Ajo Estilo Rancho Aurora   RANCHO AURORA GARLIC SOUP

This recipe is from Susana Trilling. This recipe calls for hoja santa, an herb with large, fragrant leaves. Look for it in Latin markets or grow it in your garden. If unavailable, watercress is the best substitute.

2	heads garlic, peeled and thinly sliced
½	tablespoon butter
½	tablespoon olive oil
1	large hoja santa leaf, cut into strips, or 1 bunch fresh watercress, chopped
6	cups chicken stock
1	cup cooked, shredded chicken
1	de árbol chile, left whole, or substitute a large piquín
	Salt and white pepper to taste
3	bay leaves
1	bunch celery leaves, coarsely chopped
20	toasted bread cubes
20	cubes *queso oaxaqueño*, or substitute another melting cheese

Garnish: grated Parmesan cheese

Sauté the garlic in the butter and olive oil in a soup pot until slightly browned, about 10 minutes.

Add the hoja santa and sauté for 30 seconds. Add the stock, chile, salt, pepper, and bay leaves and simmer for half an hour.

Remove the bay leaves and chile. Add the celery just before serving.

Place 5 cubes of bread and cheese in four individual soup bowls and ladle in the soup.

Sprinkle with Parmesan cheese and serve.

YIELD 4 servings   HEAT LEVEL Mild

Sopa de Lima

Even though this soup, and its many variations, is served all over Mexico, it is believed to have originated in Yucatán; it is Yucatán that provides the small, yellow, tart limes that give sopa de lima its particularly good flavor.

1	3-pound chicken, cut into 6 pieces
3	quarts water
2	teaspoons salt
3	cloves garlic, peeled and chopped
1	tablespoon Mexican oregano
3	tablespoons chopped cilantro
1 ½	cups chopped onion
2	tablespoons vegetable oil

4	serrano or jalapeño chiles, seeds and stems removed, chopped
1 ½	cups chopped tomatoes
8	Key limes or small Mexican limes, thinly sliced

Garnishes:

½	cup minced cilantro
8	corn tortillas, cut into eighths, fried and drained; or substitute tortilla chips

Lime Soup. Photograph by Wes Naman. Work for hire. Sunbelt Archives.

Wash the chicken pieces and place them in a large casserole; add the water, salt, garlic, oregano, the 3 tablespoons of cilantro, and 1 cup of the onion and bring the mixture to a boil, skimming the foam from the top. Reduce the heat to a simmer, cover, and simmer for 30 minutes.

Remove the chicken from the cooking liquid and set aside.

Strain the broth through several thicknesses of cheesecloth, return the strained broth to a clean pot, bring to a boil, reduce the heat to a light rolling boil, and cook uncovered for 20 minutes to reduce the stock.

Remove the skin and bones from the chicken and discard. Coarsely shred the meat and reserve.

Heat the oil in a small skillet, add the remaining ½ cup onion, chiles, and tomatoes, and sauté for 3 minutes.

When the stock has reduced, stir in the shredded chicken, the sautéed tomato-chile mixture, and simmer for 15 minutes.

Serve the soup in large, heated soup bowls and garnish with tortilla chips and minced cilantro.

YIELD 8 to 10 servings   HEAT LEVEL Medium

THERE'S A FUNGUS IN MEXICO CITY!

"Perhaps the most innovative dish I tried in my Mexican *haute cuisine* tastings was the *cuitlacoche* ravioli at Isadora, a dish that symbolized the philosophical flaw in the Mexican haute cuisine's culinary theory. To read the words 'cuitla-coche' ravioli' on a menu is to marvel at the stunning combination of cultures, languages, and cooking styles. *Cuitlacoche* is a highly-prized fungus that grows on ears of corn under certain wet conditions. The combination of the quintessential delicacy of the Indo-American corn culture and the semolina pasta of the European wheat cuisine made for interesting symbolism, but boring eating. *Cuitlacoche* has an incredibly smooth texture that needs the foil of something crisp. It might have worked on toast points, but the ravioli was too close in texture to the filling. The result was a gloppy mouthful of cheap pasta that masked the exotic flavor and texture of the delicate *cuitlacoche*."

ROBB WALSH / *Chile Pepper*, 1992

~~~~~~~~~~~~~~~~~~~~~~~~~~~~~

Tacos

Ask any Mexican where can you find some good tacos, and you just earned a free, fifteen-minute rant on tacos. It seems impossible for two individuals to agree on the subject. Every Mexican has a different opinion, his or hers is the most important, and he or she will defend it until you interrupt and say, "I've got to go." You will be left dizzy with more information about tacos than you bargained for.

But every once in a while you will run into a real taco expert. You can identify him right away. It's easy. After you ask him, "Where can I find some good tacos?" he will answer you with another question: "What kind would you like to have? *Al pastor*? Barbacoa? *Carnitas*? *De guisado*? *De canasta*?" Oh boy! Now you're in trouble.

One afternoon, José was at his friend Juan José´s butcher shop, and business was dead slow. The two butchers and José were just chatting idly when it occurred to José to ask for the best tacos around, since they were suppliers to a bunch of *taquerías*, and they should've known—so he thought. Well, the discussion lasted almost an hour; no one could agree with anyone else's opinion, and as it turned out, everyone knew a place—far away of course—where the tacos were worth the trip. Curiously enough, none of their recommendations were for any of their customers! The discussion turned into an ego game, a contest of descriptions intended to see the others salivate, and the one who described the experience better—and took the longest to finish his intervention—knew more than the rest and therefore would win the contest.

One beautiful thing about tacos in Mexico is the fact that whenever you're hungry, you can find a taco stand ready to serve you. It can be midday or midnight, but there's always a place to go and ease your hunger. Five in the morning? No problem, there will be one shop open where the crowd is a mix of intoxicated after-party animals in need to sober up and the early birds going to work who need to clock in at six with a full stomach.

The variety of tacos seems to be infinite. Once, José was hired to conduct a taco tour in Mexico City for a chef and a restaurateur from New York City. They were considering setting up a taco chain in the United States and wanted

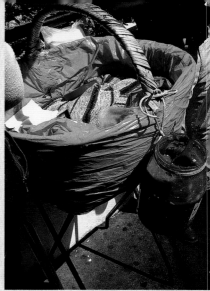

Taco sampler in Mexico City. Photograph
by Hana Brannigan from Pexels.

Popular tacos de canasta. Photograph
by José C. Marmolejo.

to know more about the subject. It seemed like a fun and easy task. The truth
is that it was difficult to decide where to start, what territory we should cover,
and how to make the best of what José thought four hours would be enough.
It turned out that they barely scratched the surface in the morning in La Merced market, concentrating on taco fillings. They took all afternoon to visit the
food stalls in the outskirts of Mexico City—they had to—in order to study
the wrappings: the different results that can be obtained between machine
and handmade tortillas; the different types of masa and mixes with industrial
and stone-ground corn flour; and the differences between fried, non-fried, and
semi-fried tortillas.

The only thing all tacos have in common is the tortilla. What goes inside
and the salsa on top of it—that's what makes the difference. The combinations
are infinite. We are referring to the countless types of tacos that can be found
in the streets of Mexico City—or more likely, on the sidewalks.

Often, foreign guests will ask José how you know what kind of tacos are
selling on the street without asking the vendor. "I'll teach you a few tricks," he
invariably responds, then he starts his dissertation with this phrase: "Think of
those golden arches you see from the distance." Then he continues, "We have,
in Mexico, many types of baskets, pots, pans, *cazuelas*, wooden and plastic boxes, etc. displayed on the street that let you know from a distance what kind of
tacos are being sold."

One of his favorite taco "signs" is the big basket—often on the back of a
bicycle—with a sky-blue plastic liner; no other color is used. It's a standard that

seems to be surreptitiously adopted by all *tacos de canasta* vendors. These guys have also adopted the same technique for displaying and dispensing the salsa: a reused commercial-size jar of mayonnaise hanging with a cord or wire from the side of the basket. By the way, *tacos de canasta* are the cheapest, greasiest, and most flavorful of mid-morning snacks. Chicharrón are José's favorites. And they're only six pesos each; that's three tacos for a bit less than a dollar.

Tacos al pastor will be available when you see a big chunk of red colored meat on a vertical grill from the distance—more often than not obstructing the sidewalk. Curiously enough, the technique—roasting on a vertical grill—was imported from the Middle East, and the pork was imported from Spain, but the seasoning on the meat is from the Yucatán Peninsula spiced up with chiles from the north of Mexico. These are the favorite tacos of all the foreigners José interviewed! They are quite affordable: eight pesos each and some places sell them "two for one"!

Another popular taco sign is a wooden box on top of a table (which is being slowly replaced by an orange plastic crate). It's hard to believe that you would sell some hot food out of a wooden box or plastic crate, but the fact is that lamb barbacoa, wrapped in agave leaves and cooked on coals in a pit or a wood-burning oven overnight, needs to be transported to the place of business. What better way than in a box or crate so long as it remains wrapped in the vegetable leaves and a piece of cloth?

Shepherd-Style Tacos for sale, a common sight on the streets in Mexico. Photograph by José C. Marmolejo.

Now, if you run into a big stainless steel frying pot that can be noticed from a distance because it's big, shiny, and has been placed ostensibly on a sidewalk, you are being welcomed to *tacos de carnitas de puerco*. The fact that the frying setup is obstructing the peaceful transit of pedestrians has a purpose. It's only a marketing trick: see, smell, purchase. Clever!

Once you have chosen the type of tacos you want to experience, other issues that are seldom addressed by Mexicans arise: the size of the tortillas and whether single or double tortilla tacos are offered. More is better, and it's not going to cost you more but will have an impact on the food cost for the *taquero*. Corn tortillas come in different sizes (between four and six inches in diameter). After an order of a few pounds, the *tortillería* master will adjust the machine to make the size and the amount the taquero requires.

This gives room for many combinations and possible cost cutting for the taquero. The smaller the tortilla, the less filling used. More tacos will be consumed, and if a double tortilla is provided you will feel satisfied at a lower food cost. Now, if you are nice to the taquero, and he gets to know and like you, he will throw an extra filling in at no charge. Needless to say, José has personally invested time and effort in getting to know a few taco masters. After José gets what he wants, he divides the filling in the two tortillas provided and makes himself two tacos for the price of one!

EARLY MEXICAN COOKBOOKS

1831 / *El Cocinero Mexicano* (The Mexican Cook), edited by Mariano Galván Rivera

1872 / *La Cocinera Poblana* (The Pueblo Cook), by Narciso Bassols

1893 / *El Libro de Cocina* (The Cookbook), by Eduardo Rodríguez y Cía

One way to get noticed—and liked—by the taquero is to ask for your tacos "light," in English, a term everybody understands nowadays. In José experience, this causes the taquero—as well as the patrons—to raise his head and eyebrows, which is José's cue to clarify: "one tortilla only!" It's a joke that makes everybody smile, since tacos are not considered "light" by anyone, and if you like tacos—like every Mexican does—you are not going to leave the taquería before you've stuffed yourself!

One fact to remember is that in Mexico there is no such thing as a taco shell, so all of the tacos in the following recipes will be soft. Note that the occasional, sparing use of lard in some of our recipes is unlikely to cause health problems.

Pork Tacos Michoacán-
Style. Photograph
by José C. Marmolejo.

115

FAMILY FAVORITES / TACOS

Tacos Carnitas de Puerco Estilo Michoacán

PORK TACOS MICHOACÁN-STYLE

2	pounds pork cut into 1-inch pieces		Water to cover
2	tablespoons lard	20	corn tortillas
2	cups orange juice		
1	bouquet garni (small bundle of fine herbs)		*Garnishes:* Salsa from chapter 2, finely chopped onion mixed with minced cilantro.
2	tablespoons salt		

Brown the meat carefully in the lard in a deep cast iron skillet over medium heat. Add the orange juice, the herbs, and the salt. Add water just to cover the meat, bring it to a boil, and then simmer for about two hours stirring frequently.

Cooking time will vary depending on water and fat content of the meat but expect at least two hours on the fire. A slow cooker would do a nice job.

Serve chopped over warm soft tortillas, garnish with finely chopped onion and cilantro, and serve with a salsa from chapter 2.

YIELD 20 tacos

HEAT LEVEL Varies according to the salsa used

Tacos de Pescado con Salsa Verde de Aguacate
FISH TACOS WITH GREEN AVOCADO SAUCE

This recipe puts the versions of fish tacos served in Mexican restaurants in the United States to shame.

TACOS DE PESCADO
Fish Tacos

2	pounds white fish fillets
	Vegetable oil as needed
¼	medium sized onion, chopped
2	serrano chiles, seeds and stems removed, chopped
2	cloves garlic, minced
1	tomato, chopped
	Salt to taste
20	corn tortillas

TO MAKE THE *tacos de pescado*

Cut the fish in bite-sized chunks and sauté lightly in a skillet while adding the chopped onion and serranos.

Once the onion is translucent, add the garlic, and 1 minute later, add the tomato. Salt to taste and remove from fire after the tomato is cooked.

All cooking should take place in about 10 minutes.

Serve over warm tortillas and dress with the green salsa.

SALSA VERDE CON AGUACATE
Green Avocado Salsa

6	tomatillos
½	medium ear cooked corn
1	clove lightly roasted garlic
3–4	chiles serranos, seeds and stems removed
1–2	sprigs cilantro
1	medium avocado
	Salt to taste

TO MAKE THE *salsa verde con aguacate*

Using the "pulse" button in your blender or food processor mix the tomatillos, onion, serranos, half of the avocado, and half of the cilantro to a rough texture. We want to replicate a rustic salsa out of a molcajete. Place the mix in a bowl.

Cut the rest of the avocado into small cubes, roughly chop the cilantro, and throw both on top of the salsa.

Add to the tacos to taste.

YIELD 20 tacos   HEAT LEVEL Medium

Fish Tacos with Green Avocado Sauce. Photograph by José C. Marmolejo.

CUISINE ARTHROPODA

"Mexican cuisine has all the colors of the rainbow and even the food has exotic names: *escamole*s (ant's eggs), *acocile*s (tiny river shrimp), *chapuline*s (grasshoppers), *gusanos de maguey* (agave worm). Scorpions are eaten in the states of Durango—famous for its large, blond ones—and Sonora. They are fried and dipped in sauce and eaten. We take off the poison sac and stinger before frying."

BEATRIZ CUEVAS CANCINO / Unpublished manuscript, 1989

Typical salsa set up in a taquería. Photograph by José C. Marmolejo.

Beef Fajita Tacos with Chipotle Salsa. Photograph by José C. Marmolejo.

Yucatecan Pescadillas

Here's another version of fish tacos, this time from Yucatán. Serve these as appetizers.

½   cup vegetable oil

1   large onion, finely chopped

2   pounds large tomatoes, blanched and chopped

5   serrano chiles, seeds and stems removed, finely chopped

2 ½   pounds marlin (or your favorite fish), cut into chunks

Chopped cilantro to taste

1   teaspoon Mexican oregano

12   corn tortillas

¾   cup vegetable oil

1   lemon, cut into wedges

Salt and pepper to taste

Heat the ½ cup of oil in a skillet and sauté the onions, tomatoes, and chiles.

Add the fish, cilantro, oregano, salt, and pepper. Cook until the fish flakes, then set aside.

Warm the tortillas and stuff them with the fish mixture.

Heat ¾ cup of oil in a separate skillet. Fry the stuffed tortillas until light brown, or until they have achieved the desired texture.

Squeeze the lemon wedges over the fish in each taco and serve.

YIELD 12 tacos   HEAT LEVEL Medium

Tacos de Arrachera con Chipotle Salsa
BEEF FAJITA TACOS WITH CHIPOTLE SALSA

A Texas restaurateur went south of the border, discovered the proper method of preparing arrachera (skirt steak), stole the technique fair and square, and fajitas were born.

2   pounds beef skirt or flank steak

4   medium avocados

Salt to taste

20   tortillas

Chipotle Salsa

On a charcoal grill using mesquite or oak charcoal, cook the meat that has been salted to your taste over coals (avoid flames).

Once the meat is ready, remove and heat the tortillas on the grill. Slice the meat thinly across the grain and make tacos, adding slices of avocado.

Serve with the chipotle salsa from chapter 2. Cerveza improves this experience.

YIELD 20 tacos   HEAT LEVEL Hot

The method of cooking al pastor, *meaning "in the style of the shepherd," actually comes from Lebanon. It's inspired by Shawarma Lebanese immigrants who moved to Mexico in the early 1900s; they brought their famous technique of spit-roasted meat, primarily lamb, with them. This version is made with pork.*

FOR THE ADOBO

4	chiles guajillos, seeds and stems removed
2	chiles de árbol, seeds and stems removed
	Water as needed
½	onion
2	cloves garlic
1	pinch fine herbs
2	ounces achiote paste (available in Latin markets or online)
4	tablespoons white vinegar

	Juice of one orange
	Juice of one lemon
2	tablespoons chicken or vegetable broth
	Salt to taste
	Water from the boiled chiles, as needed

FOR THE GRILLING

2	pounds pork loin fillets marinated in the adobo
6	slices fresh pineapple
18	corn tortillas

Boil the chiles for 3 to 5 minutes in two cups of water. Reserve the chiles and the water.

Once the chiles have cooled, mix all adobo ingredients in a blender into a uniform thick sauce. You may use the water in which you boiled the chiles to help in the blender.

Marinate the meat with the adobo for at least a couple of hours in the refrigerator.

Set up your wood or charcoal or gas grill to low heat and grill the marinated pork fillets and the whole pineapple slices.

Heat the tortillas. Chop the cooked meat and pineapple and make yourself some tacos.

Garnish with fresh onion and cilantro, and with your favorite salsa from chapter 2.

YIELD 18 tacos   HEAT LEVEL Varies according to the salsa used

Shepherd-Style Tacos. Photograph by José C. Marmolejo.

Setup for Steak and Vegetable Tacos. Photograph by fortyforks on iStock.

Tacos de Alambre

STEAK AND VEGETABLE TACOS

These are beef and vegetables tacos prepared really quickly on a griddle or in a heavy pan. Warning: the aroma will make you think you are not cooking enough meat.

Vegetable oil

2 pounds sirloin steak cut into strips

1 onion, coarsely chopped

1 red bell pepper, chopped

1 green bell pepper chopped

3 to 6 chiles serranos, seeds and stems removed, chopped

2 cloves of garlic finely chopped

Salt to taste

18 corn tortillas

In a heavy pan, use a thin layer of oil to brown the meat on medium heat.

Add the onion, peppers and the chiles, and cook for 3 to 5 minutes.

Add the garlic and salt and cook for another 3 minutes.

Heat the tortillas, make yourself some tacos and enjoy!

YIELD 18 tacos   HEAT LEVEL Medium to hot

Chorizo Taco with Cheese.
Photograph by carlosrojas20
on iStock.

Tacos de Longaniza Con Queso

CHORIZO TACOS WITH CHEESE

Longaniza is a Mexican sausage and if it is tied into small portions is called chorizo. It can be found in Mexican butcher shops or supermarkets with Mexican ingredients sections. These tacos are very easy to prepare and work wonders for breakfast, lunch, or dinner.

Vegetable oil

1 pound longaniza or Mexican chorizo

½ onion, chopped

2 to 4 chiles serranos, chopped

Vegetable oil

12 tortillas

½ pound Monterey Jack cheese, grated

Using a heavy pan, add a thin layer of oil, and sauté the longaniza/chorizo breaking it into small pieces.

Add the onions and chiles and sauté for 3 more minutes.

On a griddle, heat the tortillas and add a layer of cheese. When the cheese begins to melt add the cooked longaniza/chorizo over the cheese.

Fold the tortilla into a taco and let it sit on the griddle for a couple of minutes and serve.

YIELD 12 tacos HEAT LEVEL Medium to hot

Tacos Rellenos de Camarón

SHRIMP TACOS

Since fresh shrimp is found in abundance, shrimp tacos are popular with locals and tourists alike on all the coasts of Mexico. They are sold as street food, as well as appearing on menus at the finest restaurants. Here is a particularly tasty taco treat from Campeche.

5	*ancho* chiles, seeds and stems removed
2	tomatoes, peeled and deseeded
1	onion, chopped
¼	teaspoon salt
	Vegetable oil, as needed to fry tortillas
18	corn tortillas
2	tablespoons olive oil
2	cups finely chopped shrimp
2	tomatoes, crushed
1	onion, finely chopped
1	habanero chile, seeds and stems removed, minced
1 ½	cups finely chopped, cooked potatoes
½	teaspoon salt
	Freshly ground black pepper to taste
2	cups thinly sliced onion, soaked in ½ cup vinegar
5	cups finely shredded lettuce

Place the ancho chiles, tomatoes, onion, and salt in a food processor and process until the mixture is a smooth puree. Set the mixture aside.

Heat the oil in a deep sided skillet. Dip each tortilla in the ancho chile mixture, fry it for 3 seconds on each side, then drain on paper towels. Place the tortillas on a platter.

Heat the 2 tablespoons of olive oil in a medium skillet and add the shrimp, tomatoes, finely chopped onion, habanero chile, and potatoes. Lightly fry the mixture for 2 minutes, until the shrimp is cooked. Add the salt and pepper to taste. Stuff this mixture into the tortillas and roll up each tortilla.

Drain the onion-vinegar mixture thoroughly and sprinkle it over the tortillas, along with the shredded lettuce.

YIELD 6 servings   HEAT LEVEL Medium

123

FAMILY FAVORITES / TACOS

Shrimp Tacos. Photograph by Bhofack2 on iStock.

Grilling Pork Loin and vegetables on Skewers.

Photograph by José C. Marmolejo.

6 Outdoor Cooking
Barbacoa and Grilling

Barbacoa

Mostly unchallenged in the United States, "to barbecue" means "to cook outside," unless you face a purist from the Barbecue Belt. They will be anxious to start a discussion about what barbecue really is, but if you tell them about cooking meat "low and slow" over indirect flame you will get yourself a new friend.

Barbecue, a pre-Hispanic meat-cooking technique, can be traced on the American continent all the way back to the Mayans, who cooked wild boar and tapir in a pit. Mayans call this *pib*, meaning "hole." Today in the Yucatán Peninsula, pork is cooked in a pit more often than other meats, and *cochinita pibil*—meaning "female suckling pig cooked in a pit"—is the most representative dish of the region. Barbecue was also popular in the Caribbean islands during La Conquista and was carried north to the American continent by the Spaniards.

Barbacoa, as it is known today in Mexico, has as many variants as there are regions and cooks, but avoid telling people from the Yucatán Peninsula that cochinita pibil is a barbacoa; it will not be accepted, and it may disturb a friendship. With the meat, which could be beef in northern Mexico, mutton in central Mexico, or goat, armadillo, or iguana, in the south, plus a large variety of local herbs, spices, and chiles—all wrapped in agave or banana leaves—barbacoa is overwhelmingly diverse, with distinct and wonderful flavors owned by every region.

One of the most difficult things to accomplish in Mexican gastronomy is extracting a "cooking secret" from a traditional cook. Chefs and cooking professionals are always glad to share knowledge, the product of painful learning or long experience, but for people who inherited a recipe, method, or technique, that's another story. Jealousy prevails and society is thus denied many ancient food treasures.

As Mexicans do not know how to say no, your request to see, document, photograph, or film a gastronomic execution will end up in a "mañana" or "la semana que viene" response, which means most likely it will never happen. José, however, has been lucky enough—so he thought—to be allowed by neighbors

Heating the *pib* (or pit) for *barbacoa*. Photograph by José C. Marmolejo.

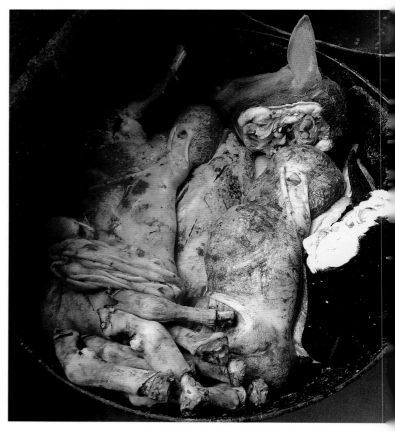

Marinating the meat.
Photograph by José C. Marmolejo.

to witness the preparation of barbacoa, a local family tradition. This didn't mean he would get all the secrets, because while they ask you to come at ten in the morning to watch the cooking project begin, when you arrive, they've already done all of the prepping! The next step—placing the meat in the pit—is at dusk, and you only get to witness how the pit is being lit. The rest of the day is spent watching the fire being maintained, and you are told there is nothing else interesting to see. The following day at dawn, the ritual calls for getting the meat out of the pit and make tacos. Done! Eat!

José arranged a visit to a second local barbacoa purveyor to verify the method and hopefully increase or complement his knowledge. That's how he got to see another procedure that was not exactly the same as the first one and left him with more questions than answers.

Since the pit-cooking technique is rather easy to understand and execute, his main interest was to decode the marinating or seasoning process. One family marinated the meat while the other seasoned it with a rub of herbs—avocado leaves included—and spices and chiles. The explanation he got from marinating was that the leftover marinade is added to water to be used for steaming, which results in a flavorful broth. In the version where the meat was seasoned with a rub, the steam also produces a broth but not as spicy or complex. He was told that seasoning a piece of meat to be cooked slowly has the purpose of preventing the meat from drying. The time and temperature of cooking results in the formation of an impervious crust that keeps the juices inside the meat, and after cooking the edible resulting membrane will serve also as a complement to the meat flavor. It is here that the difference between those two barbacoas resides.

Let's take a close look at the technique. It is basically the same as steaming meat inside of an oven, except that in pit cooking, the steamer is heated from all sides instead of over a direct flame. The cooking is uniform, at low temperature, and goes on for many hours—overnight to be precise. The meat absorbs the heat and releases its juices, which drip back into the liquid below with no place to go but back up in the form of steam, softening the tissues and keeping them moist. As the hours wear, the heat finds a way to dissipate at a slow speed, leaving meat, moisture, and juices converted into a wonderful concoction.

This could be achieved setting up a steamer inside a stove oven, but are you familiar with a slow cooker? Well, that being the case, let's use some banana leaves, wrap a seasoned piece of meat, and slow cook it overnight. That simple! Concerned about quantities? Check the recipe below, but be adventurous! Alter the herbs, spices, and chiles ad libitum. . . . Remember: it's your barbacoa, and you won't regret it!

Grilling

There must be grilling in José's genes. His attraction to fire goes back to his Boy Scout days and remains intact to this day. On weekends, when he spends a few hours outside playing with fire and food, he compares the experience to that of his dogs playing in the woods.

It is possible that cooking over an open fire started thousands of years ago with the *al pastor* technique: meat skewered on an inclined stick stuck in the ground. Sometime later, it was probably discovered that using a horizontally placed mesh—made out of green or wet sticks—was an easier and faster way to cook. Today we'll be dissecting "grilling"; the al pastor technique will have to wait.

We take it for granted. It makes so much sense, and it's so easy to use that we don't stop and think about the origin and evolution of the grill. What is the story behind that simple piece of cooking equipment that has evolved into the sophisticated grills we use today? No matter how simple or humble the grill we may have, they all basically do the same thing: hold the burning wood or charcoal separate from the food while allow the heat and flavor to pass through, improving texture, flavor, and digestibility. That little gadget, kept horizontally, gives us control over depth and speed of cooking by changing the distance between heat and food; it's the source of much pleasure and satisfaction and happiness but seldom gets any recognition. That's José's grill—a sublime invention.

We become knowledgeable about things that surround us, things we are raised with. In northern Mexico, the abundance of mesquite and cattle makes us prone to a diet based on *carne asada*, or "grilled beef." Any invitation for dinner at a house in a northern city today is bound to include carne asada. The menu may include *frijoles charros*, tortillas, guacamole, *queso fundido*, salsa, *totopos*, and with some luck, grilled vegetables or a salad, but that's pushing it to a kind of "gringo" menu, therefore subject to criticism.

The Spaniards brought cattle and their butchering method—cutting the meat lengthwise along the animal—to what is now Mexico. The British, however, introduced their butchering method to the United States: cutting across the bones (perpendicular to the length of the animal), producing what we know as steaks. While the Spaniards grilled the long boneless pieces of meat over fire, the British decided that the steaks should be cooked on a cast-iron skillet using butter, salt, and pepper. Climate contributes to cooking techniques' evolution, and humans decide where cooking takes place.

Salt and pepper—our European inheritance—have become such an unconscious habit that we find them in most recipes, and we don't question it.

José avoids black—or any other color of pepper—because in Mexico there are chiles. And many varieties of chiles, which provides an assortment of flavors and pungencies that pepper just cannot deliver. So, when cooking, José always replaces pepper with any ground or crushed dried chile he may have on hand. On special occasions, he grabs a few piquines harvested several years ago from his mother's backyard, from a bush that was planted by a bird sitting on a lemon tree. The bush prospered under the shade of the tree and a free supply of flavor and heat became available to the family. Now, with his mother deceased and house sold, he treasures those few piquines he still has, and uses them only on special occasions, those occasions when food decides to turn out superb.

Grilling meat in northern Mexico is a ritual—a long ritual. An opportunity to socialize, to play with fire, an excuse to have a tequila straight-up, chased by a *cerveza* or several, an occasion to show off your cooking skills—to feed the ego—and last but not least, to feed yourself a good piece of meat. The pleasure of consuming a good steak starts with the challenge of getting the fire started, perhaps with the secret personal challenge of using only one match and without the help of fluids—which add an undesired smell or flavor to food. It takes about thirty minutes to cook and eat a steak, but our carne asada ritual will last the whole afternoon, more often than not, well into the evening.

The journey starts with the search for the matches and wood or charcoal, only to realize there isn't enough of either or both, but we get started with a drink anyway because what is a Mexican function without a good dose of cerveza, tequila, and improvisation? And since no one is on time, it doesn't matter. Etiquette only mandates that you call to advise that you are running late—any excuse will work—but always ask if there's something else needed from the store. And there's always something needed from the store: matches, charcoal, ice, cigarettes, peanuts, more beer, among other things. Now, if you are going to be more than one hour late, you can easily be forgiven if you arrive with a special bottle of tequila or mezcal that a friend or relative brought you from a distant place—the farther the better. An abundant number of smiles will be your welcoming committee.

Back to cooking. Here's what we are looking for: the heat of coals and the smoke of an aromatic wood "burning hot"—like mesquite, oak, hickory, maple, pecan, or any fruit tree—going up through a steel mesh and cooking and impregnating the meat with desirable flavors and aromas. Simple.

Initial flames can be used to roast vegetables. Poblano chiles are my favorite grilling veggies (and the aroma is simply addictive), but any fresh chiles, bell peppers, onions, garlic, squash, and eggplant are also wonderful choices. José usually grills a week's supply of vegetables.

Vegetables before grilling.
Photograph by José C. Marmolejo.

Vegetables after gilling.
Photograph by José C. Marmolejo.

After the flames are gone, he'll have red hot coals that are ideal to sear the meat—salt and chile sprinkled on both sides—for about a minute on each side. His grilling meat is never more than one-inch thick; thicker cuts go to the smoker, but that's another story. Once searing is accomplished, he moves the coals to one side of the grill and finishes cooking the steak in the low-heat area, a few minutes each side, and medium rare is the goal. Time to eat! Buen provecho! And remember: in northern Mexico, grilling time is not just for weekends anymore, grill time is all the time. *Salud!*

THE PUZZLE OF MEXICAN CHILES

"In Oaxaca I met a lot of unfamiliar chiles, both dried red and green, and one beautiful fresh chile in its ripe, red stage, like a pimiento. Of course, I bought some of each kind and took them back to Mexico City, where I could cook with them and see if the flavor was sufficiently distinctive for me to decide if it had no substitute. All this point up the problem with chiles. One has to learn to recognize them first by their looks and only later by their names, as these vary from place to place."

ELISABETH LAMBERT ORTIZ / *The Complete Book of Mexican Cooking*, 1968

Barbacoa Casera

This is a fast-track version of a traditional dish that is widely found in Mexico. Now, can we do barbacoa at home without having to dig a hole in the yard? The answer is yes. Obviously, it will not be the same, but then again none of the barbacoas are the same, right? Well, it is possible to produce a wonderful barbacoa at home and it will be your barbacoa, like nobody else's. And you don't want to be like anybody else anyway.

2	pounds beef, lamb, or pork (a small roast)
2	ounces ground guajillo chiles or chiles de árbol
3	cloves garlic
	Fine herbs to taste
	Ground cumin to taste
	Ground black pepper to taste
¼	cup vegetable oil
	Salt to taste
	Banana leaves to wrap the meat
	Cotton cord or thick string

In a mortar or blender grind the chiles, garlic, herbs, spices, and salt with the oil into a paste. Rub the mixture generously over the meat. Toast the banana leaves lightly until they become pliable. Take care not to break them. Wrap the meat with the banana leaves and tie it with the cord. Place the wrapped meat in a slow cooker or a steamer and cook at the lowest temperature for 8 to 10 hours. Let it cool and open carefully. Enjoy!

YIELD 4 servings   HEAT LEVEL Medium

Homemade Barbacoa. Photograph by José C. Marmolejo.

The quintessential salsa for barbacoa, made with pulque (fermented agave juice), is not easily found anymore. Here is a version that can be made with beer.

20	pasilla chiles
4	cloves garlic
1	onion, sliced
¼	cup vegetable oil
1	bottle flat Mexican beer
	Salt to taste

On a griddle, toast the pasillas until they are aromatic, turning them often along with the onion and garlic.

Allow the chiles to cool and remove the stems and seeds.

In a food processor or blender, puree the pasillas with the onion, garlic, oil, salt, and beer.

Transfer the mixture to a bowl. Check and adjust for salt.

YIELD About 3 cups   HEAT LEVEL Medium

Drunken Sauce. Photograph
by BWFolsom on iStock.

Salt and dry chiles seasoning. Photograph by José C. Marmolejo.

Polvo Para Carne Asada

CARNE ASADA RUB

A simple but effective seasoning that's good for all meats going on the grill.

2 tablespoons ground chile de árbol	1 tablespoon sea salt
2 tablespoons crushed chile guajillo	Vegetable oil

In a mortar, crush the salt with the chiles to a uniform mix.

Rub the meat generously on both sides with the mix and let it rest for 12 hours refrigerated.

A few minutes before cooking, rub the meat gently with cooking oil in both sides. If more pungency is desired, increase the amount of chile de árbol powder.

YIELD ¼ cup   HEAT LEVEL Medium

This recipe was collected in Querétaro, where we were happy to find a Mexican recipe that is low in fat and high in flavor. This chicken is also wonderful cubed and served in tortillas, fajita style, with a sauce from chapter 2. Note that this recipe requires advance preparation.

2	cloves garlic, peeled
1	teaspoon dried Mexican oregano
6	ancho chiles, toasted, seeds and stems removed, chopped
3	chiles de àrbol, toasted, seeds and stems removed
3	cascabel chiles, toasted, seeds and stems removed
¾	cup apple cider vinegar

1	sour (Seville) orange, juiced; or substitute 1 orange and 1 lime
1	teaspoon Mexican oregano
2	cloves
½	teaspoon cumin
	Salt and pepper to taste
1	chicken, sectioned
	Lettuce leaves
	Avocado slices
	Tortillas

In a blender, combine the garlic, chiles, vinegar, oil, orange juice, oregano, cloves, cumin, salt, and pepper and process until it is thoroughly blended. Marinate the chicken in this mixture overnight.

Grill the chicken over hot coals or a medium gas flame until done. Or, bake uncovered in the oven at 400 degrees F for 40 minutes.

Serve with lettuce and avocados and warmed tortillas.

YIELD 4 to 6 servings   HEAT SCALE Medium

Grilled Chile-Chicken.
Photograph by palinchakjr on iStock.

7 More Spicy Meats

Carne (meat) plays an important role in the Mexican diet, with pork being the most favored and accessible variety by far. The Aztecs hunted wild peccaries, but it was the Spaniards who brought the domesticated pig to Mexico; they are credited with the popularity of pork, which has grown steadily since the introduction of pigs from the West Indies. Pigs that escaped from captivity multiplied on their own and became such nuisances that the Spanish passed laws to keep them off the streets. One quality that has certainly helped foster the pig's high profile is its willingness to eat just about anything, from garbage to grain. Literally no part of the pig is thrown away—the feet are pickled, the neck and tail are used to flavor soups, and the head is used in pozole; there are even uses for the snout!

Goats, another animal that will eat almost anything, also fared well in Mexico after their importation, but their meat was not prized as much as pork, lamb, or beef. Cattle herds began to double every two years but not because of their beef, but rather because there was a great demand back in Spain for their hides for making leather goods. Eventually, cattle ranching became most popular in the highlands of the central plateau that had been transformed into one immense grazing province. Free-range sheep were a problem because of over-grazing in the same region, turning agricultural land into near-deserts.

Mexican pig in market. Photograph by Rick Browne. Used with permission.

As one might expect, fencing the land, which became common by 1800, solved the problem as well as the incursion of livestock onto cultivated land. With so much meat available, and so many native chile peppers, a culinary collision was inevitable, as we see in the following recipes.

Ask any Mexican to name his or her favorite fruit, and chances are the answer will be el mango. *From spring until late summer, mangos are everywhere: stacked into symmetrical* montones *(mounds) in the markets, sold in the street on sticks, and sprinkled with red chile powder. Additionally, mangos are also used in cooking, especially in* la nueva cocina *(Mexican nouvelle cuisine), like this recipe. Serve this with one of the rice dishes in chapter 9.*

8	green guajillo chiles, roasted, peeled, seeds and stems removed, or substitute New Mexican chiles	¼	cup vinegar
	Pinch coriander seeds, roasted		Salt and pepper to taste
2	cloves garlic	4	pounds pork meat, cut into 1-inch cubes
1	tablespoon minced cilantro	4	ripe mangos, peeled, pitted, and cubed
1	pinch ground cumin	1	onion, sliced and separated
2	cloves, ground	6	radishes, sliced
1	cinnamon stick	1	pineapple slice, coarsely chopped
½	teaspoon fresh ginger, grated	1	head lettuce, shredded

In a food processor or heavy blender, combine the chiles, coriander, garlic, cilantro, cumin, cloves, cinnamon, ginger, and vinegar. Season with salt and pepper to taste and puree.

Place the pork in a baking dish and pour the chile mixture over the pork; top the entire mixture with the mango cubes.

Bake for about 1 hour at 275 degrees F or until done.

Garnish with the onion, radishes, sliced fruit, and lettuce.

YIELD 6 to 8 servings   HEAT LEVEL Medium

Cubed mango for the cubed pork.
Photograph by insjoy on iStock.

Pork Steaks with Pasilla Chiles. Photograph by gbh007 on iStock.

Bistec de Cerdo con Chiles Pasilla   PORK STEAKS WITH PASILLA CHILES

We collected this recipe in Zacatecas, which is also known as the "Pink City." The town received this name because of the pink sandstone used to build most of the historic homes and city buildings in the area. This simple recipe can be served with a salad and rice dish from chapter 9.

4   pasilla chiles, roasted, seeds and stems removed, and soaked in hot water

1   large clove garlic

1   teaspoon oregano

Vinegar to taste

1   teaspoon salt

8   pork steaks

Vegetable oil as needed for frying

Place the chiles, garlic, oregano, vinegar, and salt in a blender and blend until smooth.

Pound the steaks, cover with the chile sauce, and let them sit for about 2 hours.

Heat a little oil in a skillet and fry the steaks. Serve with *ensalada de guacamole*.

NOTE *Advance preparation required.*

YIELD 4 to 8 servings   HEAT LEVEL Medium

Carnero Asado con Jitomate y Chile
ROASTED BEEF WITH TOMATOES AND CHILE

This is the perfect fiesta food, in quantities large enough to offer a large helping to 20 or so guests. We suggest that you add a few tamales from "Family Favorites: Tamales" as well as some flan for dessert, and you'll have an authentic party straight from Mexico City.

2	5-pound rump roasts
	Water as needed
4	cups vinegar
3	ancho chiles, stems and seeds removed, toasted, rehydrated, and minced
3	poblano chiles, stems and seeds removed, roasted, peeled, and chopped
5	ripe tomatoes, chopped
1	head garlic, crushed and chopped
1	cup white wine

	Cloves to taste
	Cumin to taste
	Thyme to taste
	Marjoram to taste
1	bay leaf
	Oregano to taste
	Salt to taste
4	ounces ham, sliced
4	ounces bacon or salt pork, chopped
	Lemon juice to taste
1	large onion, sliced
40	tortillas

Place the beef in a large stockpot and cover with the water and vinegar. Add the chiles, tomatoes, garlic, wine, spices, and salt; let marinate for a few hours, covered, in the refrigerator.

Remove the meat from the pot and place it in a roasting dish, along with the strained ingredients from the pot, ladling the chiles over the roasts.

Place the ham and bacon on top of the roasts and insert a meat thermometer into the thickest part of the meat. Cook in the oven at 350 degrees F for 1 hour and 45 minutes, or until the meat thermometer reads 180 degrees F.

Remove from the oven and squirt lemon juice over the top of the roasts. Place the roast beef on a platter and cut into slices.

Serve with onion slices, tortillas, and the salsa of your choice from chapter 2.

NOTE *Advance preparation required.*

YIELD 20 servings   HEAT LEVEL Medium

Roast Beef. Photograph by Pixi on iStock.

Northern-Style Shredded Beef. Photograph by Bhofack2 on iStock.

Machaca Estilo Norteño

NORTHERN-STYLE SHREDDED BEEF

The word machaca *derives from the verb* machacar, *"to pound or crush," and that description of this meat dish is apt. The shredded meat, as made in Ciudad Juárez, is often used as a filling for burritos or chimichangas and is sometimes dried. Serve the meat wrapped in a flour tortilla along with shredded lettuce, chopped tomatoes, grated cheese, and sour cream, which will reduce the heat level.*

3 pound arm roast	1 cup chopped tomatoes
Water to cover	½ cup chopped onions
10 to 15 chiltepínes, crushed	2 cloves garlic, minced
1 ½ cups green New Mexican chile, roasted, peeled, with stems and seeds removed, and chopped	

Place the roast in a large pan and cover with water.

Bring to a boil, reduce the heat, cover, and simmer until tender and the meat starts to fall apart, about 3 or 4 hours. Check it periodically to make sure it doesn't burn, adding more water if necessary.

Remove the roast from the pan and remove the fat. Remove the broth from the pan, chill, and remove the fat.

Shred the roast with a fork. Return the shredded meat and the defatted broth to the pan, add the remaining ingredients, and simmer until the meat has absorbed all of the broth.

YIELD 6 to 8 servings   HEAT LEVEL Hot

Northern-Style Points of Beef. Photograph by gee1999 on iStock.

Puntas de Filete Estilo Norteño   NORTHERN-STYLE POINTS OF BEEF

Here is another northern Mexico specialty. Serve over plain white rice along with slices of mango and pineapple.

¼	cup corn oil	2	red bell peppers, sliced
½	cup olive oil	4	serrano chiles, stems and seeds removed, sliced into rings
1	large onion, sliced	6	beef fillets, cut into 1-inch wide points
2	cloves garlic, chopped		
1	green bell peppers, sliced		Salt and pepper to taste
1	yellow bell pepper, sliced		

Heat the oils in a skillet, then add the onion and fry until soft.

Add the garlic, bell peppers, and chiles and fry for another 5 minutes; then add the meat and salt and pepper to taste.

Cook until the bell peppers are soft, stirring constantly.

Serve with a bean dish from chapter 9.

YIELD 6 servings   HEAT LEVEL Medium

Filete con Salsa de Orégano

From Sinaloa, this recipe features Mexican oregano. Mexican oregano offers a much stronger flavor than Italian or Mediterranean oregano. It is Lippia graveolens, a species of flowering plant in the verbena family, while Mediterranean oregano is in the mint family.

- 2 tablespoons butter
- 3 tablespoons vegetable oil
- 2 pounds beef medallions
- 2 cups fresh Mexican oregano leaves, ground, or ⅓ cup dried
- 1 cup chicken broth
- 1 poblano chile, roasted, peeled, stem and seeds removed
- 1 cup cream
- 2 tablespoons minced onion
  Salt and pepper to taste
  Fresh Mexican oregano leaves for decoration

Heat 1 tablespoon butter and the oil in a skillet and cook the beef to taste. Once cooked, set aside and keep warm.

In a blender, combine the oregano leaves with the broth, chile, cream, and onion and puree.

Strain the mixture, then heat the remaining butter and cook the sauce for about 25 minutes, adding salt and pepper to taste, stirring constantly.

Serve the medallions on top of the sauce accompanied by roasted potatoes and a small green salad.

YIELD 6 servings   HEAT LEVEL Mild

Fillet in Oregano Sauce. Photograph by Максим Крысанов on iStock.

Chiles Anchos Encaramelados con Picadillo en Salsa de Aguacate

CARAMELIZED ANCHO CHILES WITH PICADILLO IN AVOCADO SAUCE

"This is one of my top creations regarding chiles," says Lula Bertrán. The key to this recipe is the absorption of the orange juice into the skin of the anchos, making the chiles soft enough to eat. Make sure you choose anchos that are still pliable; if they are hard as bricks, they will need to be steamed first. The presentation of the chiles is elegant on the light green avocado sauce.

THE CHILES

6	medium ancho chiles, stems left on, seeds removed
1 ½	cups orange juice
½	cup grated piloncillo, or substitute regular brown sugar or molasses
½	cup vinegar
1	teaspoon salt

THE PICADILLO

3	tablespoons vegetable oil
1	small onion, chopped fine
1	clove garlic, minced
½	pound ground beef
½	pound ground pork
¼	cup raisins
1	medium tomato, chopped
2	teaspoons minced cilantro
5	serrano chiles, seeds and stems removed, minced
½	teaspoon Mexican oregano
	Salt to taste

AVOCADO SAUCE

3	tomatillos, husks removed
2	tablespoons chopped onion
2	serrano chiles, seeds and stems removed, halved
1	clove garlic
1	tablespoon chopped cilantro
1	avocado, peeled
1	teaspoon lime juice
⅛	teaspoon sugar
½	teaspoon salt
½	cup half-and-half

TO MAKE THE CHILES

Take each ancho by the stem and, using scissors, cut a T-shaped incision that extends across the shoulders of the chile and about two-thirds down the pod. Carefully remove the seeds and membrane.

In a saucepan, bring the remaining ingredients to a boil.

Add the cleaned anchos and cook at a low boil for 15 minutes, turning once (carefully).

Remove from the heat and let cool. Remove the anchos, clean off any remaining seeds, and drain on paper towels.

TO MAKE THE PICADILLO

Heat the oil and sauté the onion and garlic.

Add the beef and pork, turn the heat to high, and brown thoroughly, stirring often.

Drain nearly all the fat and liquid from the meat mixture.

Add the remaining *picadillo* ingredients and cook over medium heat, uncovered, about 15 to 20 minutes.

TO MAKE THE AVOCADO SAUCE

Combine all of the sauce ingredients in a food processor and puree.

Add more half-and-half if necessary; the sauce should be just thin enough to pour.

Strain the sauce and heat in a saucepan, but do not boil.

To assemble dish carefully stuff the anchos with the picadillo and place each one on a plate.

Heat the plates in the oven or in the microwave. Drizzle the avocado sauce over each ancho, and serve.

YIELD 6 servings   HEAT LEVEL Medium

Picadillo to accompany the Caramelized Ancho Chiles. Photograph by athe75 on iStock.

Cabrito y Res con Chiles Anchos
BRAISED GOAT AND BEEF WITH ANCHO CHILES

Goat is often saved for celebrations in Mexico, such as a baptism or wedding. Baby goats, or kids as they are called, offer the most tender, succulent meat imaginable. This recipe from Nayarit includes beef and is flavored with ancho chiles. Serve it with the side dish of your choice from chapter 10.

5	ancho chiles, toasted, stems and seeds removed	½	cup vinegar
2	pounds tomatoes, chopped	½	cup dry red wine
1	pinch powdered ginger	2	bay leaves
8	black peppercorns	2	pounds goat meat, cut into 1-inch cubes
5	cloves garlic	2	pounds beef, cut into 1-inch cubes
½	teaspoon cumin		Tortillas
2	whole cloves		

Braised Goat and Beef with Ancho Chiles.
Photograph by Brett Hondow on iStock.

In a food processor or blender, combine the chiles, tomatoes, ginger, peppercorns, garlic, cumin, cloves, and vinegar and puree in batches.

Transfer to a bowl and add the wine and bay leaves. Place the goat and beef in a large roasting pan and pour the chile mixture over it.

Bake, covered, at 250 degrees F for 2 hours, or until done and the meat is falling apart.

Serve with tortillas and a rice dish from chapter 9 and the salsa of your choice from chapter 2.

YIELD 8 to 10 servings   HEAT LEVEL Medium

Tamales

Tamales are portable, convenient, and nutritious. They are the perfect food for travelers. On the road or on a trail, reheated in a microwave or over an open fire, tamales are gems. Since they have been steamed for at least an hour, they are practically sterile, so they will not need refrigeration and will not spoil easily. Packed in corn husks, banana leaf, or some other vegetable leaf, tamale wrappings are conveniently biodegradable. Tamales can be reheated without a pan or griddle, over a grill or directly over coals because the vegetable wrapping work as a cooking surface—and also serve as a plate. Food portioning is not a problem, as tamales come in small, medium, and large sizes. While a child can eat one or two, an adult could have half a dozen. I'm talking northern Mexico tamales because in the south they are much bigger, so adjust accordingly. They are gluten free and highly nutritious. A meat filling will supply the protein, while the masa is a good source of carbohydrates and fat—just the energy you need for a good hike. In fact, some people call tamales "Mexican energy bars." What an invention! (Note that family-size and extended family-size tamales exist; they are not steamed but baked in a pit.)

While the origin of this wonder food is disputed by many countries in the Americas, it is likely to have been invented near the place where corn was domesticated. Until they find evidence of grains of corn in a civilization previous to that of Tehuacán, Puebla, we are going to credit this region as the place of origin of tamales. From Bernardino de Sahagún, we know that the Aztecs were masters at tamale-making. A remarkable variety of tamales were served for the midday meal. They were stuffed with fruits, such as plums, pineapple, or guava; with game meat, such as deer or turkey; or with seafood, and even snails or frogs. Whole chile pods were included with the stuffing, and after steaming, the tamales were often served with a cooked chile sauce. And since Mexico is the country that has the largest variety of tamales—purportedly more than five hundred types—it is believed that they have had more time there to evolve than anywhere else.

Tamalli is a Náhuatl word that means "wrapped," and it was the origin of the words *tamal* and *tamales*—singular and plural respectively in Spanish. The word

above Tamales ready for the sauce. Photograph by Chel Beeson. Work for hire. Sunbelt Archives.

right Corn husk (top) and banana leaf tamales. Photograph by José C. Marmolejo.

"tamale" does not exist in the Spanish language. Thus, "tamal" is the name given to a dish of indigenous origin in Mexico prepared with corn dough—stuffing optional—wrapped in a vegetable leaf—dry or green corn, banana, maguey—and these days (though not recommended) could be in aluminum foil or even plastic! It can have meat and/or vegetables in the stuffing, and it could be salty, sweet, or spicy. So, there is a tamal for everyone!

After analyzing countless varieties of tamales, José feels confident that anyone can design their own tamales. There are certain rules to follow to ensure that they will come out well: the type of masa to be used, the ratio of lard/shortening to masa, and the cooking time. The rest is pure creativity—including a tamal without masa.

There are, however, some extraordinary tamales in Mexico that he wouldn't dare to try to execute. *Zacahuil* would be one of them. These extraordinary tamales are from the Huasteca region, an area comprising the southern part of the state of Tamaulipas, north of the state of Veracruz, and east of the state of San Luis Potosí and some areas bordering those states. These tamales are big: up to six feet long and weighing fifty pounds. Needless to say, a project of that magnitude surpasses his ability to prepare and consume them, but something could be done; check the recipes below. You may begin to think that such a project needs the effort of a team and can't be repeated often, and you're right. It takes a big family—perhaps some neighbors, too—and a special occasion to embark on such an adventure. But big families abound in Mexico, and excuses to celebrate do as well: birthdays, baptisms, weddings, and of course, the Day of the Dead.

As mentioned above, the type of masa is determinant. The masa used for tortillas is not the same as the one used for tamales. Masa for tamales is a coarser grind of the corn, and the masa for zacahuil is no exception. In fact, for this giant, the masa is even coarser, even granulated. Think of couscous or cooked broken grains of rice—that's the desired texture. The "filling" in this tamal is not placed at the center; it's mixed with the masa to ensure everybody gets some of it. Chicken, turkey, or pork, and a spicy sauce will flavor the zacahuil. There is also the ratio of lard or shortening to masa to consider, as previously mentioned. Two generations ago, it used to be 50 percent lard to 50 percent masa. Concerns over high-cholesterol (which genetically not all of us are susceptible to) resulted in the introduction of shortening, and so the corn meal to shortening ratios began to change to today's recommended 60 percent masa to 15 to 20 percent lard and 15 to 20 percent shortening. About the cooking time: a standard tamal takes about an hour of steaming to be ready whereas zacahuil takes between 8 and 12 hours to bake. Yes, such a tamale needs to be baked, and for that task, a big pit or an adobe oven is the solution. The zacahuil needs to be wrapped in a bunch of *papatla*—a local wild plant with wide leaves—or banana leaves. Tying up this baby properly is essential before cooking it because we don't want it to fall apart!

Corundas are another example of difficult tamales to execute. The word *k'urhunda* comes from the native language Purépecha in Michoacán and means "wrapped." These guys are so small that they fit in the palm of your hand. The width of the leaf (two inches maximum) helps to determine the shape and size of the tamales, and since they come out small, a lot of them are needed for a feast. The hard part is shaping the corundas into a pyramid using your hands and the leaves of a fresh ear of corn, although the experts who make them commercially seem to shape them faster than the human eye can register. Since the price is so low, and they can be found in the markets of Michoacán, a lot of people (like José) would rather buy them than to attempt to make them at home. Corundas may have a cheese or vegetable filling and come in three versions: covered with sour cream, with green salsa or with red salsa. They all are great as a mid-morning snack.

Now let's examine tamales without masa: *tlapiques*. These pre-Hispanic "corn husk wraps" are cooked over coals and can still be found in Mexico City in the

Commercial tamale steamer. Photograph by Steffi Victorioso on iStock.

ONE MAN'S MEAT IS ANOTHER MAN'S TAMALE

"Armadillo, venison, fish and other less identifiable animals are also sold
pre-cooked, most commonly in markets and small towns with a strong
Indian influence. In southern Mexico you may be offered *tepescuintle*.
It is a delicious meat, even if it is from the agouti, a racoon-sized rodent.
I've yet to meet a hungry carnivore who didn't love it."

CARL FRANZ / *The People's Guide to Mexico*, 1992

Xochimilco area. They can be made vegetarian—filled with cacti, seasoned with
wild herbs and chile—or can be stuffed with fish, fish roe, frog legs, or poultry
entrails. The reason José wouldn't attempt to make them is that his northern
Mexican heritage calls for masa, pork, chiles, and steam. He feels, however, that
they are an interesting piece of history—and conversation—and one of these
days he promises that he will try to make them.

One of José's favorite tamales (somebody make them for him, please) is
mucbilpollo, or *mukbilpollo*. *Muk* in the Mayan language means "to bury." Since
they are cooked in a pit they are also known as "pib." This is a family-sized
tamal made around *Hanal Pixián*, or Day of the Dead, in the Yucatán Peninsula. The fact that a hole needs to be dug in the yard in order to make this
tamal adds to the challenge, but we can cheat and make it in the kitchen oven.
It is, however, more delightful to visit the Yucatán Peninsula the first week of
November—when temperatures are pleasant—and enjoy mukbilpollo from
different vendors for several days. Their fillings vary from chicken to turkey to
pork or any combination thereof. That's a real food experience.

After reviewing steamed, roasted, baked, and pit-baked tamales, you may wish
to devote a weekend to a rare tamal-producing adventure. For the brave cooks
out there, we provide a couple of "doable" rare tamales recipes below. Scale is the
key. Any attempt to make zacahuil or mucbilpollo at home in a mini version will
be fun. We've also included a recipe to prepare *champurrado*, a chocolate-flavored
atole to accompany your homemade tamales. Muy buen provecho!

These tamales should be small, thin, but loaded with stuffing nonetheless. They will not need any salsa since the stuffing will provide the necessary moisture and flavor. The secret of spongy tamales starts with mixing the lard and shortening perfectly and later mixing the fats thoroughly with the dough. Every cubic centimeter of dough should have the same amount of fat.

40	large corn husks, soaked overnight	½	teaspoon ground cumin
1	pound cooked pork shoulder shredded (save the stock)		Salt to taste
4	guajillo chiles lightly fried. stems removed. Keep seeds and veins	10	ounces lard
2	ancho chiles lightly fried, stems removed. Keep seeds and veins	7	ounces vegetable shortening
12	ounces tomatillos boiled and ground	2	pounds coarse corn dough (prepared masa)
1	onion lightly fried	½	teaspoon baking powder
1	garlic clove lightly fried		Pork stock
			Water

Northern-Style Tamales. Photograph by Bhofack2 on iStock.

Separate the husks into leaves carefully without ripping and save the large ones. Reserve in water.

In a blender grind the chiles, tomatillos, onion, and garlic into a sauce. If needed, add some pork stock.

Melt 3 ounces lard in a saucepan and pour in the sauce. Add the cumin and salt and simmer for 20 minutes.

Add the shredded pork and cook for 10 more minutes.

Add pork stock to keep the mixture moist. Let the mixture rest overnight in a large bowl.

The next day, in another bowl, mix together the lard and shortening in two cups of hot water.

Add that and the pork stock to the corn dough to make it manageable and mix constantly with a fork.

Add the baking powder and salt and mix it some more.

To test the dough, make little balls of it randomly picked and put them in a glass of water. If they float, they are ready; if they sink, keep mixing.

Once the dough is ready, spread around 2 ounces on a corn leaf—that should be pliable by now—and add the stuffing in the middle. Fold the leaf into itself covering the stuffing with the leaf and lock everything inside by folding it again.

method is using a tortilla press, make the dough into a tortilla, place the filling in the center and fold like a turnover, then wrap and fold with the corn leaves.

Place the tamales vertically inside a steamer, so the steam can circulate around easily and evenly.

Add water, cover and cook for at least an hour. Check from time to time for water and add hot water as necessary.

After an hour you can pull a tamal out and check to see if it is done.

YIELD 30 to 40 tamales   HEAT LEVEL Medium

Tamales de Espinacas

These vegetarian tamales do not use lard—the soul of tamales—only shortening, and are wrapped in banana leaves. No further stuffing is needed here since the spinach is mixed with the dough.

FOR THE SALSA

2	pounds tomatillos
1	onion
2	garlic cloves
4	fresh jalapeños, seeds and stems removed, deveined
	Salt to taste

FOR THE TAMALES

2	pounds coarse corn dough (masa)
10	ounces shortening
½	teaspoon baking powder
1	cup vegetable stock
3	cups of julienned spinach
	Salt to taste
4	banana leaves cut in squares of 12 x 12 inches

To make the salsa, in a blender or food processor mix all salsa ingredients and puree.

To make the tamales, melt the shortening and mix it with the dough in a food processor with a dough hook. Add veggie stock and salsa to make the dough manageable. Add the spinach and the salt and keep mixing.

Divide the dough in 4-to-6- ounce portions and reserve.

Toast lightly the banana leaves squares in a griddle to make them pliable without breaking them.

Place the dough portions on the toasted squares and fold like an envelope.

Fit the tamales vertically in a steamer and cook for at least an hour.

Spinach Tamales. Photograph by Luis Echeverri Urrea on iStock.

YIELD 15 to 20 tamales   HEAT LEVEL Hot

Chilehuate

This dish is served in humid climates where the cebollina (wild onion) grows, which is what gives this dish its special flavor. Chilehuates are wonderful to include when you are serving an extensive menu of appetizers.

30	corn husks
6	jalapeño chiles, stems and seeds removed, chopped
1	pound butter
2	pounds corn masa
4	tablespoons peanut oil
2	cups cooked black beans
3	teaspoons baking powder
4	ounces shelled peanuts, ground
4	cebollinas (green onions)
2	cups squash, cubed
	Salt to taste

Soak the corn husks overnight and drain the next morning.

Place the butter in a mixing bowl and beat with an electric mixture until it doubles in size. Add the masa slowly, beating constantly. Add the salt and baking powder.

If necessary, you may add a small amount of cold water. Continue beating for 15 minutes or until a small piece will float in a glass of water.

With a mortar and pestle or in a blender, grind the cebollinas and chiles together.

Place the mixture in a frying pan along with the peanut oil and sauté quickly.

Next, add the black beans and peanuts to the mixture and stir.

Add the squash and cook for 2 minutes or until most of the liquid has cooked off.

Spread the masa over each corn husk, add some of the bean mixture, then fold each husk over. Twist the ends of each husk, making sure they are closed.

Place the folded husks in a steam cooker, cover, and cook for 45 minutes to 1 hour, or until the masa is easily removed from the husks.

NOTE *Requires advance preparation.*

YIELD 30 tamales   HEAT LEVEL Medium

Tamal with Chile and Peanuts.
Photograph by Gabriela Navarro on iStock.

Tamales con Picadillo de Pollo   CHICKEN PICADILLO TAMALES

This recipe is from Veracruz, which Cortés founded when he harbored there in 1519, before beginning his westward march to conquer the Aztecs.

1	large chicken	4	ancho chiles, softened in hot water, seeds and stems removed, chopped
3	cloves	½	cup vegetable oil
8	cups water	3	tomatoes, chopped
3	black peppercorns	30	dry corn husks
2	cups cornmeal		Salt to taste
1	large onion, chopped		
1	tablespoon chicken broth		

In a large pot, boil the chicken in 8 cups water with the salt and onion until done. Remove the meat from the bones, chop it, and place it in a skillet along with the chiles, tomatoes, cloves, peppercorns, and oil and cook for 10 minutes, stirring as needed. Add more salt if necessary.

Place the cornmeal in a separate bowl and moisten with chicken broth and oil until you create a thick masa.

Separate and soak the corn husks for about ½ hour and drain. Spread the masa on the individual husks, stuff with the chicken mixture, fold, and steam until done, about 45 minutes. Serve with a sauce from chapter 2.

YIELD 30 tamales   HEAT LEVEL Mild

Homemade Zacahuil. Photograph by José C. Marmolejo.

This is a small (for some) and fun project with guaranteed reward.

3	guajillo chiles, seeds and stems removed
4	chiles de árbol, seeds and stems removed
1	medium size onion, chopped
2 to 3	garlic cloves, peeled
1	pound cooked chicken or pork, shredded

The broth from cooking the chicken/pork

Salt to taste

2 banana leaves

Cotton cord for tying

1 ovenproof dish

In a saucepan, sauté lightly the chiles, onions, garlic, and salt in a little lard or shortening.

Once it has cooled off, put everything in a blender and add some broth and make a thick sauce. Reserve.

Pour two cups of boiling water in a bowl and add the lard and shortening and mix well with a whisk. Pour off the excess water that did not mix with the fats.

Place the flour in a bowl and add the fats little by little as you mix constantly to make a dough.

Add the baking powder and salt and mix. The secret of spongy tamales starts with mixing the lard and shortening perfectly and later mixing the fats thoroughly with the dough.

Every cubic inch of dough should have the same amount of fat. Add pork stock to the dough to make it manageable.

To test the dough, make little balls of it randomly picked and put them in a glass of water, they should float, if they sink, keep mixing.

In a large container, mix the sauce, the shredded chicken or pork with the masa to a uniform blend. If needed, add some broth to the masa to make it pliable.

Soften the banana leaves by passing them several times over a flame. This will make them pliable and easy to manage while wrapping the tamale.

Place two strings of cord forming a cross on the bottom of the ovenproof dish, long enough to tie up the tamale.

Over the cord, place the banana leaves leaving enough outside the dish to wrap the tamal. Put the masa mix inside, wrap the banana leaves and tie the cord.

Bake it for two hours at 375 degrees F. You may test readiness by inserting a toothpick, it should come out clean.

Once ready, remove the leaves, slice the cooked masa, and serve immediately.

Enjoy!

YIELD 6 servings   HEAT LEVEL Medium

This is a fast-track version to facilitate its preparation at home.

4	guajillo chiles, seeds and stems removed
4	chiles de árbol, seeds and stems removed
8	cloves garlic
1	medium size onion, chopped
2 to 3 ounces achiote paste	
8	ounces white vinegar
	Pinch of Mexican oregano
	Salt to taste

2	pounds coarse corn masa
1	pound lard and/or shortening
½	teaspoon baking powder
2	pounds cooked and roughly cut (bite size) pork or chicken
	The broth from cooking the chicken/pork
2	banana leaves
	Cotton cord for tying
1	ovenproof dish

Fry the chiles, onions, and four garlic cloves lightly in little lard or shortening.

Once it has cooled off, put everything in a blender and add some salt and broth, and make a thick sauce. Reserve it.

In a cleaned blender, mix the achiote paste, four garlic cloves, vinegar, oregano, some broth, and salt to a runny sauce. Reserve that also.

Pour two cups of boiling water in a bowl and add the lard and shortening and mix well with a whisk. Pour off the excess water that did not mix with the fats.

Place the flour in a bowl and add the fats little by little as you mix constantly to make a dough.

Add the baking powder and salt and mix. The secret of spongy tamales starts with mixing the lard and shortening perfectly and later mixing the fats thoroughly with the dough. Every cubic inch of dough should have the same amount of fat.

Mucbilpollo from Yucatán, Day of the Dead tamal. Photograph courtesy of Joaquín Mier y Terán Puerto.

Add pork stock to the dough to make it manageable. To test the dough, make little balls of it randomly picked and put them in a glass of water, they should float, if they sink, keep mixing.

In a large container, mix the sauce, the shredded chicken or pork with the masa to a uniform blend. If needed, add some broth to the masa to make it pliable.

Soften the banana leaves by passing them several times over a flame. This will make them pliable and easy to manage while wrapping the tamale.

Place two strings of cord forming a cross on the bottom of the ovenproof dish, long enough to tie up the tamale.

Over the cord, place the banana leaves leaving enough outside the dish to wrap the tamal.

Put the masa mix inside, wrap the banana leaves and tie the cord.

Bake it for two hours at 375 degrees F. You may test readiness by inserting a toothpick, it should come out clean.

Once ready, serve hot in slices. Enjoy!

YIELD 6 servings   HEAT LEVEL Medium

Champurrado   CHOCOLATE-FLAVORED ATOLE

It's a custom in Mexico to serve tamales with atole. This recipe will yield a flavorful hot drink that will please the young and the young at heart.

8	cups of water
3/4	cup of *masa harina* corn flour
2	Mexican Ibarra chocolate tablets minced

4	ounces piloncillo or 1/2 cup brown sugar
1	cinnamon stick
1	pinch of cardamom (optional)

Place 6 cups of water in a saucepan on medium heat and dissolve the piloncillo or brown sugar.

After the sweetener has dissolved, add the chocolate, cinnamon and cardamom while stirring constantly.

In a separate saucepan heat the remaining water and add little by little the corn masa until it is dissolved completely.

Add the dissolved corn masa harina to the chocolate pan while keeping the flame low.

Once the mix has dissolved completely, bring it to a boil stirring constantly with a whisk. A good froth is desired.

You may adjust sugar and masa harina for desired thickness and sweetness.

Enjoy a wonderful drink.

YIELD 8 servings

Chocolate-Flavored Atole. Photograph by Kimberly Vardeman, Creative Commons Attribution 2.0 Generic license, Wikimedia Commons.

Mexican boy selling chickens and carrots. Photograph by Mayo & Weed, Creative Commons
Attribution-Share Alike 4.0 International license, Wikimedia Commons.

8 ⦃⦃ Peppered Poultry

The Spaniards came to the New World in search of gold, but they also found a cuisine that would have a much larger impact on the world than all the riches of their dreams. Corn, beans, tomatoes, potatoes, pumpkins, and, of course, chiles, were but a few of the crops that the Spaniards and Portuguese would pass along on their travels to remake the tastes of the world. According to food historian Marilyn Tausend, writing in *México: The Beautiful Cookbook* (1991), "The true dawn of Mexican cuisine began when the Spanish allowed the subjugated Indians to have domesticated animals." Behold the chicken, whose ascent into popularity in the Western Hemisphere has been nothing short of spectacular. But before there were chickens in Mexico, the indigenous people depended on wild ducks, geese, and turkeys that were eventually domesticated.

Kennedy, in *The Cuisines of Mexico* (1986), notes, "The wild turkey, or *guajalote* is indigenous to Mexico and the New World. For centuries before the Spanish arrived, the nobility ate roasted turkey, quail and casseroles of turkey prepared with chilies, tomatoes and ground pumpkin seeds."

The turkey is still one of the most important foods in Yucatán, and every day you can eat turkey there. In fact, I became so fascinated with the variety of ways turkey could be prepared that we counted twenty-nine typical turkey recipes in one modest regional Yucatecan cookbook. And we have come to believe that no special festival is complete without *mole poblano de guajolote*. (See "Family Favorites: Moles" for a recipe.)

Noted restaurateur and Mexican food expert Rick Bayless observes in his book, *Authentic Mexican* (1987), that Muscovy ducks were domesticated by the Aztecs long before the Spanish arrived. However, "Wild-fowl specialties are not common foods in Mexico. Ducks, though not wild ones, are put on the tables of nicer restaurants in the large cities, along with the occasional quail."

William W. Dunmire, the author of *Gardens of New Spain*, writes: "Of all the imported animals, chickens appear to have been the most willingly, even eagerly accepted by Native peoples. That stands to reason, since so many tribes were accustomed to raising turkeys, parrots, and other birds. Chickens readily adapted to the wide variety of climates and must have spread through the hands

of Indian traders from village to village well in advance of Spanish settlements."
Bayless adds, "Mexican chickens are generally simmered, steamed or braised
until tender, simply because many are too tough for dry-heat roasting or frying."
Bayless also declares that "Poultry is without a doubt the most frequently eaten
meat in Mexico," and as evidence to prove that point, we present our favorite
spicy poultry dishes.

ONE VERSION OF THE INVENTION OF THE MARGARITA

"It was American Independence Day, 1942. The heat was sweltering, and
the scene was Ciudad Juárez, Mexico. Not that you couldn't celebrate
the independence of America in Mexico. During those days, just over the
bridge in Juárez's busiest commercial district, you could celebrate anything
you wanted. Pancho Morales was tending bar at Tommy's Place, a favorite
hangout for GIs from Fort Bliss. A lady walked in, sat at the bar, and ordered
a magnolia. The only thing Pancho knew about a magnolia was that it
had lemon or lime in it and some kind of liquor. So he did what any good
bartender would do—he winged it and used the most popular liquor served in
Juárez: tequila.

   With a single taste, the woman, who knew a magnolia was made of gin,
cream, lemon juice, and grenadine, realized that the drink was an imposter,
but liked it anyway because Pancho had loaded it up with enough tequila to
make anyone smile. When she asked what the new drink was called, Pancho's
brain was thinking flowers and 'm's, and had leaped from magnolia to
margarita—Spanish for daisy. And so mixology history was made, and Pancho
later immortalized the drink when he taught at the bartender's school in
Juárez before immigrating to El Paso in 1974."

ELAINE CORN / *Chile Pepper*, 1992

Pato Asado con Tequila y Salsa Chipotle
ROASTED DUCK WITH TEQUILA AND HONEY CHIPOTLE SAUCE

This recipe was contributed by John Gray, head chef at the Ritz-Carlton Hotel in Cancún. This dish is an excellent example of the sophisticated flavors that can be created with seemingly simple ingredients and one pan.

2	tablespoons olive oil
6	shallots, roughly sliced
½	cup raisins, seeded
1	tablespoon sugar
¼	cup balsamic vinegar
1	cup port wine
¾	cup chicken stock

2	chipotle chiles, rehydrated in warm water, seeds and stems removed, chopped
¼	cup tequila
¼	cup honey
1	whole duck

Preheat the oven to 300 degrees F.

Add the olive oil and shallots to a very hot sauce pan. sauté until golden, stirring constantly, then add the raisins and sugar. Allow the sugar to dissolve and lightly caramelize; do not allow it to burn.

Add the balsamic vinegar and the port wine, then reduce until thickened and about ¼ cup of the liquid remains.

Add the chicken stock to the reduced sauce, mix well and add the chipotles.

Let the sauce stand for 10 to 15 minutes, then strain. The less time the peppers are in the sauce the lighter the chipotle flavor.

Add the tequila and honey to the sauce, return to the heat and keep just warm, stirring occasionally.

In a roasting pan, uncovered, roast the whole duck for 45 minutes.

De-bone, the duck, including the skin, and cover the meat with the sauce and serve with rice or polenta and julienned vegetables or asparagus.

YIELD 4 to 6 servings   HEAT LEVEL Medium

Roasted Duck with Tequila and Honey Chipotle Sauce. Photograph by Lesyy on iStock.

Shredded Chicken Yucatan-Style. Photograph by Ceeseven, Creative Commons Attribution-Share Alike 4.0 International license, Wikimedia Commons.

Pollo en Escabeche Estilo Yucateco
SHREDDED CHICKEN YUCATAN-STYLE

Marta Figel, writing in Chile Pepper *magazine about Isla Mujeres, collected this fiery, fantastic chicken recipe. Your guests will enjoy it even more if you serve it with a round of margaritas. The drinks won't cut the heat but may help you forget how hot it is!*

10	peppercorns		Water
¼	teaspoon ground Mexican oregano	1	teaspoon salt
½	teaspoon salt	½	teaspoon ground Mexican oregano
2	cloves garlic, peeled and crushed	1	xcatic chile, stem and seeds removed or substitute yellow wax hot
1	tablespoon vinegar		
2	large red onions		
2	heads garlic	1	habanero chile, stem and seeds removed
	Juice of 3 bitter oranges, or mix 1 cup lime juice with 1/2 cup orange juice	2	serrano chiles, stems and seeds removed
3	pounds chicken legs and thighs		Flour tortillas

Place the peppercorns, oregano, and salt in a spice or coffee grinder and grind to a powder. Combine this powder with the garlic and vinegar and make a paste. Set aside.

Roast one of the onions and both heads of garlic in a 350 degree oven for 20 minutes. Let cool.

Peel the remaining onion, slice it into rings, and marinate it in the bitter orange juice.

Place the chicken in a stockpot with water to cover, salt and oregano, and simmer until the chicken is tender, about 30 minutes.

Drain the chicken, reserving the broth, and transfer it to an ovenproof dish. Add the peppercorn paste, 2 tablespoons of the bitter orange juice, and bake uncovered at 350 degrees until golden brown, about 30 minutes.

Peel the roasted onions and garlic and combine them with the reserved chicken stock. Add the chiles and simmer for 5 minutes. Add the marinated onion, bring to a boil, and remove from the heat immediately.

Drain the broth and reserve both the broth and the chiles and onions. Separate the chiles from the onion and coarsely chop them.

Skin the chicken and shred the meat from the bones. Add the chopped chiles and the onion to the chicken and mix well. Reduce the stock by boiling to 1 1/2 cups and add it to the chicken mixture until the mixture is moist but not soupy.

Serve the chicken with rice and a favorite salsa from chapter 2 on the side.

YIELD 4 servings   HEAT LEVEL Hot

THE HIDDEN CACHE OF CHILES

"Mexico City, 1910. Elegant Mexicans eat in French. They prefer the *crêpe* to its poor relation of native birth, the corn tortilla. *Oeufs en cocotte* to the humble [*huevos*] *rancheros*. They find *béchamel* sauce more worthy than guacamole, that delicious but excessively indigenous mixture of avocados, tomatoes, and chile. Faced with foreign peppers or Mexican chiles, the gentry rejected the chile, although later they sneak back to the family kitchen and devour it secretly, ground or whole, side dish or main dish, stuffed or plain, unpeeled or naked."

EDUARDO GALEANO / *Memory of Fire: Century of the Wind*, 1988

This recipe was contributed by our friends Nancy and Jeff Gerlach, who have traveled in Mexico extensively. Although they were served this dish on both sides of Mexico, it does come from Yucatán, where it is available in nearly every restaurant. In Cancún, there are even pollo pibil *take-out stands!* Pibil *refers to the method of cooking marinated meats wrapped in banana leaves in a rock-lined pit. Banana leaves were abundant in the central* mercado *in Cozumel, but since they are rare in the United States, use aluminum foil instead. Bitter or Seville oranges are also hard to find, but mixing orange, grapefruit, and lime juices makes an acceptable substitute.*

¼	cup recado rojo (see recipe, chapter 2)	1	medium onion, sliced
2	tablespoons lime juice	3	xcatic or banana chiles, chopped, or substitute yellow wax hot
1	tablespoon orange juice	2	tablespoons vegetable oil
1	tablespoon grapefruit juice	4	large banana leaves or aluminum foil
4	chicken breasts		

Mix the recado with the fruit juices. Marinate the chicken in the mixture for 4 hours or overnight in the refrigerator.

Sauté the onion and chiles in one tablespoon of the oil until soft.

Brush the banana leaf or foil with oil. Place one chicken breast in the center, pour ¼ of the marinade over the chicken, and top with the onion mixture. Fold the foil over and tightly secure the seams.

Place the packages on a pan, and bake for one hour at 350 degrees.

Remove the foil and drain off any excess liquid. Serve with refried black beans and habanero salsa.

NOTE *This recipe requires advanced preparation.*

YIELD 4 servings   HEAT LEVEL Mild

Pibil-Style Chicken. Photograph by ArtEvent ET, on iStock.

Chicken and Sausage with Chipotle Chiles. Photograph by Akchamczuk, on iStock.

Pollo con Salchichas en Chile Chipotle
CHICKEN AND SAUSAGE WITH CHIPOTLE CHILES

This hearty dish offers a smoky taste that comes from both the sausages and the chipotles. You might like to start this dish with ensalada de guacamole. See the recipe in chapter 4. If you can't find chipotles en adobo *in cans, rehydrate dried chipotles in hot vinegar.*

1	2-pound chicken, sectioned	½	clove garlic
1	clove garlic	2	tablespoons vegetable oil
1	small onion	1	medium onion, sliced
	Water to cover	5	slices sausage
1	pound tomatoes, chopped		Salt to taste
4	chipotle chiles in adobo, chopped		

In a large pan, cover the chicken with water, add the garlic and onion and cook it over high heat until the chicken is tender, about 45 minutes.

In a separate pan, cook the tomatoes, then add the chiles and garlic.

Fry the sliced onion in the oil and add the tomato mixture. Cook over a low heat for about 10 minutes. Add the chicken, sausage and salt to taste. Cook over a low heat for another 10 minutes and serve with rice.

YIELD 4 to 6 servings   HEAT LEVEL Medium

Hen in Walnut Sauce.
Photograph by Максим
Крысанов, on iStock.

Gallina en Nogada

HEN IN WALNUT SAUCE

This recipe requires you to grind spices in a coffee grinder or spice mill. If you have a coffee grinder, don't worry about removing the leftover spices after you're done. Simply grind white rice in the grinder and then wipe out with a wet paper towel. The rice will remove all spices, ensuring you won't have chile coffee!

6	tablespoons butter	2	onions
1	piece white bread	4	ancho chiles, seeds and stems removed, rehydrated in hot water
¼	cup peanuts, peeled	¾	cup chicken broth
¼	cup walnuts	1	large chicken, separated and cooked in 3 cups of water with salt and pepper to taste for 45 minutes
1	stick cinnamon		
2	cloves		
3	piquín chiles, stems removed		
2	cloves garlic		

Heat the butter in a skillet and fry the bread, peanuts and walnuts for about 5 minutes. Remove and puree in a food processor or blender. Reserve.

In a spice mill, combine the cinnamon stick, cloves, and piquín chiles and grind to a powder. Combine this powder with the garlic, onions, ancho chiles, and chicken broth in a food processor or blender and puree.

Remove to a saucepan, add the pureed nuts and cooked chicken parts and let this cook until the flavors blend. Serve over white rice.

YIELD 6 to 8 servings   HEAT LEVEL Medium

The Oaxaca marketplace is famous for its incredible selection of chiles and other locally grown produce. This recipe features the ancho chile. Serve with a side dish from chapter 10.

1	medium chicken, sectioned	2	cloves garlic
	Salt and pepper to taste	1	medium onion
	Corn oil as needed for frying	6	black peppercorns
3	ancho chiles, stems and seeds removed	3	cloves
		1	cinnamon stick
½	cup ground almonds	½	*bolillo* (or small French roll) crumbs
4	tomatoes, roasted, peeled and seeded	2	tablespoons sugar
		4	cups chicken broth

In a large skillet, salt and pepper the chicken and fry it in the oil making sure it doesn't burn or stick, then remove the chicken from the pan and drain.

In the same oil, fry the chiles, all but 2 tablespoons of the almonds, tomatoes, garlic, onion, peppercorns, cloves, cinnamon and bread crumbs. Pour the mixture into a blender and blend until smooth. If necessary, add a little broth. Return the mixture to the pan and cook at a low temperature. Add the chicken, sugar, and chicken broth and cover.

Cook at a low temperature until the chicken is tender. Before serving, add the remaining almonds.

YIELD 4 to 6 servings   HEAT LEVEL Medium

Almond Chicken Oaxacan-Style.
Photograph by ALLEKO on iStock.

This recipe from Hidalgo calls for nine cloves of garlic. We know, you're thinking that's a lot of garlic! But Mexicans love their garlic in many different forms. In Baja, garlic is found in the form of crispy garlic—coarsely or finely chopped garlic sautéed until crisp and golden and used as a topping for various dishes. This imparts an earthy, gentle flavor that enhances the primary components of the dish.

1	large chicken, sectioned		5	ancho chiles, stems and seeds removed, rehydrated in hot water
	Salt to taste		2	pasilla chiles, stems and seeds removed, rehydrated in hot water
1	onion			
1	clove garlic		8	cloves garlic
	Water to cover		½	teaspoon cumin
			¼	cup butter for frying

In a large pot, simmer the chicken with the salt, onion and garlic until done, about 45 minutes.

Grind the chiles with the garlic and cumin in a mortar and pestle, then fry the paste in a frying pan with the butter for about 5 minutes, stirring constantly.

Add the chicken and some of the broth and let it cook until the flavors marry. Serve with white rice.

YIELD 4 to 6 servings   HEAT LEVEL Medium

Garlic and Cumin Chicken.
Photograph by SGAFotoStudio
on iStock.

Barbacoa de Pollo

The Mexican barbacoa has much more in common with the Hawaiian luau than the Americanized version of barbecue, which has come to mean cooking meat over hot coals with a tangy sauce. In Mexico, the meat is wrapped in banana leaves or corn husks and then steamed.

8	guajillo chiles, stems and seeds removed, or substitute New Mexican		2	heads garlic
			3	black peppercorns
2	chipotle chiles, stems and seeds removed		2	bay leaves
			2	cups vinegar
2	ancho chiles, stems and seeds removed		4	pounds chicken meat
			10	chopped corn husks
2	tablespoons cumin			Red chile powder
				Salt to taste

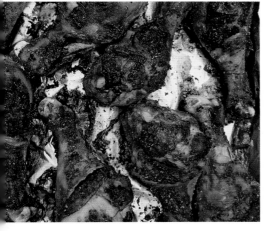

Barbecued Chicken. Photograph by SEASTOCK on iStock.

Toast the chiles on a baking sheet in a 200-degree F oven, then soak them in hot water until they become soft.

Place the chiles in a blender with the cumin, garlic, peppercorns, and bay leaves. Once this mixture is blended, place it in a bowl, add the vinegar and mix well.

Place the chicken in a deep dish and cover it with the chile mix and salt to taste, then let it marinate overnight in the refrigerator, so the meat absorbs the flavors. Place the marinated chicken in the corn husks and sprinkle with a little ground chile, then wrap well and tie the ends.

Place the wrapped meat in a skillet with a little water or a steamer, cover and cook at a low temperature for one or two hours, or until done.

Serve with lettuce, avocado, and a green sauce from chapter 2.

NOTE *This recipe requires advance preparation.*

YIELD 8 servings   HEAT LEVEL Medium

Chicken Breasts in Chipotle-Pineapple Sauce. Photograph by EzumeImages on iStock.

Pechugas en Salsa de Chipotle con Piña
CHICKEN BREASTS IN CHIPOTLE-PINEAPPLE SAUCE

Pineapples thrive in the tropical terrains of Mexico. This fruity-hot dish was collected in Mazatlán, while full of college students and tourists, is still home to fine traditional Mexican cooking.

1 ½   pounds tomatoes, cooked and peeled

1   medium onion

2   cloves garlic

4   *chipotle* chiles in adobo
    Salt and pepper to taste

2   tablespoons vegetable oil

3   chicken breasts, boned and pounded

1   can pineapple in heavy syrup

1   cup chicken broth

Combine the tomatoes, onion, garlic, chiles, salt and pepper in a food processor and pulse until just blended.

In a large pan, fry the mixture in the oil. When done, add the chicken, pineapple, and chicken broth.

Cook until done, uncovered, for about 40 minutes. Stir occasionally. Serve with white rice, or a spiced rice from chapter 9.

YIELD 4 to 6 servings   HEAT LEVEL Medium

Pollo en Chile Verde

It's easy to see how this traditional Mexican recipe for the state of Chihuahua received its name; more than half of the ingredients are green, including both poblanos and serranos, which offer high heat when combined.

14	tomatillos, chopped
4	serrano chiles, stems and seeds removed
2	poblano chiles, stems and seeds removed
2	cloves garlic
½	medium onion
1	small bunch cilantro
1	chicken, sectioned
	Salt and pepper to taste
½	cup water

Cook the tomatillos in a splash of vegetable oil until soft in a large sauté pan, and set aside.

Grind the chiles, garlic, onion and cilantro together in a blender. Add the chile mixture to the tomatillos, then add the chicken parts, salt and pepper to taste.

Add the hot water to the skillet and cook over medium heat for 1 hour and 15 minutes, or until done. Serve with white rice.

YIELD 4 to 5 servings   HEAT LEVEL Medium

Green Chile Chicken.
Photograph by Satriady
Utomos on iStock.

Querétaro-Style Enchiladas. Photograph by bhofack2 on iStock.

Enchiladas

All enchiladas start with the simple corn tortilla.

"No es enchilame otra" states an old Mexican saying. Literally, "It's not like making me another enchilada." This popular truism is based on the fact that there is nothing easier than making an enchilada.

Enchilada is a short name for *tortilla enchilada*, which it is a tortilla covered with chile sauce on both sides, fried, then rolled or folded with no filling. That's an enchilada alright. Without frying, it's pre-Hispanic food, a tradition that remains alive with very poor people. In other words, a simple, economical, and flavorful way to appease hunger and please the palate—soul food that is. But somewhere along the line, someone decided that the humble tortilla enchilada should be fried, and it evolved into a more nutritional and sophisticated dish. It was decided that folded or rolled, it should have a filling. Cheese or chicken would be appropriate, and this dish became popular among all income levels. How about beef enchiladas? They are popular in the United States but rare in Mexico. Wild mushroom enchiladas? Well, I make them at home.

A digression is needed here: it's time to define a quesadilla. You will see further down why. A quesadilla is a folded tortilla stuffed with cheese that can be heated on a griddle or fried until the cheese melts. In central Mexico, however, this statement will cause an endless debate because in this region it's stuffed with anything you can think of, cheese included. A set of three quesadillas could be covered with a hot and fiery sauce or salsa, and *mira, unas enchiladas*! So we have now another method of making enchiladas with any cooking sauce or salsa but without the splattering of frying a tortilla covered with sauce.

Often, we find *enchiladas de mole* in restaurants. These are fried quesadillas, folded or rolled, stuffed with cheese or chicken (your choice), and covered with mole sauce. A few restaurants will call them *enmoladas*—a more appropriate name we think—and they are always a favorite. And you will find *enfrijoladas* also; as you can easily guess, they are fried quesadillas covered with bean sauce. And then there are *entomatadas*—quesadillas covered with tomato sauce (no chiles please). The enchilada universe is big, very big.

Growing up, *enchiladas rojas* were José's favorites. For Don Alfonso, his father,

Tortilla-making in a Mexican village. Photograph by Kieran Lamb, Creative Commons Attribution 2.0 Generic license, Wikimedia Commons.

that wasn't real food, or at least he didn't consider them serious food. For him, a real meal had to include meat, so, enchiladas were some sort of a cheap appetizer, but to José they were a treat. The best thing about enchiladas rojas at home was that his mother would make some extra that became leftovers, which the following day would be reheated and turned into a good casserole. It didn't look as attractive as the day before, but the flavor was better, the sauce had penetrated completely into the tortillas, the cheese had melted twice, and somehow, the flavor had matured. This practice gave way to *enchiladas al horno*—baked enchiladas. Inspired by the reheated enchiladas, his mother then decided to cut the tortillas in half, cover them in chile sauce, fry and arrange them in an oven dish with cheese in layers like we make lasagna. Guess what? The appearance surpassed that of the casserole but the flavor did not. The reheating trick was the secret answer and needed to be done—and so it was done.

One day José was introduced to *enchiladas verdes*. This was before GMOs. To-

CHILES FOR THE SPIRIT WORLD

Among the descendants of the Maya, chile is regarded as a powerful agent to ward off spells. For the Tzotzil Indians of the Chiapas highlands, chile assists in both life and death. The hot pods are rubbed on the lips of newborn infants and are burned during the funeral ceremonies of *viejos* (old ones) to defeat evil spirits that might be around. The Huastec tribe of San Carlos Potosi and Vera Cruz treat victims of the "evil eye" with chile peppers. An egg is dipped in ground chile, then rubbed on the victim's body to return the pain to the malefactor.

matillos were small and tart, and sour cream was the fix. His palate adapted, and he fell in love with enchiladas verdes. From a purist's perspective, they should be called fried quesadillas covered with tomatillo and serrano sauce—with onion and garlic for sure, heavy on the cilantro, and sour cream to taste.

Legend says that a gringo came to Mexico and wanted to try enchiladas but didn't want them to be pungent. Enchiladas verdes were suggested. They were, however, too spicy for the visitor and the cook in turn "fixed" the "problem" by spreading sour cream all over the green panorama. Another version of the legend says that the foreigner was from Switzerland, and knowing he would be sensitive to a fiery sauce, someone made him entomatadas with sour cream on top to resemble the colors of his flag. The tourist loved the plate, and a new dish was born. From that day they were called *enchiladas suizas*, or "Swiss enchiladas," which are made without chiles. Should they still be called enchiladas? You decide. Today we even have sour-cream enchiladas with little or no capsaicin, which I think should be called *encremadas*. So, enchiladas without chiles? José vows, "I shall not touch them with my fork or my keyboard! In fact, last night I made some entomatadas, but I couldn't help adding some red habaneros."

A versatile dish, today we find an infinite variety of enchiladas depending on the restaurant, the city or region, and the type of chile used to make the sauce. José's favorite red enchilada sauce is made with ancho chiles, bitter for some, but he has a secret that he inherited from his mother, which he gladly shares with you in the recipe below: Enchiladas Doña Luz.

NOTE *In making enchiladas, preparing the sauce first is recommended. The three recipes below require quesadillas. Make them with corn tortillas and cheese on a griddle, then fry them lightly. Serve and cover generously with the sauce. Top them with sour cream, chopped onions, roasted vegetables, more cheese, etc. Any enchilada sauce leftover will be great on top of fried eggs the following morning.*

Enchiladas Doña Luz

José notes, "My favorite enchiladas 24/7. Can a fried egg be put on top? You bet!"

12	cheese quesadillas
3	ancho chiles
1	fried corn tortilla
¼	onion
2	cloves garlic
	Pinch of Mexican oregano
	Salt to taste
	Sour cream to taste

Garnish: Chopped onions

Remove the stems from anchos and cut them open. Shake off loose seeds, keep veins and seeds attached to veins, rinse. Boil the chiles for three minutes and let them cool off in the water.

In a blender puree the chiles, fried tortilla, onion, garlic, oregano and salt with a little water used to boil the chiles. Look for a thick sauce that will still pour. The fried tortilla will help balance the bitterness of anchos.

Boil the sauce 3 minutes and serve over warmed quesadillas.

Top with sour cream and chopped onions.

YIELD 4 servings   HEAT LEVEL Medium

Enchiladas Doña Luz. Photograph by José C. Marmolejo.

Green Enchiladas
with roasted peppers
and onions. Photograph
by José C. Marmolejo.

Enchiladas Verdes   GREEN ENCHILADAS

These can be found all over Mexico with no trouble and with no one claiming a patent on them.

12	cheese quesadillas
1	pound tomatillos
4 to 6 chiles serranos
¼	onion
2	cloves garlic
1	sprig cilantro

Salt to taste

Sour cream to taste

Garnish:

Chopped onions for garnish

Chopped cilantro for garnish

Wash the tomatillos with dish soap to remove natural wax. Remove stems from serranos, seeding and deveining optional.

Using a blender make salsa with vegetables and salt. Save some cilantro for garnishing. Some water could be added to help the blending.

Boil the sauce 3 minutes and serve over quesadillas. Add sour cream and chopped cilantro on top. Beans on the side? Sure.

YIELD 4 servings   HEAT LEVEL Medium

Chile Poblano Enchiladas. Photograph by José C. Marmolejo.

Enchiladas de Chiles Poblanos

CHILE POBLANO ENCHILADAS

Fire-roasted poblanos are a delicacy and a sauce based on them is refined and sophisticated. The best use of this dish is to impress your guests.

12	cheese quesadillas
6	poblano chiles, roasted, peeled, seeds and stems removed; remove the veins if gringos are guests
¼	onion, roasted in a pan
2	cloves garlic, roasted in a pan
	Salt to taste
	Vegetable or chicken stock
	Sour cream

Garnish: Edible flowers for garnish

In a blender, puree the poblanos, onion, garlic and salt with stock needed to make it a thick but pourable sauce.

In a pan with little oil heat the sauce. Correct for thickness with stock and check for salt. If the sauce turned out too fiery add some sour cream.

Boil the sauce 3 minutes and serve over quesadillas.

Squirt your signature with sour cream on top and garnish with flowers. *Ooh là là!*

YIELD 4 servings   HEAT LEVEL Medium

Enchiladas Sonorenses

These enchiladas are not the same as those served north of the border. The main differences are the use of freshly made, thick corn tortillas and the fact that the enchiladas are not baked. Dave and Mary Jane dined on these enchiladas one night in Tucson as they were prepared by Cindy Castillo, a friend of the Durán family, who is well-versed in Sonoran cookery. They took detailed notes in order to re-create Cindy's dish here.

THE SAUCE

- 15 to 20 chiltepínes, crushed
- 15 dried red New Mexican chiles, seeds and stems removed
- 3 cloves garlic
- 1 teaspoon salt
- 1 teaspoon vegetable oil
- 1 teaspoon flour

THE TORTILLAS

- 2 cups masa harina
- 1 egg
- 1 teaspoon baking powder
- 1 teaspoon salt
- Water
- Vegetable oil for deep frying

TO ASSEMBLE AND SERVE

- 3 to 4 scallions, minced (white part only)
- 2 cups grated queso blanco or Monterey Jack cheese
- Shredded lettuce

To make the sauce, combine the chiles, salt, and enough water to cover them in a saucepan. Boil for 10 or 15 minutes or until the chiles are quite soft. Allow the chiles to cool and then puree them in a blender along with the garlic. Strain the mixture, mash the pulp through the strainer, and discard the skins. Heat the oil in a saucepan, add the flour, and brown, taking care that it does not burn. Add the chile puree and boil for 5 or 10 minutes until the sauce has thickened slightly. Set aside and keep warm.

To make the tortillas, mix the first four ingredients together thoroughly, adding enough water to make dough. Using a tortilla press, make the tortillas. Deep fry each tortilla until it puffs up and turns slightly brown. Remove and drain on paper towels and keep warm.

To assemble and serve, place a tortilla on each plate and spoon a generous amount of sauce over it. Top with the cheese, lettuce, and onions.

YIELD 4 to 6 servings   HEAT LEVEL Hot

Thick tortilla for making Sonoran enchiladas. Photograph by Alejandro Linares. Garcia. Creative Commons Attribution-Share Alike 3.0 Unported license, Wikimedia Commons.

Enchiladas Estilo Querétaro   QUERÉTARO-STYLE ENCHILADAS

This recipe calls for chile-infused vinegar, which has become fairly easy to find in the past few years. However, if you can't find any in your local hot shop or gourmet store, search the internet and sources will be revealed. You can make your own by steeping chopped serrano chiles in vinegar for a day or two.

2	cups water
10	ancho chiles, seeds and stems removed, chopped
2	cloves garlic, peeled and chopped
½	teaspoon oregano
2	cloves
½	teaspoon cinnamon
	Salt to taste
24	corn tortillas
5 ½	ounces chorizo, fried

3	potatoes, peeled and chopped into small pieces, cooked, and fried
4	carrots, chopped, cooked and fried
1 ⅓	cups vegetable oil
¼	cup chile-infused vinegar
1 ½	cups asadero cheese, grated (a mild Cheddar cheese, or Monterey Jack, may be substituted)
1	onion, chopped
½	head lettuce, chopped
	Salt to taste

Pour the 2 cups of water into a large saucepan. Next, add the chiles, garlic, oregano, cloves, cinnamon, and salt and boil for 5 minutes.

Remove the pan from the heat, transfer the mixture to a blender, and process it until smooth.

Place the tortillas on two large baking sheets with sides, and carefully put 1 tablespoon of the chile mixture onto the center of each tortilla.

Combine the chorizo, potatoes, and carrots. Spoon some of the mixture on top of the chile paste on each tortilla. Starting at one end, roll each tortilla into a cylinder and set aside.

Pour the oil and chile infused vinegar into a large skillet and heat until the oil is hot. Place the enchiladas in the oil and fry quickly until almost crisp.

Drain the enchiladas on paper towels.

Place the fried enchiladas on a platter and cover them with the cheese, onion, and lettuce and serve.

YIELD 24 enchiladas   HEAT LEVEL Medium

Papadazules ENCHILADAS WITH PUMPKIN SEED SAUCE AND EGGS

Translated, the name of this filling dish means "food for the lords." It is a Mayan dish that originated on the Yucatán Peninsula. When served with scrambled eggs, it makes a great breakfast dish.

CHILTOMATE

- 4 tomatoes, grilled and peeled
- 1 habanero chile, stem and seeds removed, finely minced
- 1 tablespoon butter or corn oil
- 1 onion, chopped

  Salt and pepper to taste

PUMPKIN SEED SAUCE

- 12 ounces pumpkin seeds, toasted
- 1 bunch epazote, soaked in water and ground and salt
- ¼ cup olive oil
- 24 corn tortillas
- 2 cups grated Monterey Jack Cheese

To prepare the *chiltomate*, grind the tomatoes and chile together with a mortar and pestle. Heat the butter in a skillet and sauté the onion, then add the tomato-chile mixture, and the salt and pepper. Mix well and set aside.

To make the pumpkin seed sauce, in a blender, liquefy the pumpkin seed along with the epazote and water until you create a salsa with a thick consistency.

In a medium-sized frying pan, heat the oil over high heat. Fry the tortillas in the oil for 3 seconds a side, remove, and drain.

Next, coat one side of the tortillas in the pumpkin seed salsa. Salsa side up, fill each tortilla with cheese and roll them. Arrange the tortillas on a plate and pour the rest of the salsa over them. Pour the chiltomate on top of the salsa and serve.

YIELD 24 enchiladas   HEAT LEVEL Hot

Enchiladas with Pumpkin Seed Sauce and Eggs. Photograph by Slevinr, Creative Commons Attribution-Share Alike 3.0 Unported license, Wikimedia Commons.

Mexican seafood market. Photograph by Rick Browne.
Used with Permission.

9 Stone Soup, Mexican Sashimi, and Other Spicy Seafood

With nearly six thousand miles of coastline, plus numerous lakes, rivers, and streams, it's no surprise that seafood is enormously popular in Mexico. And fortunately, much of it is combined with Mexican chile peppers of all heat levels.

The Birth of Mexican Seafood

The True Story of the Conquest of New Spain was written by Bernal Díaz del Castillo, a Spanish soldier in the conquistadors' army. He finished writing his book in 1568 and died sixteen years later in 1584 in what is today Guatemala. However, his book wasn't published until 1632, in Spain, forty-eight years after his death. Since he didn't proofread the final version of his work, it was most likely subject to alterations, which may have introduced a number of errors. In this work, Díaz del Castillo describes vividly, among other things, the dishes Moctezuma II had at his disposal on a daily basis. He discusses about thirty different dishes, three hundred servings of which were prepared daily. The food was presented on white tablecloths with beautiful women doing the table service and providing water, tortillas, and clean towels. This display of sophistication and complexity in the cooking and serving was unexpected and astonishing to the Spaniards.

The extravagance of these banquets undoubtedly led to many legends. A popular one is that fresh fish was brought to Moctezuma II's table from the Gulf of Mexico to Tenochtitlán, some 250 miles away. This feat was accomplished through a team of relay runners called *painanis*. Seafood was not the only thing these runners transported; exotic fruits and vegetables were also moved through this method, as well as messages—drawings made on cotton paper. It's said that these runners were used to announce to Moctezuma II that the mysterious Spaniards had arrived.

Five hundred years after these events, a relay foot race was organized from the Port of Veracruz to Teotihuacán, in the outskirts of Mexico City. It was some twenty miles less than the original distance to avoid the hassle of entering the capital's downtown. Even though the original route was adjusted for logistical reasons and was a bit shorter, it took the winning team thirty-four hours to arrive at the finish line. With 1,200 participants, the event proved to be a success, but it also proved that the Moctezuma II story is only a myth. It is impossible to transport fresh seafood from the Port of Veracruz to Mexico City on foot without refrigeration and avoiding spoilage. And considering the shaking involved in running for two days, this most definitely had ruined the texture of the fish. While Moctezuma II definitely ate fish, it came from around his own city: Tenochtitlán, which was built in the middle of a lake.

With the presence of immigrants from Spain (and their African slaves), and later from France, the Middle East, and China, among other countries, Mexican gastronomy expanded significantly with the influence of imported ingredients, recipes, and techniques. The seafood arena was no exception. The variety of seafood found in Mexico resulted in an incredible new assortment of dishes. And we must not forget that seafood is an impressively versatile family of foods that can be boiled, fried, grilled, baked, roasted, smoked, or eaten raw! As one can see, the Mexican seafood equation has many variables, all contributing to the immense variety of dishes we have today.

In the 1500s the Port of Veracruz became entry point of European culture into Mexico. Gastronomy was only one manifestation of it—a very important one—and the books on Veracruz cuisine show a pattern of imported ingredients, such as olive oil, olives, capers, oregano, cloves, and cinnamon, among others.

During José's days as a student in France, he made an effort to try at least one dish representative of every region he visited. In the Côte d'Azur, he went with some friends to a decent restaurant—no budget for fancy places—to try the famous bouillabaisse. To his shocking surprise, it tasted the same as his mother's *sopa de pescado a la veracruzana*! José was a bit disillusioned, having spent precious travel money on something he was very familiar with. Many "Mexican" dishes thus were born abroad; many are the result of the marriage of foreign ingredients, while others are completely original. And the famous sopa de pescado a la veracruzana is just one more debt Mexico owes to France.

As proud as they are of their cuisine, people from Veracruz should not forget that it represents, unmistakably, the fusion of two cultures, perhaps more so because some of those ingredients arrived in Europe from Africa, the Middle East, and Asia before the Spaniards embarked to America. Veracruz, however, was the place where those ingredients were married—a marriage that has lasted more than five hundred years—and the birthplace of a cuisine in La Nueva España: the Mexican seafood cuisine.

Mexican Sashimi

Dave and chef Dany Lamote of the Hotel California in Todos Santos, Baja California Sur, were fishing with fourth-generation professionals off the Pacific coast. There was no dock nor fancy yacht. The tackle was old and weather-beaten. But this was real fishing, not a tourist trip from a resort.

They had a captain and a pilot aboard the twenty-two-foot, wide-beam *ponga* boat that launched from the beach using a line to a puller ponga that was already in the water. It was cool and cloudy on that March day, with frigate birds cruising above them, sea lions on the rocky cliffs, pelicans diving, and unknown fish in the depths below.

They were trolling with large, jointed Rapala lures when Dany got the first strike—and a good one. His rod bent severely and the line streamed out as the fish made a run. Dany had fished this way many times, so after about a seven-minute fight the pilot gaffed the fish, which turned out to be a twelve-pound grouper. Dave had always fished for grouper by anchoring near a reef and sending down a baited hook, but when they're hungry enough, groupers will leave the coral and swim upward to take a lure.

The captain only joined the action when his guests were landing a fish; otherwise, he was searching the ocean for jumping fish that were hunting bait fish and scanning the skies for pelicans, gulls, and terns diving or skimming the ocean for fish.

They caught one more grouper and then tied into a school of yellowtails, which are really jacks and closely related to amberjacks. People confuse them with yellow-tailed snapper and yellowfin tuna, but these yellowtails are the same prized fish that are sushi bar favorites called *hamachi* in Japanese. Soon, everyone had a fish except for Dave, and it was time to head back to the beach. But on the way, the captain pointed, the pilot made a sharp turn to starboard, and the guys fishing soon tangled with another school of yellowtails. Dave finally caught his fish, a sixteen-pounder that took nearly fifteen minutes to land.

The return was dramatic. Like a surfer (and there are plenty of them off nearby beaches) the captain waited near the shore for the perfect wave, and then they rode it in, going about twenty knots per hour, to a perfect, gliding landing on the beach. Everyone hopped out of the ponga, and a truck came down to pull the boat up the beach and beyond the tide line.

Dany instructed the captain about the fish, and soon thirty-three pounds of clean fillets were delivered to Dany's new restaurant, Santo Vino, at the Hotel California. In a matter of minutes, Dany had invited eighteen lucky people to a private, evening feast of fish that were only five or six hours out of the ocean.

The first course was Mexican sashimi, as Dave called it, and he had never seen so much raw fish devoured so quickly. That was soon followed by grilled grouper topped with a savory sauce. The wine flowed, the bilingual conversations were animated, and it was the perfect end to a truly wonderful day of fishing.

The Mexican coastlines of the Pacific, the Sea of Cortez, the Gulf of Mexico, and the Caribbean yield an amazing quantity and variety of fish and seafood. Early in the morning, the market stalls are piled high with the fresh catch, and, in a few hours, the fresh fish, shrimp, and shellfish find their way into restaurants and homes. Most of the *pescados y mariscos* used in the following recipes are available in the United States; for those not as readily available, we have suggested substitutes so it will be easy to prepare the recipes.

CEVICHE LORE

"I love ceviche, but some of my friends won't even taste it because they think it's raw fish. It's true that ceviche is not cooked fish; however, it's not raw, like the fish in sashimi and sushi. When you cook fish, the protein muscle fibers coagulate. This is a chemical process which changes the fish from soft and slightly translucent to firm and opaque. The fish in ceviche is also firm and opaque but the same chemical process is accomplished by marinating it in lime juice, in the refrigerator. Ceviche is "cold-cooked" fish.

Will marinating fish eliminate parasites? Deep-sea fish are relatively free of parasites, but freshwater fish and fish such as salmon, that spend part of their lives in fresh water, may be contaminated with roundworms or tapeworm larvae. Cooking fish with heat kills these parasites, but marinating in lime juice may not. When in doubt, freeze the fish, keeping it at zero degrees Fahrenheit for three days. This will kill the parasites making the defrosted fish safe to be eaten cold-cooked or raw."

KATHY GALLANTINE / *Chile Pepper*, 1992

Mexican Sashimi. Photograph by T.Tseng, Creative Commons Attribution 2.0 Generic license, Wikimedia Commons.

Mexican Sashimi

Dave watched chef Dany prepare this colorful sashimi, and we've attempted to reconstruct it here, but it probably isn't exact. No matter. It will be delicious if you pick the freshest fish you can find! You can also make this dish with cooked yellowtail, and it will still be great.

16	thin yellowtail fillets (hamachi) or other mild, raw fish
1	serrano chile, minced
¼	onion, sliced and separated
½	avocado, sliced
⅓	cucumber, chopped
1	lime, sliced in half lengthwise
1	tablespoon soy sauce

Place the fillets on a serving plate. In a bowl, combine all the remaining ingredients and mix well. With your fingers, drop the bowl ingredients over the fillets and serve immediately.

YIELD 6 to 8 servings   HEAT LEVEL Mild to Medium

Stone Soup, Chinoteco-Style

Down at the tip of the Baja California Peninsula, Dave stumbled across a pre-Hispanic chile pepper and fish soup recipe that uses river stones as the heat for cooking. The Chinoteco tribe of Pueblo San Felipe Usila was a fishing-based culture, and their fishermen used guajes, *or "gourd pots," told hold their fresh water while ocean fishing. To make the* guajes, *fresh gourds are used. The seeds and any flesh is removed and the gourds are dried in the sun.*

After the catch, they used the guajes *as pots for cooking their fish chowder because the gourds could not be placed over an open flame. They heated smooth stones in a fire to accomplish this according to the recipe below. It was totally ingenious, and you can replicate it today. The river stones used to cook the soup are smooth, usually polished over centuries by moving water, that are about four inches wide and two inches thick. Similar stones are sold by nurseries as garden decorations. Use your barbecue grill to heat the stones as hot as you can get them and use long tongs with wooden handles to transfer them to the cooking bowl.*

6	river stones, heated as hot as you can get them on the grill
6	large dried gourds cut like bowls or other large bowls
2	pounds snapper or other white fish, cut into ¾-inch cubes
1	medium onion, finely chopped
2	sprigs cilantro
2	springs epazote
2	ripe tomatoes, finely chopped
4	cloves garlic, chopped
4	serrano chiles, finely chopped
	Fish or clam broth as needed

Mix all of the soup ingredients except the water or broth in a large bowl, and then divide it evenly among the 6 bowls. Add the water or broth until each bowl is ¾ full. Add a stone to each bowl and let the soup boil for 4 to 5 minutes. Remove the stones and serve the soup carefully.

YIELD 6 servings   HEAT SCALE Medium

Stone Soup Chinoteco-Style awaiting the snapper and other ingredients. Photograph by Qù F Meltingcardford, Creative Commons Attribution-Share Alike 3.0 Unported license, Wikimedia Commons.

Salmon with Smoked Tomato Pasilla Chile Vinaigrette. Photograph by DragonFly, on iStock.

Salmon Estilo Ritz-Carlton Cancún

SALMON WITH SMOKED TOMATO PASILLA CHILE VINAIGRETTE

Chef John Gray of the Ritz Carlton Cancún presents one of his terrific fish recipes. The pasilla chiles and the balsamic vinegar add a spicy and herbal edge to the grilled salmon. Chef Gray suggests serving this dish with mashed potatoes with serrano chiles and roasted onions.

½	cup finely chopped shallots		Pinch of basil to taste
½	cup dried pasilla chiles, seeds and stems removed, julienned	1	cup, plus 2 tablespoons balsamic vinegar
1	medium tomato, peeled	2	cups olive oil
	Salt and pepper to taste	4	salmon steaks

To prepare the dressing, in a pan, roast the shallots and pasilla chiles until the shallots are golden.

Peel the tomato and smoke it for 5 minutes over charcoal with wood shavings; after smoking, deseed and dice the tomato. Add the tomato to the chiles and shallots. Add salt and pepper to taste; this seasons the tomatoes instead of the dressing.

Allow the mixture to sit for 5 minutes, then add the basil, balsamic vinegar, 1 3/4 cups of the olive oil, and additional salt and fresh cracked pepper to taste.

Brush the salmon steaks with 1/4 cup olive oil and grill the steaks for 3 to 5 minutes per side. Arrange the finished salmon on a heated platter and cover with the reserved vinaigrette.

YIELD 4 servings   HEAT LEVEL Mild

Mero Estilo Tikin Xic

MAYAN-STYLE GROUPER

We again thank chef John Gray of the Ritz-Carlton Hotel in Cancún for this recipe. We cooked this on the beach for a demo of the documentary Heat Up Your Life. *The habanero chile adds just a little heat to this fish dish. As in many Cancún resorts, the guests are "gently" introduced to the flaming chiles of the area; many of these tourists have probably never eaten chiles before, so the chefs tend to use a light and judicious hand with them. Serve this with a rice dish and a salad from chapter 10. This ideally should be cooked in a pellet smoker where the temperature can be steadily maintained automatically.*

2	pound whole grouper, butterflied
1	cup recado rojo (see recipe in chapter 2)
1	cup orange juice
½	cup water
¼	cup plus 2 tablespoons fresh lemon juice
¼	cup plus 2 tablespoons vinegar

2	cloves garlic, chopped
1	medium onion, sliced
1	medium tomato, sliced
2	tablespoons minced habanero chiles
	Salt to taste
	Banana leaves for steaming

Marinate the whole butterflied grouper in a mixture of recado rojo, orange juice, water, lemon juice, vinegar, and garlic for 1 hour.

Cover the fish with the slices of onion and tomato, sprinkle the chiles on top, and then lightly salt the fish.

Layer a grill or smoker with banana leaves. Place the fish on the leaves and layer heavily with more leaves, covering the entire grill.

Bake at 325 degrees F under the leaves for 20 minutes per pound.

YIELD 4 servings HEAT LEVEL Medium

Fish filet "Tikin Xic" made on stovetop.
Photograph by José C. Marmolejo.

For fish and garlic lovers, this recipe from Campeche is the one to cook. The roasted garlic and onion, along with the cumin, vinegar, and chiles, adds a burst of flavor.

2	medium onions, cut in half
8	cloves garlic, unpeeled
1	teaspoon butter
2	tablespoons dry white wine
½	teaspoon ground achiote
1	teaspoon Mexican oregano
1 ½	teaspoons ground cumin
5	whole cloves, ground in a processor
1	teaspoon whole black peppercorns, ground in a spice mill
3	large jalapeño chiles, roasted, peeled, seeds and stems removed

½	cup olive oil
¼	cup fresh lemon juice or lime juice
½	cup vinegar
½	teaspoon salt
1	large banana leaf
4	8-ounce snapper or grouper fillets or steaks
3	tomatoes, sliced
4	*güero* chiles or substitute yellow wax hots, seeds and stems removed and chopped.

Place the onions and garlic in a small ovenproof glass covered casserole dish (or use a terra-cotta garlic roaster), dot them with the butter, and pour in the wine. Roast in a 400 degree F oven for 50 minutes, or until the cloves are soft. Carefully squeeze the cloves out of the peels and place them in a blender along with the onion.

Add to the blender the achiote, oregano, cumin, ground cloves, ground black peppercorns, chiles, oil, lemon juice, vinegar, and salt and puree until the mixture is smooth.

Lightly oil a shallow baking pan, spread the banana leaf in it, and pour 1/2 of the pureed mixture over the banana leaf. Place the fish in a single layer toward the middle of the leaf, and pour the remaining puree over the fish.

Arrange the tomatoes and the chiles over the puree, wrap the leaf over the mixture and secure the leaf with a toothpick.

Bake the fish at 350 degrees F for 25 minutes, or until the fish is tender.

YIELD 4 servings   HEAT LEVEL Medium

Ceviche de Palapa Adriana—Estilo Acapulquito

ACAPULCO-STYLE CEVICHE FROM PALAPA ADRIANA

This recipe is from Kathy Gallantine, who wrote about ceviche in Chile Pepper magazine in her article, "My Search for the Perfect Ceviche." "If you wish to try Acapulquito-Style ceviche at Palapa Adriana," she wrote, "a restaurant on the Malecón in La Paz, Baja California Sur, you must specially request it. The ceviche listed on the menu is served without the peas, carrots, and serrano chiles. Serve this dish for a light lunch or a light dinner on hot nights when you don't even want to turn on an oven!"

1 ½ pounds of any white fish fillet, chopped

8 Mexican (Key) limes, juiced

2 serrano chiles, stems and seeds removed, minced

1 tomato, finely chopped

½ onion, finely chopped

¼ cup canned peas

¼ cup finely diced cooked carrots

2 teaspoons minced fresh cilantro

Salt and black pepper to taste

8 to 10 corn tortillas, fried flat and very crisp

Acapulco-Style Ceviche from Palapa Adriana. Photograph by Proformabooks on iStock.

Place the chopped fish in a shallow container. Pour the lime juice over the fish, cover, and refrigerate the mixture for about two hours, stirring occasionally, until the fish is opaque.

Just before serving the ceviche, stir in the tomato, onion, peas, carrots, and cilantro. Add the salt and pepper to taste. With a slotted spoon, heap the ceviche onto the crisp tortillas and serve.

VARIATION Use tiny cocktail shrimp or sliced bay scallops in place of the white fish. Reduce the marinating time to 30 minutes or less.

YIELD 3 to 4 servings   HEAT LEVEL Mild

Mexican-Style Clams. Photograph by Fudio on iStock.

Almejas a la Mexicana — MEXICAN-STYLE CLAMS

Since the Baja California coastline is thousands of miles long, it is no wonder that everyone partakes in the wonderful varieties of fish and seafood. Serve these spicy clams over an equally spicy pasta or a rice dish from chapter 10.

6	dozen clams		5	*serrano* chiles, seeds and stems removed and chopped
1	cup water		¼	cup chopped cilantro
1	cup dry white wine		1	teaspoon salt
½	cup olive oil		½	teaspoon freshly ground black pepper
1	large onion, chopped			
3	cups peeled and chopped tomatoes			Cotija cheese (or substitute Parmesan), grated

Thoroughly clean the clams.

Put all of the remaining ingredients in a large stock pot, bring the mixture to a light rolling boil, reduce the heat to a simmer, add the clams, cover, and steam until the shells open, about 10 minutes. Discard any unopened shells.

Combine the remaining ingredients except for the cheese in a bowl to make a salsa.

Serve the clams with the salsa ladled over them and a little cheese grated over them.

VARIATION *Serve the clams over a spicy pasta covered with a warm tomato salsa.*

YIELD 6 to 7 servings   HEAT LEVEL Medium

Conch Ceviche. Photograph by shalamov on iStock.

Ceviche de Caracol del Mar

CONCH CEVICHE

This dish is one where you get to beat the heck out of the conch with a meat tenderizing mallet! If you don't, you'll still be chewing it three years from now. It is tough, but it is also extremely tasty, much like abalone. Serve this dish from Yucatán on chopped mixed greens and include some grated radish. Garnish with warm corn chips and lime slices.

1	pound fresh conch, pounded to tenderize and cut into bite size pieces
¼	cup fresh lime juice
¾	cup fresh lemon juice
1	habanero chile, seeds and stem removed and minced
1	cup finely chopped onion
¼	cup chopped cilantro
1	cup peeled and chopped tomato
¼	cup olive oil
1	teaspoon salt
¼	teaspoon freshly ground black pepper

Put the cut-up conch in a shallow glass pan and cover with the lime and lemon juice. Marinate in the refrigerator for 5 hours. Drain the conch and place it in a mixing bowl.

Add the chile, onion, cilantro, tomato, olive oil, salt, and black pepper, mix, and serve.

NOTE *This recipe requires advance preparation.*

YIELD 3 to 4 servings   HEAT LEVEL Hot

Jaiba a la Veracruzana

Another delicious recipe from beautiful Veracruz! If fresh, whole crabs are not available, cook crab legs, remove the meat, and then serve the final mixture in small, ovenproof, shell-shaped individual serving dishes. This entree is easy to prepare and makes an elegant presentation.

12	fresh whole crabs, cooked and meat removed and shells reserved (or, substitute 3 pounds freshly cooked crab legs)
¼	cup olive oil
1	cup minced onions
3	cloves garlic, minced
1 ½	cups peeled, chopped tomatoes
4	serrano chiles, minced, seeds and stems removed
2	tablespoons minced parsley
½	teaspoon salt
¼	teaspoon freshly ground black pepper
¾	cup coarsely chopped green olives
⅔	cup dry bread crumbs
1	egg, thoroughly whisked

Garnishes: Thinly sliced lemons or limes

Minced parsley

Coarsely chop the crab meat and set aside. Heat the oil in a medium size sauté pan and sauté the onions and the garlic for 1 minute. Add the tomatoes, chiles, parsley, salt, and black pepper and sauté for another minute, stirring and tossing the mixture.

Then, mix the reserved crab, olives, and bread crumbs into the sautéed mixture. Mound this mixture into lightly oiled crab shells or oven proof shell ramekins.

Pour about 1 teaspoon of the whisked egg and a few drops of olive oil over each portion. Place the shells on a baking sheet and bake for 20 minutes in an oven pre-heated to 350 degree F, or until golden. Garnish and serve immediately.

YIELD 6 to 8 servings HEAT LEVEL Medium

Veracruz-Style Crab.
Photograph by nobtis on iStock.

If you can't find mulato chiles, substitute an extra ancho or pasilla chile. Serve this chile shrimp from Baja California with hot rice and complement the dish with sautéed baby vegetables.

2	dozen large, fresh shrimp		1	onion, cut into eighths
1	mulato chile, stem and seeds removed		2	cloves garlic
			½	teaspoon salt
1	ancho chile, stem and seeds removed		2	teaspoons Mexican oregano
			2	tablespoons white wine vinegar
1	pasilla chile, stem and seeds removed		2	tablespoons olive oil

Bring a small pot of water to a boil, rinse the shrimp in cold water, and add the shrimp to the water. Boil for 3 minutes or until the shrimp turns pink. Drain the shrimp and peel them when they are cool enough to handle and set aside.

Toast the chiles in a skillet, over a low heat, for 1 minute, tossing them and taking care that they don't burn. Remove the pan from the heat, cover the chiles with hot water, soak them for 10 minutes, and then drain the chiles.

Place the chiles and the soaking water in a blender and add the onion, garlic, salt, oregano, white wine vinegar, and puree until smooth.

Heat the oil in a small skillet and pour in the pureed chile mixture and simmer for 5 minutes, adding more water if the mixture gets too thick. Add the shrimp, mix it with the chile sauce, and simmer for 30 seconds.

Pour the shrimp mixture into a lightly oiled, small casserole dish and bake in a 350 degree F preheated oven and bake for 5 minutes. Serve the shrimp hot from the oven over rice.

YIELD 4 servings   HEAT LEVEL Medium

Baja-Style Chile Shrimp.
Photograph by ALLEKO on iStock.

Camarones Adobados Estilo Veracruz

ADOBO SHRIMP VERACRUZ-STYLE

This Veracruz-style dish involves sautéing the shrimp rather than boiling it, as in the Baja-style. The chiles and cider vinegar add the spark to this recipe. Serve with warm tortillas and a shredded lettuce, tomato, and jícama salad with an oil and vinegar dressing.

4	tablespoons corn or canola oil		2	cloves garlic
1	pound fresh shrimp, peeled		1	teaspoon ground black pepper
5	pasilla chiles, seeds and stems removed, roasted		⅓	cup apple cider vinegar
1	onion, cut into eighths		½	teaspoon whole cumin seeds, crushed

Heat 2 tablespoons of the oil in a medium sauté skillet, add the shrimp, and sauté for 2 minutes. Using a slotted spoon, place the shrimp in a small bowl and set aside.

Add 1 tablespoon of the oil to the shrimp pan and sauté the onion and garlic for 1 minute. Remove the pan from the heat and stir in the chiles, black pepper, vinegar, and the cumin. Allow the mixture to cool for a few minutes and then put the mixture into a blender and puree until smooth.

Heat the remaining tablespoon of oil in the sauté pan, add the pureed chile mixture, and simmer for 15 minutes, stirring frequently and adding enough water to keep the mixture thick and heavy and to avoid burning.

Add the reserved shrimp to the sauce and simmer for 2 minutes, only long enough to heat the mixture and to allow the chile flavor to infuse the shrimp. Serve hot.

Adobo Shrimp Veracruz-Style.
Photograph by javarman3 on iStock.

VARIATION *Serve the shrimp over a spicy pasta covered with a warm tomato salsa.*

YIELD 2 to 3 servings   HEAT LEVEL Medium

A bowl of mole poblano sauce.
Photograph by Juanmonino at iStock.

Muchos Moles

Someone once said, "There are as many recipes for salsas as households in Mexico." We submit the same goes for moles. While in the United States, standardization may be the goal, in Mexico, flavor uniqueness, personality, or "household signature flavor" is the aim. Nevertheless, somehow we are permanently looking for that fabulous, original, authentic, pure, one-in-a-million recipe that is going to transport us to heaven more than once. We can make the search our life's purpose, but when we find it, is almost impossible to retain. The experience as a rule—with its due exemptions—can never be repeated.

José shares the following mole experience: I once found a *mole verde* in a humble *fonda* (inn) in the market of Valle de Bravo—a beautiful town about eighty miles west of Mexico City—that I enjoyed immensely. One day driving from Zitácuaro, Michoacán, to Mexico City with Diana Kennedy, we took a detour to see my weekend property which we used for about twenty years for ecological education purposes, and Diana, an environmental activist, was curious to see. While in Valle de Bravo, I suggested that we go for lunch to try that mole verde. The place was named La Fonda de Toño, but guess what? That day, the mole was not perfect, and Diana, as usual, did not hesitate to fully express it. However, she also vocally appreciated the extraordinary cleanliness and beauty of the place. She loved to see all the pots and pans hanging, perfectly arranged and spotless, inside the little establishment's open kitchen. She told me that someone who takes pride in displaying his cooking tools must be a good cook, but the magic of the mole verde that we were after just wasn't there that day. Sometime later, I went back again by myself, looking for that memorable mole verde, and Toño, the cook and owner of the little establishment, had passed away.

In my perspective, mole is a sauce that usually has the following groups of ingredients: chiles, fruits (fresh and/or dried), seeds, herbs, and spices plus sugar and salt. Any mole thus can have easily a dozen or dozens of ingredients! Having said that, you can now imagine the infinite combinations of those ingredients, and you can begin to see the magnitude of the universe of the different moles that are possible and that do exist! To further complicate the mole equation, add the flavors—take your pick— of turkey, pork, goat, chicken, insects, worms,

SECRETS OF MOLE

"A *mole* recipe is not something dashed off on a file card and handed
to an appreciative dinner guest. It is a family treasure, and in some cases
a family secret. A visitor certainly can ask for the recipe and the flattered
cook may begin ticking off the ingredients of the fingers of both hands,
sometimes two or three times over. But ask the cook to specify proportions
of ingredients and the steps to create the *mole*, and the conversation
suddenly can become vague."

William Stockton, *The Albuquerque Tribune*, December 12, 1985

and seafood, and the result is nothing short of mind boggling. And we must not forget that the stock we use also has an important role in the final flavor of the product. As you can see, "the chocolate sauce"—as I often hear it referred to in the United States—is a very limited concept, since chocolate can be only one of multiple ingredients a mole can have—if present, since it is not always the case.

Moles can be sweet, fruity, spicy, salty, fiery, and much more depending on the accent a specific ingredient can impart. This is decided by the mind and the hands of the cook, and his or her mood that day. The combination of chiles, herbs, spices, nuts, and chocolate can produce unimaginable flavors! Here resides the element of surprise. In addition, mole ingredients have an effect on the brain. So, it is just not the look, flavor, smell, or texture that affects our senses and determines our experience, some substances in the mole go to our brain to release endorphins that make us feel very good, crave for more, and, at times, reach ecstasy. Just think how amazing a mix of endorphins produced by chiles, chocolate, and sugar will make you feel!

Many of us have heard the legend of the "Siete Moles de Oaxaca"—seven moles that belong to each of the seven regions of that beautiful state. The legend is a strong symbol of a rich cultural heritage (Oaxaca is the state in Mexico with the highest percentage of its population speaking native languages); it is an expression of pride that is also reflected in their attire, crafts, customs, festivals, and food, among other traits. Politically, the state of Oaxaca today is divided in eight regions: Cañada, Costa, Istmo, Mixteca, Papaloapan, Sierra Sur, Sierra Norte, and Valles Centrales, where you can find 570 municipalities and more than eleven thousand communities. Due to the diversity in topography, climate, and ecosystems, you could say that there are eight states and cultures within Oaxaca, as the culture of the mountains has nothing to do with the culture of the Valles Centrales or that of the Isthmus of Tehuantepec. Even though those *siete* moles have been adopted to represent different regional cultures, there are other, lesser-known moles that, due to the isolation of small towns hidden in the mountains where access is limited, have not traveled to Oaxaca to be widely known. There are claims that Oaxaca already has around twenty different moles; in my view, it's a world yet to be discovered.

Making mole is not rocket science. It is sold as a mix, in a paste or powder form. The mix is dissolved with animal or vegetable stock, and the sauce is ready. You can then customize the concoction by adding one or more ingredients to your liking and give your preparation a distinct personality or your "household signature flavor." This is both easy and fun. Our advice is to get some mole in a paste or powder form and prepare it according to its instructions. Then see if you like it and begin to add, bit by bit, chipotles en adobo or ground chile de árbol to make it spicier, chile pasilla for sophistication, brown sugar to make it sweeter, herbs and spices to achieve a more complex flavor, nuts for a more refined taste, or chocolate to please easy palates.

José once bought red mole powder in bulk at around $2.75 per pound, and was going to make some mole, but he felt like trying a prune flavor. So he bought some prunes, ground them in a blender with some stock, and added them, little by little, to his mole pot until he reached the flavor he was looking for. Easy, right?

If you travel to Mexico, try muchos moles (don´t hesitate to ask for tastings before ordering one), and when you find an outstanding creation, enjoy it as much as possible, ask for seconds, try to get the recipe, and keep in mind that most likely the experience can't be repeated. If this is the case, you just had a once in a lifetime experience. Buen provecho!

This recipe is from Susana Trilling. She writes in her article, "My Search for the Seventh Mole": "*I have suggested chile substitutions here to reflect varieties more commonly available north of the border. You can use vegetable oil instead of lard, but the flavor will change dramatically. In our pueblo, people use chicken or turkey, which is traditional, and also add pork meat and a piece of beef to enhance the flavor.*"

1	whole chicken, cut into eight serving pieces
6	cups chicken stock
5	chilhuacle negro chiles, stems and seeds removed (or substitute ancho chiles)
5	guajillo chiles, stems and seeds removed (save the seeds) or red New Mexican chiles
4	pasilla chiles, stems and seeds removed (save the seeds)
4	mulato chiles, stems and seeds removed (save the seeds) or ancho chiles
2	chipotle chiles, stems and seeds removed (save the seeds)
1	medium white onion, quartered
6	cloves garlic
2	tablespoons whole almonds
2	tablespoons shelled and skinned peanuts

2 to 4 tablespoons lard or vegetable oil

2	teaspoons raisins
1	slice of bread (challah or egg-rich bread is best)
1	small ripe plantain, sliced or substitute a banana
½	cup sesame seeds
2	pecan halves
1	1-inch cinnamon stick, Mexican preferred
2	whole peppercorns
2	whole cloves
2	medium tomatoes, chopped
5	fresh tomatillos, chopped
1/2	teaspoon dried oregano
½	teaspoon dried thyme
1	avocado leaf, omit if not available or substitute bay leaf
1	bar or to taste Mexican chocolate, Ibarra preferred

Salt to taste

Plenty of fresh tortillas

Simmer the chicken in the stock until tender, about 1/2 hour. Remove the chicken and keep warm and reserve the stock.

In a large frying pan or comal, toast the chiles, turning once until darkened, but not burned or, as some oaxaqueñas prefer, fry the chiles in lard.

Oaxacan Black Mole. Photograph by Esdelval on iStock.

Place the chiles in a bowl and cover with hot water to soak for 1/2 hour to soften. Remove the chiles and place in a blender or food processor and puree, adding a little chile water if necessary, to form a paste.

In the same pan, roast the onions and garlic cloves until slightly browned, remove. Then toast the almonds and peanuts slightly, remove. Finally, toast the chile seeds, taking care to make them dark but not burned.

Heat 2 tablespoons of lard in the skillet and fry the raisins until plumped, remove and drain on paper towels. Next fry the bread until browned, remove and drain. Repeat with the plantains. Add more lard if necessary, lower the heat and fry the sesame seeds slowly, stirring often. When they are slightly browned, add the pecans and brown, remove and drain.

Toast the cinnamon, peppercorns, and cloves lightly in a dry pan. Cool and grind in a molcajete or spice grinder.

In a food processor or blender, puree the nuts, bread, sesame seeds, and pecans in small batches, remove. Add the onions, garlic, plantains and puree, remove. Finally, add and puree the tomatoes and tomatillos.

In a large *cazuela* (heavy pot) heat the remaining lard and fry the chile paste, stirring constantly so it will not burn. When it is "dry" (when the chiles have absorbed most of the liquid) add the tomato puree and fry until the liquid has evaporated. Add the ground spices, the nut-bread mixture, the pureed onion mixture, and the oregano and thyme.

Heat, stirring constantly, to a simmer and add the chocolate to the mole. Toast the avocado leaf for a second over the open flame and add. Slowly add some of the reserved chicken stock to the mole until the mixture is just thick enough to lightly coat a spoon and salt to taste. Continue to simmer for 5 minutes, return the chicken to the mole and heat through. Serve with plenty of sauce and hot tortillas.

YIELD 4 to 6 servings   HEAT LEVEL Hot

Oaxacan Little Red Mole. Photograph by Alejandro Linares Garcia, GNU Free Documentation License, Version 1.2, Wikimedia Commons.

Mole Coloradito Oaxaqueño

OAXACAN LITTLE RED MOLE

This recipe is also from Susanna Trilling. She notes that there are still many señoras in the small pueblos who insist on using their molcajetes for the tedious grinding of the ingredients used in this celebrated dish!

1	whole chicken, cut into eight serving pieces
6	cups chicken stock
5	ancho chiles, stems and seeds removed
2	guajillo chiles, stems and seeds removed, or substitute dried red New Mexican chiles
5	whole peppercorns
5	whole cloves
2	2-inch cinnamon sticks, Mexican preferred
1	white onion, peeled and quartered
10	cloves garlic
3	tablespoons lard or vegetable oil
1	small French roll, sliced
1	small plantain or substitute a banana
2	tablespoons raisins
¼	cup sesame seeds
10	whole almonds
2	medium tomatoes, quartered
3	sprigs fresh marjoram or oregano
1	bar or to taste Mexican chocolate, such as Ibarra
1 or 2	avocado leaves or substitute bay leaves
	Salt to taste

Simmer the chicken in the stock until tender, about ½ hour. Remove the chicken and keep warm and reserve the stock.

In a large frying pan or comal, toast the chiles, turning once until darkened, but not burned. Toast the guajillos a little longer because of their tougher skins. Place the chiles in a bowl and cover with hot water to soak for ½ hour to soften.

Remove the chiles and place in a blender or food processor and puree, adding a little chile water if necessary, strain.

Toast the peppercorns, cloves, and lightly in a dry pan or comal. Cool and grind in a molcajete or spice grinder.

In the same pan, roast the onions and garlic cloves until slightly browned. Cool and place in a blender or food processor and puree with a little water.

Heat the lard in the pan until smoking hot, and fry the bread until lightly brown, remove and drain on paper towels.

Fry the plantain on both sides until browned, remove and drain. Quickly fry the raisins, remove. Lower the heat and add the sesame seeds, stirring constantly for a couple of minutes then add the almonds and continue to fry until both are well browned. Remove, drain, and combine with the bread, plantain, and raisins, reserving bit of the sesame seeds for garnish.

Place in a blender or food processor and puree, adding a little water if necessary. Wipe out the skillet with a cloth and add 1 tablespoon lard. When hot, add the tomatoes and fry well. Place in a blender or food processor and puree until smooth, remove.

Heat a tablespoon of lard in a cazuela or heavy pot until smoking. Add the chile puree and fry, stirring constantly, so it will not burn. It tends to splatter about, so be careful! Fry for a couple of minutes, add the tomato puree, the ground spices, and the marjoram and heat through.

Stir in the bread mixture and continue to heat, stirring constantly. Add the chocolate and avocado leaves, thin with the reserved chicken stock, and continue to simmer for 30 minutes.

Add the chicken, adjust the salt, and heat through. Serve with black beans, rice, and tortillas.

YIELD 4 to 6 servings   HEAT LEVEL Medium

This recipe was collected in Jalisco, where cooks combine pasillas, cascabels, and pickled jalapeños to form their trilogy of chiles. This is certainly one of the simplest mole recipes we've come across. It's also very tasty.

1	chicken, sectioned
	Water to cover
2	medium onions, sliced
	Salt to taste
1 ½	cups rice, cleaned and soaked
4	pasilla chiles, seeds and stems removed
3	cascabel chiles, seeds and stems removed
4	tablespoons vegetable oil
1	teaspoon cumin
6	black peppercorns
4	cloves garlic, crushed
4	green tomatoes, chopped
S	alt to taste
½ to 1	head lettuce, shredded
	Pickled jalapeños to taste

Place the chicken parts in a pan, cover with water, and add the onions and salt to taste. Cook the chicken until it is tender, 45 minutes to 1 hour. Once cooked, remove the chicken from the broth, keep it warm, and set the broth aside.

Measure the broth to 3 cups, adding more water if necessary. Cook the rice in the broth until done, stirring occasionally to make sure it doesn't stick.

In a separate pan, fry the dried chiles in a little oil, then add the cumin, peppercorns, garlic, onions, tomatoes, and green tomatoes until the chiles become soft. Remove to a blender and puree, then return to the pan. Add the rice and cook for a few minutes.

Serve the rice with the chicken and decorate with the lettuce and jalapeños.

YIELD 6 servings HEAT LEVEL Medium

Chicken in mole with rice.
Photograph by carlosrojas20 on iStock.

Chichilo Oaxaqueño

Susana Trilling observes in her article, "My Search for the Seventh Mole": Here is the legendary seventh mole from Oaxaca, my friend Celia's famous mole chichilo."

THE MEAT AND BEEF STOCK

1 ½	pounds beef bones with meat; meat cut off the bones
2	quarts water
1	onion, chopped
8	cloves garlic
1	bay leaf
1	chile de árbol or substitute large piquín or *santaka* chile
5	whole peppercorns
2	carrots, chopped
2	stalks celery, chopped
1	whole allspice berry
1	whole clove
½	pound pork butt, cut in 1-inch cubes

Chilhuacle negro pods in the Oaxacan market. Photograph by Dave DeWitt.

THE CHILE PUREE

5	chilhuacle negro chiles, stems and seeds removed (save the seeds) or substitute anchos
6	guajillo chiles, stems and seeds removed, (save the seeds) or substitute red New Mexican chiles
1	corn tortilla, torn into strips
1	sprig fresh oregano
1	sprig fresh thyme
2	allspice berries
1	whole clove
1	teaspoon cumin seeds
1	stick cinnamon, 2-inches long, Mexican preferred
	Tomato puree
4	large tomatoes, quartered
3	fresh tomatillos, halved
1	clove garlic
1	small onion, roasted
2	chayotes or substitute zucchini, sliced thin
½	pound green beans, chopped
5	small potatoes, peeled and quartered
3	tablespoons lard or vegetable oil
2 to 3	avocado leaves, or substitute bay leaves
	Salt to taste

Garnish: Sliced onion and lime

To make the meat and beef stock, in a large stock pot, cover the beef bones with cold water, bring to a boil, and boil for 20 minutes, skimming off any foam that forms. Lower the heat and add the onion, garlic, bay leaf, chile de árbol, peppercorns, carrots, celery stalks, cloves, allspice, clove and cook for 5 minutes. Add the beef and pork cubes, lower the heat and simmer, covered, for 1 hour. Strain the stock, cool in the refrigerator, and skim off any fat that rises to the top.

To make the chile puree, in a large frying pan or comal, toast the chiles, turning once until darkened, but not burned. Place the chiles in a bowl and cover with hot water to soak for 1/2 hour to soften.

Toast the tortilla strips on the comal until they blacken, remove. Toast the saved chile seeds on the comal and heat until the seeds are blackened. Remove the seeds and place in water to soak. Change the water after 5 minutes, and soak again for another 5 minutes. Drain.

Drain the chiles and place in a blender or food processor along with the tortillas, blackened seeds, oregano, thyme, allspice, clove, cumin, cinnamon, and a little water and puree to a paste.

To make the tomato puree and finish, roast the tomatoes and tomatillos on the comal until soft, and remove. Then roast the onion and garlic. Place them in the blender and puree.

Bring 3 cups of the reserved stock to a boil and the chayote, beans, and potatoes. Reduce the heat, and simmer until the potato is easily pierced with a fork. Drain and reserve the vegetables.

Heat the lard or oil in a heavy pot or cazuela and fry the chile puree. Add the tomato mixture and fry for a couple of minutes. Stir in just enough of the beef stock to thin the mixture and salt to taste. Toast the avocado leaves and add.

Add the vegetables to the mole and heat through. Garnish the mole with the sliced onion and a lime slice and serve.

YIELD 4 to 6 servings   HEAT LEVEL Medium

MEXICAN MOLE SAYINGS

"Don't tell me you ate mole without wiping your mustache."

"When you grind and grind, not even the metate is left."

"There is no mole if there's no metate."

"If you didn't put chile in it, don't pretend to know."

"Mole, mole, give them mole."

"You are the sesame seed of my mole."

Mole Poblano con Pollo

MOLE POBLANO WITH CHICKEN

This recipe is from our friend Jim Peyton, who has written two books on the foods of the border country and has also contributed to Chile Pepper *magazine. He says that as with most Mexican dishes, there are probably as many recipes for mole poblano as there are cooks who have prepared it. According to Jim, the mole recipe presented here is an amalgamation and is as elaborate as this recipe gets in terms of the number of different ingredients. There are no poblano chiles used in this recipe, but the dried version of them, the ancho, is used instead. This means that the name of the mole is not derived from the fresh chile pod. Rather, mole poblano means, specifically, "the mole from the state or city of Puebla." Note: Turkey or duck may be substituted for the chicken.*

CHILE PASTE

1 dried mulato chile, stem and seeds removed

1 dried ancho chile, stem and seeds removed

2 pasilla chiles, stems and seeds removed

1 chipotle chile, stem removed

1 tablespoon vegetable oil, optional

SPICE MIXTURE

4 fresh tomatillos, husks removed

3 tablespoons vegetable oil

1 tomato, roasted and peeled

½ teaspoon coriander seeds

½ teaspoon chile seeds

3 tablespoons sesame seeds

¼ teaspoon anise

2 whole cloves

½ inch stick cinnamon

¼ teaspoon whole black peppercorns

3 tablespoons pumpkin seeds

2 tablespoons peanuts

2 tablespoons almonds

2 tablespoons raisins

3 tablespoons dried, chopped prunes

1 3-inch piece plantain, or substitute a banana

½ corn tortilla

½ piece white bread

1 to 2 cups chicken broth, homemade preferred

THE CHICKEN AND FINISHING THE DISH

2 to 3 tablespoons vegetable oil

4 boneless skinless chicken breasts, cut in half

1 to 2 cups chicken broth

1 tablespoon sugar

1 ounce Mexican or bittersweet chocolate

Garnish: 2 to 3 tablespoons sesame seeds

Mole Poblano with Chicken. Photograph by Marcos Elihu Castillo Ramirez on iStock.

To make the chile paste, either fry the chiles, except the chipotle, in a little oil or toast in a 250 degree oven until they just begin to brown and become fragrant, taking care that they do not burn.

Place the toasted chiles and the chipotle in 2 cups hot water and soak for 15 minutes or until soft.

Place the chiles and a little of the water they were soaking in, in a blender and puree to a paste. Strain the paste.

To make the spice mixture, fry the tomatillo in a tablespoon of the oil until just soft, about 5 minutes, drain, and place in a blender. Add the tomatoes.

Toast the seeds, anise, cloves, cinnamon, and peppercorns in a heavy skillet over a low heat, stirring constantly until the sesame seeds just begin to brown—about 3 to 5 minutes. Allow the seeds to cool and place in a coffee or spice grinder and grind until a fine powder is achieved. Add to the tomatillos and tomatoes.

Fry the pumpkin seeds in a tablespoon of oil until they puff up. Be careful, as they will pop and spatter as they brown. Drain and add to the blender.

Fry the nuts, raisins, and prunes in a tablespoon of oil for about 2 minutes or until the raisins are puffed. Remove and add to the blender.

Fry the plantain until it begins to brown. Remove and add to the blender.

Finally, fry the tortilla and bread until the tortilla is softened, adding more oil if necessary. Remove, drain, and coarsely chop. Add to the blender.

Blend the spice mixture, adding just enough chicken broth to make a thick paste. Remove the paste to a bowl.

To make the chicken and finish the mole, heat the oil in a skillet and quickly brown the chicken breasts; remove and keep warm.

Add the chile paste to the skillet and simmer for 5 minutes. Next add the spice mixture and continue simmering for an additional 5 minutes. Stir in enough broth to produce a sauce that just coats a spoon or about as thick as a thin milkshake.

Add the sugar and chocolate to the sauce and stir to dissolve. Return the chicken breasts and simmer, uncovered, for 5 to 10 minutes or until just cooked through.

Garnish with the sesame seeds and serve.

VARIATION *To prepare mole enchiladas, simply wrap shredded chicken in corn tortillas that have been softened in hot oil, top with the sauce and garnish, and heat at 350 degrees F for 10 minutes.*

YIELD 4 servings HEAT LEVEL Medium

Mole de Olla con Epazote

Mole is not only a sauce but a thick soup, too. If you have a taste for mole but very little time, try this quick and easy recipe from Tlaxcala. Serve the chicken with hot rice and an avocado salad.

5 tomatoes

8 to 10 chipotle chiles, seeds and stems removed

2 cloves garlic

4 tablespoons vegetable oil

1 3-pound chicken, cut into 6 or 8 pieces

½ cup water

½ cup chicken broth

1 teaspoon salt

¼ cup chopped epazote

Roast the tomatoes in a skillet until the skins blister; allow them to cool slightly and then peel and cut the tomatoes in half.

Tear or cut the chiles into strips, cover with hot water, and rehydrate them for 20 minutes. Place the chiles and the soaking water into a blender; add the tomatoes and the garlic, and puree until the mixture is smooth.

Heat 2 tablespoons of the oil in a small skillet, pour in the pureed mixture, and sauté for 5 minutes.

Heat the remaining oil in a medium size skillet, lightly brown the chicken, add the water, chicken stock, and salt, and bring to a boil. Reduce the heat and simmer for 20 minutes, covered.

Pour the sautéed chile mixture over the chicken, cover, and simmer for 15 minutes. Add the epazote and simmer for 10 minutes more. Serve hot with rice.

YIELD 6 servings   HEAT LEVEL Medium

Pot Mole with Epazote. Photograph by UAwiki, Creative Commons Attribution 2.0 Generic license, Wikimedia Commons.

A "hotluck" celebration at the Fiery Foods Show. Photograph by Wes Naman. Work for hire. Sunbelt Archives.

10){ Fiery Accompaniments and a Few Desserts

Vegetables and side dishes are what we all bring to potluck parties. Think of spicy Mexico, with all of its herbs, spices, and chiles, and you too can create something so dynamic that it will outshine the standard potluck entrée and make it a "hotluck" delight!

Fruits and Vegetables

The New World vegetables that were cultivated in Mexico sustained both rich and poor alike. Corn, beans, squash, and chiles were nutritious and valuable as commodities. Maize (corn) and squash are reputed to be the first cultivated crops in the ancient Valley of Mexico, circa 7000 BC. Squash is available to everyone, but fresh squash blossoms, piled high in the markets, are some of the most fragrant and delectable parts used in special recipes. You may be able to find squash blossoms in farmer's markets, or you can harvest the male flowers from your own garden—they're the ones with no baby squashes attached to them.

FLAVORFUL MONEY

"Chocolate was so expensive that is could hardly have been the drink of poor peasants. It was used in Mexico as a currency instead of the coinage that the Aztecs had never originated. The pods of the cacao were made up into packs of 24,000 pods as a standard unit of currency."
Carson Ritchie, *Food in Civilization*, 1991

Ensalada de Flor de Calabaza con Vinagre Enchilado

SQUASH BLOSSOM SALAD WITH CHILE VINEGAR

According to Lula Bertrán, "We use squash blossoms very often in our recipes. We think they are very Mexican. What I wanted to do in this recipe was use my vinegar because everyone loves it so much. The vinegar will work in any kind of salad." Note that the vinegar must sit for at least two days.

THE VINEGAR

1	cup apple cider vinegar
2	cloves garlic
6	black peppercorns
6	white peppercorns
6	green peppercorns
1	chile de árbol or substitute ½ New Mexican chile
4	chiltepínes or substitute chile piquines
1	serrano chile, seeds and stem removed, halved
1	sprig fresh basil
2	sprigs fresh rosemary
1	bay leaf

THE SQUASH BLOSSOM SALAD

1 ½	cups julienned jicama
1	cup watercress
1	cup mixed lettuce leaves
8	large squash blossoms, or substitute other edible flowers, minced
½	cup sesame oil
½	teaspoon roasted sesame seeds
½	cup Chile Vinegar
	Salt and freshly ground pepper to taste
½	cup grated goat cheese

Combine all ingredients for the vinegar in a bottle. Cover and let sit in a cool place for at least two days and preferably one month.

Squash blossoms for the salad.
Photograph by MahirAtes on iStock.

To assemble the salad, place the julienned jicama in a cross-hatched pattern on the center of each of four salad plates. Cover partially with the watercress and lettuce leaves. Sprinkle on the minced squash blossoms.

In a jar, mix together the sesame oil, sesame seeds, chile vinegar, and salt and pepper. Lightly pour the dressing over the salads and top with the goat cheese.

NOTE *This recipe requires advance preparation.*

YIELD 1 cup vinegar; 4 servings of salad
HEAT LEVEL Mild

Chayote squash. Photograph by debaird, Creative Commons Attribution 2.0 Generic license, Wikimedia Commons.

Chayotes Exquisitos

EXQUISITE CHAYOTES

Squash is one of the staples of the New World foods, and in this recipe from Hidalgo, chayote squash plays the starring role. Chayote has a delicate taste and takes well to any type of seasoning. Serve this side dish with a spicy pork recipe from chapter 6 or 7.

4 poblano chiles, roasted, peeled, seeds and stems removed	1 ½ cups whole corn kernels, preferably fresh off the cob
1 tablespoon vegetable oil	Water as needed
2 tablespoons butter	½ cup milk
1 cup chopped onion	½ teaspoon salt
5 chayotes, washed and cut into eighths	¼ teaspoon freshly grated black pepper
	1 cup grated Monterey Jack cheese

Cut the roasted chile into 1 inch square pieces and set aside.

Heat the oil and the butter in a sauté skillet, add the onion, and sauté for 1 minute. Then, add the chayote squash and the corn and sauté over a low heat for 2 minutes. If the mixture starts to dry out, add a few tablespoons of water.

Stir in the cubed chile, milk, salt, and pepper and simmer until the chayote has softened.

Remove the sautéed mixture to a small glass baking dish, cover with the cheese, and bake at 350 degrees F for 10 minutes, or until the cheese has melted.

YIELD 6 servings   HEAT LEVEL Mild

When you eat chayote squash, you are eating a part of history, starting with the Aztecs and the Mayas. Chayote was one of the mainstays of their diet. The squash has a delicate taste and takes well to high seasoning. This side dish from Sinaloa goes well with any meat, poultry, or seafood dish.

2	ancho chiles, seeds and stems removed
	Hot water
3	garlic cloves
1	teaspoon dried thyme
¼	teaspoon ground cumin
½	teaspoon salt

2	teaspoons butter or vegetable oil
¼	cup chopped onion
3	tablespoons dried bread crumbs
2	tablespoons cider vinegar
1	pound chayote squash, peeled and sliced into ¼ inch slices

Squash in Adobo Sauce. Photograph by porosolka on iStock.

Tear the ancho chile into strips, put them into a small dish, add 1 cup of hot water, and let the chile rehydrate for 20 minutes.

Pour the chiles and water into a blender and add the garlic, thyme, cumin, salt, and puree until smooth. Set aside.

Heat the butter in a sauté skillet and sauté the onion for 1 minute. Add the chile puree to the onion, along with the bread crumbs and cider vinegar, cover and simmer for 10 minutes. Stir the mixture and add more water or stock if the mixture gets too thick.

While the sauce is simmering, steam the chayote squash in 1/2 cup water for 8 minutes. Drain and then add to the simmering sauce. Serve immediately.

YIELD 5 to 6 servings HEAT LEVEL Mild

Chickpea Salad with Poblanos. Photograph by nata_vkusidey on iStock.

Ensalada de Garbanzos con Poblanos
CHICKPEA SALAD WITH POBLANOS

Serve this delicious Sonoran-style dish over shredded mixed greens to accompany one of the fish dishes from chapter 9. We recommend using freshly cooked chickpeas, but the canned variety will also work if the peas are thoroughly rinsed.

Juice of 1 lemon

Juice of 2 limes

¼ cup minced cilantro

¼ cup olive oil

¾ cup minced onion

2 ½ cups cooked chickpeas

6 ounces cream cheese, softened

2 poblano chiles, roasted and peeled, seeds and stems removed, chopped fine

Mixed greens

Mix the citrus juices, cilantro, olive oil, and the onion in a medium size glass bowl. Allow to stand at room temperature for 3 hours.

In a small bowl, combine the cooked chickpeas, softened cream cheese, and the chiles and mix thoroughly.

Add this mixture to the marinated citrus mixture and mix thoroughly.

Serve the mixture over shredded, mixed greens.

YIELD 4 servings   HEAT LEVEL Mild

Elote con Crema y Chiles Serranos
SPICY CREAMED CORN AND SERRANO CHILES

The state of Morelos is beautiful and diverse. Dave's wife Mary Jane lived in Cuernavaca for three months while going to summer school language classes and ate herself silly the entire time! This rich side dish is very typical of the area, and we suggest serving it with a simple, spicy grilled meat from chapter 6.

Spicy Creamed Corn and Serrano Chiles.
Photograph by amberleeknight on iStock.

5	ears fresh corn, steamed for 3 minutes
2	tablespoons butter or vegetable oil
¼	cup minced onion
4	serrano chiles, seeds and stems removed, minced
¼	cup chopped epazote
2	tablespoons water
¼	cup milk
½	teaspoon salt
¼	teaspoon freshly grated black pepper
¾	cup cream, warmed
½	cup grated sharp cheddar cheese

When the corn has cooled enough to handle, cut the kernels from the ears and set aside.

Heat the butter in a small sauté pan and add the onion, chile, epazote, and sauté for 30 seconds.

Then, add the water, milk, salt, black pepper, and the reserved corn and bring the mixture to a light boil. Reduce the heat to a simmer and add the cream and the cheese; simmer only until heated through, and the cheese is melted, and do not let the mixture boil.

YIELD 4 servings   HEAT LEVEL Medium

All the flavors of Yucatán are found in this dish. The cilantro, habanero chiles, and epazote all come together here. The diner has a choice of green or red sauce over the poached eggs. Cook the sauces first, so that they are ready when the eggs are done.

GREEN SAUCE

1	teaspoon vegetable oil
4	epazote leaves, chopped
10	tomatillos or 8 green tomatoes, coarsely chopped 3/4 to 1 cup water
1	habanero chile, seeds and stems removed, halved
4	tablespoons coarsely chopped cilantro
½	teaspoon salt
2	teaspoons coarsely chopped epazote

RED SAUCE

1	teaspoon vegetable oil
8	tomatoes, roasted and peeled and quartered
½	cup coarsely chopped onion
¼	cup coarsely chopped cilantro
½	teaspoon salt
1	habanero chile, seeds and stem removed and cut in half
2	tablespoons chopped cilantro

THE EGGS

12	fresh eggs, poached in molds or in a large skillet with 2 tablespoons vinegar added to the water

Uxmal-Style Eggs. Photograph by NataBene on iStock.

To make the green sauce, heat the oil in a small skillet and sauté the epazote and the tomatillos for 1 minute, or until the tomatillos are softened. Allow the mixture to cool for a few minutes, and then place it in a blender with the water, habanero chile, cilantro, salt, bell pepper, and the epazote and puree the mixture. Return this mixture to the skillet and keep it warm.

To make the red sauce, heat the oil in a small skillet and add the tomatoes, onion, cilantro, salt, and the chile and sauté for 1 minute. Allow the mixture to cool slightly and then pour it into a blender and puree. Return this mixture to a small saucepan, add the 2 tablespoons chopped cilantro, and keep the sauce warm.

Place 2 poached eggs on a warm dinner plate and serve with the red and/or green sauce.

YIELD 6 servings   HEAT LEVEL Medium

Six varieties of beans. Photograph by José C. Marmolejo.

The Versatile Beans

A clay pot with boiling beans is a common fixture in the kitchens of Mexico. When more water is needed, it is added to the beans from a deep clay saucer on top of the pot. It's right there, and it's hot from the steam of the boiling beans. The saucer thus acts as a pot cover and a hot water supplier. This is how beans—called *frijoles de la olla*, literally "out of the pot"—are cooked in Mexico. My grandmother and my mother cooked beans in the same way. Once ready, they can be eaten immediately, or the beans can embark in a journey toward becoming *frijoles guisados*—which can take many forms—or ending as *frijoles refritos, enfrijoladas*, or *sopa tarasca*.

There are about fifty varieties of commercially produced beans and countless native varieties produced by sustenance farmers in Mexico. Tastes, preferences, and climate determine where and what varieties are produced and consumed among the different regions of Mexico. The annual consumption of beans in Mexico is around twenty-two pounds per capita, an amount that makes beans a staple. As we've discussed previously the milpa in chapter 3, beans are one of the foundations of Mexican cuisines. Notwithstanding the diversity, my local dry beans supplier regularly carries only six varieties: *negro de Veracruz, canario, bayo*, *flor de mayo*, *flor de junio*, and pinto. Buyers—mostly women—decide which one to buy considering only two factors: taste and cooking time. Six varieties in a store are enough to satisfy any local preferences. Wholesalers in Mercado La Merced and Central de Abasto carry more varieties, and some arrive in Mexico City only to be shipped somewhere else. Local consumption is thus limited to a few varieties.

Frijoles de la olla are a delicacy in themselves, and if a few fixings are available they can be glorious. Look for my favorite prep of frijoles de la olla in the recipes below. Once beans are cooked, they can take many forms. After a day or two frijoles de la olla—whatever amount is left from the batch—can be fried to preserve them and give them a twist in flavor. Garlic, onions, chiles, and cheese could be added at this time; if they remain watery, they are called frijoles guisados. From here, immediately or after a few days, frijoles guisados can be mashed to a paste and fried again to obtain frijoles refritos. At this last stage, they can be served as a side dish or used as a spread on tostadas, quesadillas, and the countless forms corn creations can take. Frijoles guisados can also be run through a blender to produce a sauce for enfrijoladas or to make sopa tarasca. The results of cooking this versatile legume are endless.

Frijoles de la olla can also take what we call "the pork route." By adding cooked pork and sautéed vegetables the result is a completely different dish. The delicious combination of beans and pork is an offspring of the marriage of Mesoamerican and European cuisines, where America provided the beans, and Spain provided the pork. *Frijol con puerco* is an old tradition in the Yucatán Peninsula—eaten on Mondays, don't ask me why! *Frijoles charros* is a tradition in northern Mexico—recipe below—and the side dish of choice is carne asada. Other traditions, including *cassoulet* in France, *fabada* in Spain, and *feijoada* in Portugal, are expressions of what I think was a common situation: poverty and scarcity. Almost forgot two others! *Pasta e fagioli* in Italy—Italian sausage added—and salt-pork rich Boston baked beans should complement my point. All those dishes are beans and pork in principle, and if you go to a country that has suffered war, famine, or an epidemic you will find a local version of it.

If scarcity and poverty were the driving forces behind a pot of beans that was transformed by adding whatever was available or leftover in the kitchen from previous days and boiled again, fried, or refried, well, what a blessing in disguise those circumstances were!

In his book *El Arte de Cocinar con Chile* (1986), Arturo Lomelí states that chile is "the soul of the Mexicans." If this is the case then what are corn and beans to the Mexicans? I think if chiles are the soul, corn must be the body and beans the mind . . . or vice versa?

Plate of pot beans and fixings. Photograph by José C. Marmolejo.

Frijoles de la Olla

POT BEANS

This is where the beans universe begins. A good pot of boiled beans is a treasure that can be consumed as is or elevated to more complex concoctions. Here is José's personal preparation method.

1 pound your choice of black, pinto, or
    bayo dry beans

2 quarts hot water

1/2 onion

2 cloves garlic

1 sprig epazote (optional)

2 tsp sea salt

1 avocado in small cubes, finely chopped
    onion, cilantro and chile serrano,
    and sour cream for toppings

By hand, clean the beans of debris. Rinse them in hot water to remove any dust. Soak the beans in hot water for one hour in a covered container. Strain and begin boiling them using the 2 quarts of hot water.

Boil the beans for one hour, then add the onion, garlic, epazote, and salt; boil for 10 more minutes. Check the beans for softness, boil longer if necessary.

Serve the beans hot and add the toppings. Flour or corn tortillas or tostadas is the way to go. Good for breakfast, lunch and dinner

YIELD 8 servings   HEAT SCALE Varies according to the amount of serranos used

Frijoles Charros

MEXICAN COWBOY BEANS

Simple and inexpensive to make, here's one of our favorite recipes including our "secret" ingredient: lard!

1/2 pound chicharrón (pork rinds)

Vegetable oil

1 to 2 ounces lard

2 tomatoes, chopped

1 onion, chopped

2 to 4 chiles serranos, chopped

2 pounds cooked frijoles de la olla, as above, without the toppings

1 sprig of cilantro, roughly chopped

Cut the chicharrón into bite sizes and fry it in oil to render any fat in it. Add the lard and keep frying for 3 minutes over a low flame. Lard is as delicate as butter; don't let it burn. Add the vegetables (except for the cilantro) and fry for 3 minutes. Add the cooked beans and boil for 15 minutes. Add the cilantro and hot water as needed. Simmer for 10 minutes and they are ready!

YIELD 10 servings   HEAT SCALE Hot

Mexican Cowboy Beans. Photograph by José C. Marmolejo.

Wedding Roast and Beans with "Poison." Photograph by José C. Marmolejo.

Asado de Boda

WEDDING ROAST

This dish is frequently served in rural weddings in Northern Mexico. It's basically pork cooked in lard and chiles and has no relationship to carne asada or Argentinian asado. This dish produces enough flavored fat that we shouldn't waste it. You can use it to prepare frijoles con veneno (beans with poison) featured in the recipe below.

6 guajillo chiles, stems and seeds removed	1 pound pork ribs, cut parallel to the bones
6 ancho chiles, stems and seeds removed	1 pound pork loin, cut in bite size chunks
4 garlic cloves	4 ounces lard
1 onion, quartered	Pinch of oregano
	2 bay leaves
	Pinch of ground cumin
	Salt to taste

Boil the chiles for 3 minutes and put them in a blender along with the onion and garlic. Using the water in which the chiles were boiled, run the blender to make a runny sauce. Brown the meat in the lard and add the chile sauce. Bring it to a boil and simmer for 30 minutes. Add the salt, oregano, bay leaves, and cumin; simmer for 15 more minutes. Remove the bay leaves. Let the dish cool off to allow the separation of fat. At this time you can skim the fat you will need to refry the beans in the following recipe. Serve hot with white rice on the side and with frijoles con veneno.

YIELD 6 servings   HEAT SCALE Medium

Frijoles con Veneno   BEANS WITH POISON

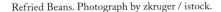

This is a quick way to prepare refried beans. Using the excess fat from the previous dish, which contains flavors from the herbs, spices and chiles to be transferred through the fat into the beans.

2 pounds cooked beans

The excess fat from the asado de boda.

Heat the fat in a pan and add the beans. Mash the beans thoroughly while heating them. Once you have a uniform mass, serve as an accompaniment to the asado de boda.

YIELD 8 to 10 servings   HEAT LEVEL medium

Refried Beans. Photograph by zkruger / istock.

Fungi / Mushrooms and Huitlacoche

Mid-May marks the beginning of the rainy season in Mexico. It lasts six months in central Mexico, and that is the time when forest fires give way to green lush foliage, cooler temperatures, and lots of wild mushrooms. It takes about a month or so for the soil to be saturated with rainwater, and by the end of June or beginning of July it is possible to go out and harvest some wild mushrooms. One must go accompanied by someone who can distinguish the edible from the toxic and the *locos* (*Psilocybe mexicana*)—psilocybin or magic mushrooms. But more important is to know whether the edibles are green, ripe, or *pasados* (overripe) and this is when a guide's help really comes in handy. And from the sustainable point of view, one must not harvest them all. Some healthy ones should be left alone to reproduce. Well, José has refused to learn the intricacies of mushroom lore. Instead, he hires a guide and lets him or her do the work while he enjoys the walk, nature, and the clean air so absent in the big city.

When it is not possible to escape the city, wild mushrooms can be bought in neighborhood traditional markets around Mexico City during the rainy season and with some luck dehydrated some time afterward. There are about fifty different species of them, but not all of them appear at the same time. As the season comes to an end, the rare, the precious, the valuable begin to appear. While all have a distinctive flavor, some are much more sought after than others. Morels are a good example of that, since the French have made them famous and therefore desirable. Yes, you can find morels in central Mexico in the wild.

For the people in need, a mixture of fresh edible mushrooms will suffice to make *sopa de hongos*, a chicken stock-based soup sprinkled with the sautéed harvest of the day. Also popular and inexpensive are the *quesadillas de hongos*. Contrary to common sense and common belief, there's no cheese in the quesadillas in central Mexico, unless you request it to be added—and you will be charged extra for it. Are we saying that a quesadilla can exist without cheese? Most definitely they can in central

Mexican wild mushrooms.
Photograph by José C. Marmolejo.

Mexico. In fact, there is an endless discussion about it—and an ancient rivalry perhaps—between people from the north of Mexico and *chilangos* (residents of Mexico City) that never seems to end. Well, it stopped recently, and here's how it happened: during the September 2017 earthquake in Mexico City, people were asked to scratch out the bar codes on the labels of their food donations to prevent their sale. People were also asked to write encouraging messages on the packages, and some food coming from Monterrey was labeled "because of your bravery and service to victims of the earthquake, we let you get away with having quesadillas without cheese." Aid, encouragement, and humor all at the same time. Where else but in Mexico?

Back to our delicious wild mushrooms. Once they are harvested and rinsed, they can be blanched and/or sautéed in butter and garlic for the perfect filling of a quesadilla, taco, or omelet. One must use only one type of mushroom to appreciate its delicate and distinct flavor. A mixture of several mushrooms will taste good also, but if you train your palate first eating one species at a time, perhaps later you can create a combination where the result is greater than the sum of its parts. This is an endless task, and that's what good chefs do best. So, get out there, find your mushrooms, use the recipes below, and enjoy!

An Aztec legend holds that before Quetzalcóatl—the feathered snake god— arrived in the "Land of the Aztecs," the people fed themselves with only wild herbs and wild animals, and corn was hidden behind tall mountains. Quetzal-cóatl then turned himself into an ant and carried a grain of corn to his people, and so agriculture began, and a corn civilization was born. As nature always works its magic, a fungal spore found its way into an ear of corn during the Aztec age and thrived. The corn was destroyed by the fungus, but someone must have decided not to throw it away. The fungus-infected ear of corn was cooked, seasoned, and named *huitlacoche* (pronounced "WEET-la-co-chay," with the emphasis on the first syllable). This part is *not* a legend: a corn plant disease really did become an Aztec delicacy, worthy of emperors!

At one time, huitlacoche (also spelled *cuitlacoche*) could be harvested during the rainy season but never "planted". The right conditions for its existence— humidity and temperature—are indispensable, not to mention the availability of a young ear of corn. About ten years ago, scientists isolated the fungus and reproduced it in vitro, and the controlled production of the spores and the inoculum took off. Much sought after today, huitlacoche can be found in Mexico year-round thanks to the climate of central Mexico, modern agricultural practices, and a growing demand. Research is now oriented towards the production of huitlacoche in greenhouse conditions, but only the seasonal prices will determine the financial viability of this endeavor.

Recently, José visited his local vegetable purveyor for three days in a row in order to buy huitlacoche. The vendor kept saying "mañana" when José asked for the delicacy but finally produced a beautiful basket of fresh huitlacoche. The price was 20 pesos per kilo, but since he had to go there three times to get it, the vendor, kind of embarrassed, dropped the price for José to eighteen pesos without having to bargain. This is roughly fifty cents per pound.

Fresh huitlacoche in an open market. Photograph by José C. Marmolejo.

A real bargain, but even with those low prices, it's more profitable for small farmers to produce the fungus than the corn.

Huitlacoche, known as *le charbon du maïs* in France and "corn smut" in the United States, smells earthy, almost smoky, and somewhat like truffles and the finest fungi, but its flavor is more intense than any other mushroom. It's been said that fungi project the smell and flavor of the soil where they grow, but huitlacoche is "aerial," growing on live tender kernels of corn on the cob. It's a parasite! In a recent tasting of *mole negro de huitlacoche* (recipe below), José asked a friend his opinion of the flavor of the mole. He only wanted to know if more huitlacoche should be added to the recipe because he thought so. Most of his friends said no—they considered it to be well balanced. However, one of his friends, Guillermo, commented that the mole tasted like corn. This comment was amusing to everyone present, since the dish was, in reality, full of corn!

Ustilago maydis (the scientific name of the fungus) has been researched at several universities around Mexico. Some researchers are looking for medical applications, while others have discovered that huitlacoche is rich in antioxidants, amino acids, soluble carbohydrates, vitamins, and minerals. What I have observed—and tested—is that once cooked, huitlacoche is great with tortillas, salsas, pasta, rice, chiles and practically everything else. Well, buen provecho, year-round, then!

Fresh huitlacoche is available in the United States. It's not fifty cents a pound but more like $12.50 a pound from OregonMushrooms.com. It's also available canned from MexGrocer.com.

MUSHROOM RECIPES

NOTE *These recipes work with all species of commercially grown mushrooms, too. Hard-textured mushrooms should be cooked a bit longer.*

Sopa de Hongos Silvestres   WILD MUSHROOM SOUP

1 pound fresh wild mushrooms

1/2 onion, julienned

1 clove garlic, finely chopped

1 chipotle chile or chile de árbol

1 tablespoon vegetable oil

1 quart of chicken stock, fat removed

1 sprig of cilantro

Wash the mushrooms thoroughly and slice them thinly.

In a pot, sauté the onion, garlic, and the chile in the oil. Add the sliced mushrooms and cook lightly for about 2 minutes.

Add the stock and cilantro and boil for 5 to 10 minutes.

YIELD 4 servings   HEAT SCALE Medium

Wild Mushroom
Soup. Photograph
by José C. Marmolejo.

Wild Mushroom Pâté.
Photograph
by José C. Marmolejo.

Pâté de Hongos Silvestres

WILD MUSHROOM PÂTÉ

This mixture can be served on crackers or toasted French bread.

1	pound wild mushrooms
½	onion, chopped
4 to 6	cloves garlic, minced
1	ounce ground almonds or pecans
1	sprig cilantro or parsley
1	pinch *herbes de Provence*

A splash or two of port wine,
      brandy, or cognac (optional)

Salt to taste

Wash the mushrooms thoroughly and mix them along with the onion, then sauté them for 2 to 3 minutes in olive oil.

Add the garlic and sauté for 1 more minute. Let the mushrooms and onions' sweat.

Add the port wine (if applicable) and the herbs and reduce.

On a hot pan, toast the almonds or pecans and place them on a grinder with salt to taste. Add to the sautéed mix and grind it until you reach the texture of pâté.

Yield About 2 cups

For the following recipes here is the first step: rinse the fresh or canned huitlacoche a couple of times. A black residue after a couple of rinses is okay: it's actually what we are looking for. Some "corn silk" in the mix is okay too; it is only fiber. Sauté a chopped onion and a minced garlic clove in vegetable oil. Finely chopped serrano chiles to your taste may be added at this time. Add 2 cups of the cleaned huitlacoche and cook it for about 15 minutes until soft, then mash it like potatoes. Add epazote or cilantro and simmer for about 5 minutes. You've now have cooked huitlacoche, ready to make tacos, quesadillas, omelets, and so on. For the recipes that call for huitlacoche sauce, just place the cooked huitlacoche in a blender with a splash of water or light chicken stock, and you have a wonderful dark, silky, and flavorful sauce.

Crepas de Huitlacoche

CORN FUNGUS CRÊPES

	Vegetable oil	1 or 2	fresh serrano chiles, minced (optional)
1	pound fresh huitlacoche, cleaned as above		A sprig of epazote or cilantro
¼	onion, chopped	1	cup of sour cream or shredded Monterey jack or Muenster cheese
2	cloves garlic	12	crêpes

In a skillet, heat the oil and sauté the onion, garlic, and chiles for 5 minutes. Transfer to a blender, add the huitlacoche and water to cover. Blend until a sauce is made. Reserve.

Stuff the crêpes with cheese and roll up, place on serving plate, and cover with huitlacoche sauce. Sign your dish with sour cream or sprinkle more cheese on top and place it in the oven at 425 degrees F for about 5 minutes. Garnish with the cilantro and serve.

YIELD 12 crêpes   HEAT SCALE Medium

Corn Fungus Crêpes. Photograph by a nata_zhekova on iStock.

Spaghetti with Corn
Fungus and Tomatillo
Sauce. Photograph
by José C. Marmolejo.

Pasta con Huitlacoche y Tomatillo Sauce
SPAGHETTI WITH CORN FUNGUS AND TOMATILLO SAUCE

1	pound of your favorite spaghetti or linguine
	Parmesan cheese to sprinkle
2	cups of huitlacoche sauce (see above)
2	cups of tomatillo sauce
8	ounces fresh tomatillos, chopped
½	onion, chopped

1 or 2 cloves garlic, minced

1 or 2 fresh serrano or habanero chiles, finely chopped

A sprig of cilantro

Salt to taste

While cooking the pasta, in a blender, blend the tomatillos with the onion, garlic, chiles, cilantro and salt. Heat the mix and you have the tomatillo sauce. Heat the huitlacoche sauce. Everything should be ready at the same time. Serve the tomatillo sauce in half of the serving plate. Serve the huitlacoche sauce on the other half of the serving plate. Place the pasta in the middle of the plate over the two sauces. Sprinkle the Parmesan over the pasta.

YIELD 4 servings   HEAT SCALE Medium

QUELITES / EDIBLE WILD GREENS

After a long day without lunch while working at José's father's farm, José and his father left for home hoping for a big dinner, only to get caught in a rare rainstorm, and their truck got stuck in the mud. It doesn't rain much in northern Mexico, but when it rains, it pours. After the two of them were rescued by a neighbor's farmworker equipped with chains and a tractor, they found themselves, late at night, in his small adobe house with a dirt floor and no electricity. There was, however, a fogón, a three-foot-high fireplace, which serves as a wood-burning stove, heating system, and a source of light. Not enough comfort for contemporary standards, but for the late 1950s, it was very cozy.

They were graciously offered dinner and were seated around a table in front of tin enamel plates full of warm quelites. There was also a big stack of hand-made corn tortillas that had been reheated on a griddle—made out of a fifty-five-gallon steel drum cap—sitting on top of a few stones over the wood fire. No silverware was present. The tortillas—cut in halves and folded—acted as spoons. José never had tasted quelites before and found them outstanding. We all have memorable meals; but for José, this one was one of the most special.

Quelites are edible wild greens. When found in the middle of a modern field of crops, they are weeds and need to be rooted out. Around the milpa, their presence is desirable. Abundant in the rainy season, peasants pick and carry them home to feed the chickens and pigs, while others clean and sauté them for human consumption. Onions, garlic, and fresh or dry chiles make their perfect seasoning.

At the beginning of civilization, all the greens that we find today in the supermarket were quelites, including lettuce, spinach, and kale. Early agriculture made it possible to produce vegetables as needed, and modern agriculture allows us to have them available year-round.

Watercress or *berro* (*Nasturtium officinale*), hoja santa or *acuyo* (*Piper sanctum*), chard or *acelga* (*Beta vulgaris*), and purslane or *verdolaga* (*Portulaca oleracea*) are examples of greens available in American supermarkets today as well as street markets in Mexico, where they are consumed the same way they were hundreds of years ago.

According to the National Commission on Biodiversity in Mexico, there are around 360 species considered to be quelites, but only about thirty of these can be found in the street markets today. The word "quelite" comes from the Náhuatl term *quilitl*, which means "edible weed," and they have been known and consumed by all Mesoamerican civilizations for countless generations. Quelites are also used to wrap food like hoja santa, perfume it like cilantro, and for condiments like epazote. Some have medicinal uses too, and their nutritional value is remarkable. Besides being an excellent source of fiber, they are rich in minerals and vitamins, and others may contain healing substances. A true vegetarian treasure!

José recalls that before he tried quelites for the first time in the house of the poor farmworker, he had read a short story in an elementary school book that revolved around a dish called *quelites con queso* (recipe below). He now considers that book the first "food book" he ever read. He doesn't remember exactly what that particular story was about, but this dish name came up so many times that it seemed like every other sentence claimed how delicious it was. Even though he had never eaten quelites con queso, because of the story, he felt like he was familiar with the dish—or at least he thought so.

After the dinner, José and his father left for home, about half an hour drive from where they got stuck in the mud, and fortunately, there were no more incidents. With no cell—or any other type of phone available—they found José's mother worried when they arrived. She knew it had been a long day. She also knew that they had run into trouble and most definitely, she knew that they had not carried food along. Immediately she asked if they had eaten. José answered, "We had dinner. We had some delicious quelites con queso." It was an announcement he was prepared and anxious to make, to which his father added: "Yes, we ate, yes they were quelites, but they didn't have any cheese. . . . They were rotten sour." Poor José, just a kid, thinking that he knew about quelites con queso and not realizing that the acidic flavor on the dinner didn't come from melted cheese but from spoiled food!

NOTE *All quelites need to be rinsed only in cold water before proceeding to cook them, as hot water would prematurely extract their delicate flavor.*

MEXICAN TRUFFLES

Cuitlacoche is variously called "maize mushrooms," "corn smut," and "Mexican truffles," and these varied terms illustrate the fact that some farmers hate it, but chefs love it. Basically, it's a dark gray fungus (*Ustilago maydis*) that grows on corn and has become a delicacy in both Mexico and the United States. Although it infests corn and ruins some crops, some farmers in both countries are deliberately infecting their crops to harvest and can the fungus. While corn only brings pennies a pound, *cuitacoche* can be sold for up to two dollars a pound. It's used in tortilla casseroles, with zucchini to stuff tacos, and as a flavor base for sauces, soups, and meats. "It's the ugly duckling of the mushroom kingdom," commented *cuitlacoche* distributor Cristina Arnold, "but you don't consume it for its looks, you consume it for its earthy flavor."

Greens with Cheese. Photograph by José C. Marmolejo.

Quelites con Queso   GREENS WITH CHEESE

This easy and versatile dish can be made into tacos, served as a side dish and even be prepared as a fondue for dipping tortilla chips.

10   ounces quelites of your choice, coarsely chopped. Spinach or purslane are recommended.

½   onion, finely chopped

1   clove garlic, finely chopped

½   pound Monterey Jack cheese, grated

Cooking oil

Garnish: 1 to 2 fresh red jalapeño chiles, finely chopped

In a skillet, sauté the onions and garlic in a little oil. Lower the flame and add the cheese, stirring constantly until all cheese is melted. Add the quelites and stir for 3 to 5 minutes. Garnish with the jalapeños. Serve on corn or flour tortillas, or as a side dish to meats, or to accompany rice or pasta.

YIELD 2 servings   HEAT LEVEL Medium

Fettuccine with *Cenizo*

This recipe is a courtesy of José's daughter, Natalia. He tried it while he was visiting her in Milano, Italy. She makes it with cima di rapa *(broccoli rabe) but it can be made with mustard greens, kale, chard, or spinach.*

8   ounces dry pasta or 16 ounces of fresh pasta, cooked

10   ounces cenizo (*Chenopodium berlandieri*). Substitute purslane, spinach, kale, or chard

2   cloves garlic, finely chopped

Butter

Olive oil

¼   cup sour cream

Juice of 1 lemon

Lemon zest to taste

Salt to taste

Garnish: Grated Parmesan cheese (optional)

Sauté the quelites in butter with the garlic and salt until soft. Remove and reserve.

In the same sautéing pan, sauté the pasta lightly with some olive oil.

Add the sour cream, the lemon juice, and some of its zest, too. Add salt to taste.

Serve the quelites over the pasta and garnish with cheese.

YIELD 4 Servings

Fettuccine with
Cenizo. Photograph
by José C. Marmolejo.

Leek, Potato, Poblanos, and Quelites Soup. Photograph by José C. Marmolejo.

Sopa de Poro, Papa, Poblanos y Quelites
LEEK, POTATO, POBLANO, AND QUELITES SOUP

Leek and potato soup is a classic from the Old World, to which chef Stephen Pyles added poblano chiles, making it one of José's favorite soups. In the rainy season, the abundance of quelites suggests adding them to this soup for a change on a cold afternoon.

3	medium-size cooked potatoes cut in small cubes. Save the water in which the potatoes were boiled.
3	roasted poblano chiles stemmed, seeded. Deveining is optional.
1	leek
10	ounces of quelites of your choice. Spinach or purslane are recommended.
2	cloves garlic, finely chopped
	Olive oil
	Salt to taste

Cut the leek in ¼-inch thick slices and sauté in the olive oil in the pot where you are going to boil the soup. After the leek has changed color, add the garlic and finish sautéing. Reserve.

In a blender, mix half of the potatoes, poblanos, and leek with garlic to a texture of your choice using the water in which the potatoes were boiled. Pour the mix into the cooking pot, add the other half of the potato cubes, and boil for 5 minutes. Add the quelites and salt and boil for 3 additional minutes.

YIELD 4 servings   HEAT LEVEL Medium

Like beans, rice is featured in Mexican cuisine. Introduced into Mexico in the 1600s, rice has been a popular foodstuff ever since. Ironically, Mexican cuisine focuses heavily on rice, while potatoes, which are native to the New World, have largely been ignored. Mexican rice recipes probably outnumber potato recipes five to one—but we will attempt to remedy that!

Arroz con Chiles Poblanos Rojos RICE WITH RED POBLANO CHILES

This rice recipe from Nuevo León is unusual because of the addition of green tomatoes (really tomatillos) and sliced hard boiled eggs. The roasted red poblano chile adds the color and a dash of heat. Serve the rice with a chicken dish from chapter 8.

3	tablespoons olive oil	½	teaspoon ground cumin
2	cups rice	½	teaspoon salt
1	cup minced onion	¼	teaspoon freshly ground black pepper
2	cloves garlic, minced		
2	jalapeño chiles, seeds and stems removed, cut into thin rings	4	cups chicken or beef stock
		2	red poblano chiles, roasted, peeled, seeds and stems removed, chopped
1	cup chopped tomatillos or substitute green tomatoes		

Heat the oil in a medium saucepan and sauté the rice, onion, garlic, jalapeño chiles, tomatillos, cumin, salt, and black pepper for 2 minutes, or until the rice turns golden. Stir in the broth, bring the mixture to a boil, cover, and reduce the heat to low. Cook the rice for 20 minutes.

Stir in the red poblano chiles and serve.

YIELD 4 to 6 servings HEAT LEVEL Medium

Rice with Red Poblano Chiles. Photograph by Eric Bobrie on iStock.

Potatoes with Chile. Photograph by Wes Naman. Work for hire. Sunbelt Archives.

Papitas con Chile

POTATOES WITH CHILE

This recipe is extremely hot and very typical of Sonora, where people make salsa casera (chapter 1) with 2 to 3 cups of chiltepínes! To reduce the heat, add fewer chiltepínes. Serve this with a mild fish entree from chapter 9.

3	tablespoons butter
3	tablespoons olive oil
2	pounds gold potatoes, peeled and cut into ½-inch cubes
5	cloves garlic
1	teaspoon crushed chiltepínes
1	cup water
½	teaspoon salt

Heat the butter and olive oil in a large sauté skillet and add the diced potatoes. Toss and turn the potatoes with a spatula for 1 minute. Reduce the heat to a simmer, add 3 tablespoons of water, and cook the potatoes at a low heat while you are making the chile sauce.

Place the garlic, peppers, water, and salt in a blender and puree thoroughly. Pour this mixture over the potatoes and simmer for 10 to 15 minutes, or until the potatoes are tender.

YIELD 4 servings HEAT LEVEL Extremely Hot

Chile-Spiced Potato Salad. Photograph by MSPhotographic on iStock.

Barbacoa de Papa   CHILE-SPICED POTATO SALAD

Potatoes, one of the New World crops, star in this recipe from Tlaxcala. It's a new twist to warm potato salad, redolent with chile, herbs, and spices; serve it at your next hot and spicy Mexican barbecue (chapter 6).

3	tablespoons vegetable oil
1	cup chopped onions
3	cloves garlic, minced
¼	teaspoon cinnamon
2	whole cloves, ground in processor
½	teaspoon ground cumin
1	teaspoon dried thyme
1	teaspoon Mexican oregano
½	teaspoon salt
2	whole bay leaves
¼	cup chopped fresh mint
2	teaspoons hot chile powder, such as cayenne
	Water as needed
4	cups cubed potatoes, cut in 1/2-inch cubes
½	cup mayonnaise or more if needed

Heat the oil in a medium-size skillet and sauté the onion and garlic for 1 minute.

Add the cinnamon, ground cloves, cumin, thyme, oregano, salt, bay leaves, mint, half of the chile powder, and water to cover and simmer for 2 minutes. If the mixture starts to get too thick, add a few tablespoons of water.

Add the cubed potatoes and coat with the chile mixture. Cover and simmer the potatoes for 15 to 20 minutes, or until the potatoes are tender.

Remove the whole bay leaves and place the potatoes in a bowl. Mix in mayonnaise and serve warm, sprinkled with the remaining chile powder.

YIELD 4 to 5 servings   HEAT LEVEL Medium

Tamales de Postre

Sweet in flavor and pink in color—optional—these tamales are a treat for breakfast or after a light dinner.

1 ¼   cup lard

½   teaspoon baking powder

1   tablespoon red chile powder

2   pounds coarse corn dough

1 ½   cups warm water

1   cup sugar

¼   cup raisins or blueberries

1   teaspoon ground cinnamon

¼   teaspoon of red vegetable food colorant (optional)

20 to 24 corn husks

In a food processor mix the lard with the baking powder and red chile powder and beat for at least 3 minutes.

Add the dough with the water and process until a homogeneous mixture is obtained.

Add the sugar, raisins and/or berries, and the coloring (if desired) and mix. Place between 4 and 5 ounces of dough on a corn husk and spread.

Fold and close like an envelope. Place the tamales vertically in a steamer arranging them so the tamales do not block the steam up.

Steam the tamales for an hour. After that pull one out and check to see if they are ready.

YIELD 20 to 24 sweet tamales   HEAT LEVEL Mild

Dessert Tamales. Photograph by Marcos Elihu Castillo Ramirez on iStock.

above San Genaro, a gourmet market in Mexico City. Photograph by José C. Marmolejo.

right Game and insects menu at a restaurant inside Mercado San Juan Pugibet in Mexico City. Photograph by José C. Marmolejo.

José's Brunch *The Evolution of Gourmet Markets and Supermarkets in Mexico*

Coauthor José C. Marmolejo reports from Mexico City.

The renewed interest in both Mexican and international gastronomy by the young, educated, and curious class of Mexicans has created the demand for a new market concept in Mexico City. While traditional markets in Mexico are hot, crowded, and smelly, along with the ever-present threat of pickpockets and not exactly honest vendors, it takes the right attitude to have a pleasant experience in them. But today, Mexico City offers a new breed of markets: spaces where you can have a feast of prepared foods and can take home a good loaf of bread or a dozen churros, an organic marmalade, or a kilo of organic coffee from a distant region. They are called gourmet markets—locations where twenty, thirty, or more small food vendors thrive. A place where you can find as many different menus as the vendors present. And they offer all types of beer, wine, coffee, and juices among other beverages. Think of a food court in a shopping center but more resembling Chelsea Market in New York City. I call them specialty markets.

There are around ten of these establishments—and growing in Mexico City. Other Mexican cities have followed suit and have opened their own. The gourmet, or specialty market allows people with discerning food requirements—and gluttons alike—to find a satisfactory experience. They also allow people who dream of owning a restaurant to start one almost overnight: rent the space, set up the kitchen, cook, and serve over a bar. It's an inexpensive option to test a food idea or menu, to create a job for yourself, or to position your food business to fly high.

With all those vendors, you can go by yourself or in a group and find something for everyone's taste and enjoy it around a communal table. These places are clean, with business images well defined and in harmony with the design and decor of the locale. One would think that this experience would be pricey; however, the food is generally inexpensive to moderately priced.

The first market of this kind was Mercado Roma, a project conceived by architect Michel Rojkind in 2013 for the Roma neighborhood in Mexico City.

Lunch crowd at Molière gourmet market in Mexico City. Photograph courtesy of Mercado Molière.

As the saying goes, "those who hit first, hit twice," and its original success translated into a second venture in the traditional neighborhood of Coyoacan.

Another market worth visiting is Mercado Molière. Located a few blocks from the Polanco district, it is home to seventeen vendors. It may seem like a small venture, but they offer everything from Argentinian-style steak to *torta ahogada* to tacos Sinaloa-style. Any of these three choices can be had for less than eight dollars. Can't beat that! The beauty of Mercado Molière is that once you place your order, you can go up to the second floor to sit in an airy bar with a terrace. There, you can order your favorite beer and your food will be brought to your table. What an experience!

By contrast, Mercado San Genaro has fifty-two vendors. I went there for a Sunday brunch, but I ended up stopping at several different places: coffee in one spot, a pastry in another, huevos rancheros somewhere else, tacos de mole poblano in another, and to top everything else, *birria de marlin*!

Birria is a delicious dish that merits its own paragraph. It is in Jalisco where this stew on steroids was born. The meat (or fish) is cooked, and the stock is reserved and skimmed. Then a sauce is made with three different chiles, tomatoes, onions, garlic, herbs, and spices. The blend is just wonderful and distinctive. Originally, birria was made with goat meat, but I have tasted birria in other states made from lamb or beef. In the neighboring states of Jalisco, Nayarit, and Sinaloa, located on the Pacific Ocean have an abundance of fish, especially marlin, which is easily found found in smoked form as *marlin ahumado*. Well, someone had the terrific idea to make birria de marlin. It is one of my favorite stews and is not so easy to find in Mexico City. Mandu Todo de Marlin in San Genaro market has it on its menu, and it is the best birria de marlin I've ever had. We share an excellent recipe below.

Birria de Marlin

1	pound marlin ahumado or other smoked fish	2	cloves	

1   pound marlin ahumado or
other smoked fish

2   chiles anchos

3   chiles guajillos

3   chiles cascabel

3   chiles de árbol (if a spicier version
is desired)

4   skillet-roasted tomatoes

¼   skillet-roasted onion

2   cloves roasted garlic

¼   cup white vinegar

2   cloves

3   black peppercorns

1   pinch cumin

½   teaspoon of herbes de Provence

     Salt to taste

4 to 5 cups of skimmed chicken or beef
stock

     chopped cilantro or Italian parsley
to taste, chopped white onion to
taste, and lemon slices.

Remove the seeds and stems from all the chiles and boil them in a large pot for 3 to 5 minutes and let them rest for 10 minutes.

Drain them, saving the water. In a blender, grind the chiles with the vinegar, the herbs, and the spices; the roasted tomatoes, onions, and garlic; and a cup or two as needed of the water in which the chiles were boiled.

A thick sauce will be the result; strain it and fry it with little vegetable oil for about 5 minutes.

Add the shredded fish along with the stock and simmer for 15 minutes. Add salt to taste.

Serve with chopped cilantro/parsley, onion, and a slice of lemon to garnish. I recommend tasting the stew before garnishing it. You may find it doesn't need much.

YIELD 4 to 6 servings   HEAT LEVEL Medium

Birria de Marlin. Photograph
by José C. Marmolejo.

Tacos de Pescado Sinaloa   FISH TACOS SINALOA STYLE

This is a simple, tasty, and healthy recipe for fish fillets. It's very common to find vendors of grilled fish on a stick or in tacos along the coasts of Jalisco, Nayarit, Sinaloa, and Sonora. The flavor of fresh fish that's been marinated and grilled on wood or charcoal is just remarkable.

2 pounds fish fillets

6 guajillo chiles, seeds and stems removed

3 chiles de árbol, seeds and stems removed

1 ounce achiote paste

2 cloves garlic

1/4 white onion

Juice of two lemons

Juice of two oranges

Pinch of herbes de Provence

Salt to taste

20 corn tortillas

Clean and boil the chiles for 3 to 5 minutes and let them rest for 10 minutes, then drain. In a blender, grind them with the achiote paste, onion, garlic, orange juice, lemon juice, herbs, and the salt. Transfer to a bowl, add the fish, and marinate for 30 to 60 minutes in the refrigerator. Grill the marinated fish and taste it. Make your tacos with hot grill-heated tortillas. Dress your tacos with your favorite vegetables and salsa.

YIELD 20 tacos   HEAT SCALE Medium

While I searched for my ideal brunch, I thought about the dramatic culinary changes in Mexico's supermarkets. Focused on improving customer service, these establishments have widened their inventories, supplying more imported foods and ingredients, installing coffee shops and restaurants in their premises, and training their employees to advise customers on wines, cheeses, cooking utensils, and condiments among other areas.

One of my favorite places in Mexico City for coffee, beer, tapas, or fresh seafood cocktails is a supermarket. I even call it "my office." I meet there with people socially and for business. In fact, I do some of my writing there. It's a store where they also bake my favorite sourdough bread and offer the best croissants in town. Alas, no coupons, discount prices, or special offers are found there, and you pay for parking. The store, however, was an instant success the day they opened. How did we get here?

Today you can order your groceries over the phone or online and have them delivered to your doorstep or pick them up at a drive-thru in the store parking

Assortment of desserts at a pâtisserie department at City Market Santa Fe. *Photograph by José C. Marmolejo.*

lot. But if you do that, you will be missing among other things, such as fancy meat aging rooms, a French patisserie, a chocolatier, a European bakery, and a full-blown Mexican *tortilleria*. You'll also miss out on such rarities as a fifteen dollar Kopi Luwak espresso—the coffee beans of which are eaten in cherry form and fermented in the digestive tract of an Asian palm civet!

While I may have favorites among supermarkets, there are other stores that compete for that title. Some have the best assortment of wines or the best sommelier, the best prices for mezcal, or an Illy coffee bar or a tea bar with a different variety of tea for every week of the year.

There are also places that offer fresh-baked pizza, brought to your table with full restaurant service, including the bottle of wine of your choice from the store shelves, opened for you and served at store prices. Do you feel like champagne, prosecco, or cava? No problem, pick it from the shelves and request service; a fast-chilling machine will have your espumante cold within minutes and brought to your table in a bucket of ice with flutes and napkins! All of the above on top of salad bars, sushi bars, ceviche bars, sandwiches bars—the choices are overwhelming.

What happened to the supermarkets with free parking, some weekday special offers, and discount coupons? They still exist but continue to cater to another segment of the big market. Market segmentation, however, has brought variety, sophistication, and eccentricities.

Department stores have also jumped on the bandwagon. One store in particular leases space to several food vendors, serving among other things, *churros con chocolate*, Middle Eastern food, and to top it all, a wide selection of tequila, mezcal, and beer. Now, the Mexican gents have an amicable place to wait while the ladies shop.

This didn't happen overnight. It took years of research, trial and error, pricing exercises, changes and more changes, but in the end, that work has produced today's food shopping experience that can offer you three-hundred different olive oils in one place, among other eccentricities.

Recently, while I was visiting the supermarket, I saw packets of tamarind pulp (with seeds) and suddenly had a desire to eat *mole de tamarindo*, or "tamarind mole." So, it was time to search for that old recipe that my friend Nushie Chancellor and I "reverse engineered" in Austin, Texas, some twenty years ago. Nushie's daughter had purchased an order of mole de tamarindo "to go" in Mexico City and brought it all the way to us in Austin, Texas. After a few trial runs, we worked out a plausible recipe—below is an adapted version—that was later published in the book *The Mexican Gourmet* (1995) by Dolores Torres Yzabal and Shelton Wiseman.

Time to go to the market—this time in Mexico City—to get the tamarind pulp, the chiles, seeds, nuts, and spices needed for the project. I first went to Mercado La Merced where notwithstanding its extraordinary size, I could not find

Tuna cut to your liking at Mercado San Juan Pugibet in Mexico City. Photograph by José C. Marmolejo.

There are around 120 brands of beer at City Market Santa Fe, Mexico City. Photograph by José C. Marmolejo.

A typical cheese and cold cuts establishment in Mercado San Juan Pugibet in Mexico City. Photograph by José C. Marmolejo.

the tamarind pulp, and the mulato chiles were not the quality I wanted, but went home with my anchos, pasillas, seeds, nuts and chocolate. Now, where should I go next to find my tamarind pulp and my mulatos? The obvious answer was El Mercado de San Juan Pugibet. Everything edible that you cannot find anywhere else in Mexico can be found there. It is a true gourmet, or specialty market.

Are you looking for fresh tuna, bison, ostrich, edible scorpions, tarantulas, worms, ants, or mosquito eggs? Asian or European vegetables or exotic fruits? Fresh turkey, piglet, rabbit, or *cabrito* (baby goat)? Eccentric, but this is the place. Would you like to taste an exotic meat burger made from venison, duck, or alligator? It is possible in some of the food stalls, notably El Gran Cazador, which also has a spot where you can sit and order an appetizer made from agave worms, *chapulines* (grasshoppers), or *escamoles* (ant eggs). If you're looking for an out-of-the-ordinary experience while in Mexico City, think of El Mercado de San Juan Pugibet.

Aside from its exotic array of foods, El Mercado de San Juan Pugibet offers a *comida corrida* (a humble three- or four-course freshly prepared meal for about three to four dollars) or tapas made with the best Mexican and imported cheeses and cold meats. They can also prepare you a sandwich, baguette, or panino to your liking, along with a good glass of wine or a fine beer. And if you are lucky, spontaneously, your cheese purveyor (La Holandesa, with its forty-to-fifty-foot-long display of cold meats and cheeses) will set you up with a *table à fromages* with excellent bread, a glass of wine—you can bring your own—or an imported beer just as an excuse to make conversation and obviously and deliberately to make a customer. It's "standing room only," but this can be a memorable experience, provided you have the luck, the time, and good company.

After my visit, I went home with a satisfied stomach, my tamarind pulp, some of the best mulatos I've ever seen, and the rest of ingredients I needed, plus some that I wasn't looking for. After all that searching in dozens of great markets from tiny to gigantic, this was my chosen brunch after my visit to El Mercado de San Juan Pugibet.

Mole de Tamarindo   PORK IN TAMARIND MOLE

FOR THE MEAT

8   serving pieces of chicken, turkey, or pork

½   onion, chopped

1 to 2 cloves garlic, minced

Salt to taste

FOR THE MOLE

2   ounces tamarind pulp

2   cups water

2   ancho chiles

2   mulato chiles

1   pasilla chile

Vegetable oil

2   cups of the chosen meat stock

½   tomato, chopped

¼   onion, chopped

1   clove garlic, minced

1   ounce each almonds, pecans, and peanuts

½   ounce each sesame seeds and raisins

2   ounces dried prunes

1   clove

1   pinch cinnamon

1   teaspoon sugar

1   ounce Mexican chocolate or bittersweet (dark) with cinnamon

Prepared white rice and corn tortillas

Salt to taste

Water

To cook the meat, place it in a stock pot and cover it with water. Add the onion, garlic and salt and bring it to a boil. Reduce the heat and simmer for 20 minutes. Reserve both the meat and stock.

For the mole, soak the tamarind pulp in water for about an hour. Meanwhile remove the stems and loose seeds from the chiles and fry them lightly in a bit of vegetable oil until soft but not crisp. Drain and save the oil. Soak the chiles in the stock for about 30 minutes.

Reheat the oil and fry the tomato, onion, and garlic over medium heat for about 5 minutes. Puree the mixture in a blender and pour in a large saucepan coated with a little vegetable oil.

On a griddle toast lightly the almonds, pecans, peanuts, and sesame seeds. Place them in a blender and puree, adding enough stock to make a thick sauce. Add the mixture to the saucepan.

Place the chiles and their stock in a blender and puree. Add more stock if needed to make a smooth sauce. Pour this mixture into the saucepan.

Puree the tamarind pulp and water with the raisins and the prunes in a blender. Add to the saucepan. Add salt to taste.

Bring the mixture in the saucepan to a slow boil and cook for 5 minutes. Add the clove, cinnamon, sugar, salt, and chocolate. If the mole is too thick add stock. Simmer for 15 minutes stirring constantly to avoid burning the sugar.

Heat the meat in the sauce and serve with rice and corn tortillas.

YIELD 6 to 8 servings   HEAT LEVEL Medium

Pork in Tamarind Mole with rice.
Photograph by José C. Marmolejo.

THE FIRST NEW WORLD RESTAURANT

The first inn and restaurant in North America was opened in Mexico City on December 1, 1525. A settler by the name of Pedro Hernández was authorized by the mayor and city council to establish an inn that also served food and drink. The proprietor was required to list the rates for his services, and overcharging was punished by a fine of four times the overcharge.

Jabalí con Verdolagas en Salsa de Tomatillo
WILD BOAR WITH PURSLANE IN TOMATILLO SAUCE

Here is another dish served at El Mercado de San Juan Pugibet. This simple recipe yields a strong complex flavor that is soul food to me. Use pork if you can't find wild boar and spinach if you can't find purslane. Purslane is a common garden weed with succulent leaves.

2 pounds wild boar loin cut in bite-size
   pieces, or substitute pork loin

Vegetable oil

1 pound tomatillos

1 onion, cut into quarters

2 cloves garlic

Salt to taste

4 serrano or morita chiles, seeds and
   stems removed

1 sprig cilantro

1 pound purslane, chopped

Prepared rice and corn tortillas

In a saucepan, brown the meat in the oil. Cover it with water. Add the onion, garlic, and salt and bring it to a boil. Reduce the heat and simmer for 20 minutes. Drain. Keep the meat in the saucepan. Reserve the stock.

In a blender combine the tomatillos, onion, chiles, cilantro, garlic, and salt. Add a cup of stock and puree. Pour this sauce into the saucepan with the meat. Simmer for 10 to 15 minutes, adding stock to make a stew. Five minutes before turning off the fire, add the purslane. Serve with rice and corn tortillas.

YIELD 8 servings   HEAT LEVEL Medium

Wild Boar with Purslane in Tomatillo Sauce.
Photograph by José C. Marmolejo.

Glossary of Mexican Chiles

Mexican chiles are available on line and can be found in natural foods markets, Latin markets, and some supermarkets in the west and southwest and in large cities in the east. Unless otherwise specified, the chiles defined here are of the species *Capsicum annuum*. Researchers and cooks alike should be forewarned that the chile nomenclature of Mexico is often confusing, mainly due to the different names given to the same chile in different regions. Some of varieties have multiple names, and some names are used to describe multiple varieties. We have attempted to sort it out below.

achocolatado: "Chocolatey"; another name for pasilla, probably a reference to its dark brown color.

acorchado: "Corky"; A cultivated variety of jalapeño. The name is a reference to the "corking," or brown streaks on the pod.

ahumado: "Smoked-cured"; referring to chipotle chiles.

Altamira: A cultivated variety of serrano.

amarillo: Any yellow chile, but specifically *chilcoxtle*.

amash: A *piquín* chile that grows wild in Tabasco, Chiapas, and Yucatán. Very hot and consumed in the green form.

amomo: A variety of piquín chile. This is a botanical name referring to the resemblance to grains of paradise, or *malegueta* pepper.

Anaheim: See New Mexican.

ancho: "Wide" or "broad"; a dried poblano chile. It is a large, broad, mild chile with a raisin-like aroma and flavor. Confusingly, ancho is called pasilla in Morelia, Michoacán, and *chile joto* in Aguascalientes. It is also called pasilla in some northern states and in California.

Apaseo: A cultivated variety of pasilla.

balín: "Bullet"; a cultivated variety of serrano chile.

bandeño: In the state of Guerrero, a name for the green *costeño*. The name refers to the bank of a river.

bola: "Ball" or "marble"; see *cascabel*. Also, in Jalisco, a word for a round piquín.

bolita: "Little ball"; see cascabel.

boludo: "Bumpy"; see cascabel.

bravo: "Brave, wild, savage"; a local name of *chile de árbol*.

caballo: "Horse"; another name for *rocoto*.

cambray: A long, narrow chile grown in San Luis Potosí and marketed in Monterrey.

canario: "Canary"; a yellow variety of the rocoto, or *chile manzano*. *Capsicum pubescens*

candelaria: A cultivated variety of jalapeño.

capon: An emasculated chile; one with the seeds removed.

caribe: A variety of *güero* grown in Aguascalientes; usually found fresh, it has a conical shape, is about 1 1/2 inches long and is colored yellow.

carricillo: A name in central Mexico for the güero.

cascabel: "Jingle bell" or "rattle"; an allusion to the seeds rattling in the pods of this round chile about 1 1/2 inches in diameter and dark red in the dried form. In the fresh form it is called *bola*, *bolita*, and *boludo*. Dried, cascabels are also known as *coras* and *guajones*. Grown in Jalisco and Guerrero.

casero: "Homemade"; in the state of Guerrero, a name for the green costeño.

Catarina: A dried chile from the state of Aguas Calientes; it is 1 to 2 inches long, 1/2 inch wide, and the seeds rattle in the pods. Possibly a variety of de árbol.

Chiapas: A name for the chiltepín in Chiapas.

chilaca: Fresh form of the pasilla chile. This term is also used to refer to New Mexican types grown in Mexico.

chilacate: A chile eaten both fresh and dry in Jalisco that resembles a small New Mexican type. Also called *tierra*.

chilaile: See *mora*.

chilcoxle: A dried yellow chile used in the *mole amarillo* of Oaxaca. Also spelled *chilcostle* and *chilcoxtle*.

chile colorado: Generally, any red chile; usually guajillo.

chile seco: Any dried chile; in various states of Mexico they refer to different chiles. For example, in the state of Colima, the term most often

refers to guajillos. In other parts of Mexico it refers to chipotles.

chilhuacle: A Oaxacan chile primarily used in moles. Some sources say that it is a regional variety of guajillo, but to our eyes it more closely resembles a small poblano. There are three forms, *amarillo*, *rojo*, and *negro*. Also spelled *chilguacle*.

chililo: "Little chile"; a variety of *piquín* in Yucatán.

chilpaya: A variety of chiltepín in Veracruz.

chiltecpín: "Flea chile" in Náhuatl.

chiltepín: A spherical wild chile varying from 1/4 inch to 1/2 inch in diameter. Extremely hot. Also spelled *tepín*, *chiltepe*, and *chiltipín*. Also called *chilpaya*. They are pickled when fresh or added to soups and stews. Dried, they are a year-round spice.

chino: Another term for a dried poblano chile, especially in central Mexico and San Luis Potosí.

chipotle: Any smoked chile, but most often used to refer to a jalapeño that is smoked until it is very dark and stiff. Also spelled *chilpotle* and *chipocle*. A typical chipotle sold in North American markets is a jalapeño that is smoked while green, rather than red, and thus has a whitish-tan color. They are often so dehydrated that they need to be reconstituted by soaking in hot water.

cola de rata: "Rat's tail"; a term for a long, thin variety of chile de árbol in Nayarit.

colorado: Another term for a dried red New Mexican chile.

comapeño: A small, orange chile consumed both fresh and dry in Veracruz. Also called *ozulyamero*.

Cora: A cultivated variety of *cascabel* grown in Nayarit, where it is also called Acaponeta and *cuerudo*. It is eaten both fresh and dry. The name is also the same as an Indian tribe.

corazón: A spicy, heart-shaped poblano grown in Durango.

corriente: In the state of Guerrero, a name for the green *costeño*.

costeño: A small dried red chile about an inch long that is a variety of chile de árbol. Commonly found in the states of Veracruz, Oaxaca, and Guerrero. Also spelled *costeña*. Other regional terms for this chile are *bandeño*, *casero*, *criollo*, and *corriente*.

cotaxtla: A cultivated variety of serrano.

cuaresmeño: See jalapeño. The name refers to Lent, probably an allusion to the agriculture of the chile at that time of year.

cuauhchilli: In Jalisco, Nayarit, and Aguascalientes, a variety of de árbol.

cuicatleco: A variety of chile consumed by the indigenous people of the district of Cuicatlán, Oaxaca.

de agua: "Water chile"; a fairly long (to 4 inches) conical chile that grows erect on plants in Oaxaca. It is used both in its green and dried red forms in sauces and stews. Some sources say it is a variety of poblano, but that is doubtful.

de árbol: "Tree chile"; the bush resembles a small tree. The hot pods are red and about 1/4 inch wide by 1 1/2 inches long. Also called *cuauhchill*, *alfilerillo*, *pico de pájaro*, and *cola de rata*. Grown primarily in Jalisco and Nayarit.

de chorro: "Irrigated chile"; a variety of poblano that is so named because each plant is irrigated separately. Grown only in Guanajuato and Durango. The pods are used only in the green form.

de color: "Of color." There are two types:

chile paser, a dried poblano that is left on the plant until the pods turn red and then are removed and dried in the sun, and *chile de secadora*, which is a green poblano that is removed from the bush are dried in a dehydrator.

de la tierra: Another term for a dried red New Mexican chile.

de monte: "Hilly chile." A general term for wild chiles, the chiltepínes.

de onza: "By the ounce"; a small dried, brick-red Oaxacan chile about 3 inches long and 1/2 inch wide. It is used in moles.

de siete caldos: A chile from Chiapas that is supposedly so hot that one is enough to spice up seven pots of soup.

diente de tlacuache: "Opossum tooth"; the name for chiltepín in Tamaulipas.

dulce: "Sweet"; a term for bell peppers and pimiento.

Esmeralda. "Emerald"; a cultivated variety of poblano.

espinateco: "Spiny"; a cultivated variety of jalapeño.

flor de pabellón: "Flower of the Pavilion"; a cultivated variety of poblano.

gachupín: Name for piquín in Veracruz.

guajillo: A common chile in Northern and Central Mexico, it resembles a small dried red New Mexican chile. It is used primarily in sauces. Grown primarily in Zacatecas, Durango, and Aguascalientes.

güero: "Blonde"; a generic term for yellow chiles. See Xcatic. Other terms are *carricillo*, *cristal*, and *cristalino*.

habanero: "From Havana"; formerly considered to be the hottest chile in the world, this pod is of the species *Capsicum chinense*. The fresh pods, usually orange, are about an inch wide and an inch and a half long, with a distinct aroma reminiscent of apricots. Grown in the Yucatán Peninsula. *Capsicum chinense.*

huachinango: Another term for a large jalapeño; term for chipotle in Oaxaca. A variety developed by the Instituto Nacional de Investigaciones Agrícolas (National Agricultural Research Institute).

INIA: A cultivated variety of habanero. A variety developed by the Instituto Nacional de Investigaciones Agrícolas (National Agricultural Research Institute).

jalapeño: The familiar small green chile about 3/4 inch wide and 1 1/2 to 2 inches long. Of medium heat, it is often called chipotl*e* in its dried, smoked form. Also spelled *xalapeño.* Also called *cuaresmeño.*

Japón: "Japan"; a small, pointed chile grown in Veracruz and San Luis Potosí.

joto: The term for *chile ancho* in Aguascalientes.

la blanca: "The white one"; a cultivated variety of *mirasol.*

loco: "Crazy"; a term for mutants and hybrids, especially those chiles hotter than normal.

largo: "Long or large"; a cultivated variety of serrano.

Loreto 74: A cultivated variety of mirasol.

macho: "Manly"; another name for piquín.

manzano or *manzana*: "Apple"; of the species *Capsicum pubescens.* Grown in the states of Michoacán, Chiapas, Guerrero, and Mexico, these chiles resemble small apples and are usually used in the red form. One variety is yellow and is termed *canario.* They have thick flesh and black seeds. The variety is also called *ciruelo* in

Queretaro. The manzano is also called *cera*, Malinalco, and rocoto.

max or *mash*: Another name for piquín in Yucatán.

meco: A blackish-red smoked jalapeño.

Miahuateco: Grown only in the states of Puebla and Oaxaca, this large variety of poblano is used only in its green form.

mirasol: "Looking at the sun"; the erect (sometimes pendant) pods are 2 to 4 inches long, are quite hot, and are used both fresh and dry. It is primarily grown in Zacatecas. Also called *miracielo.*

mora: "Mulberry" or "blackberry"; a smoked red serrano or jalapeño that is pliable. Also called *morita* in many parts of Mexico and *chilaile* in Quintana Roo.

morelia: A variety of *poblano* that is grown only in Queréndaro, Michoacán. The pods dry to a black color, so it is also known as *chile negro.* Named for the capital of Michoacán.

morita: A cultivated variety of jalapeño.

morrón: Generally, a bell pepper but also another name for *pimiento.*

mosquito: "Mosquito chile"; another name for the piquín.

mulato: A variety of dried poblano chile that has very dark brown—almost black—pods. Grown primarily in Jalisco, Guanajuato, and Puebla.

negro: "black"; see Morelia. Also sometimes refers to a dark *pasilla* chile.

New Mexican: Formerly called Anaheim, this pod type is grown in Chihuahua and other northern states and then imported into the United States. It is a long (to 8 inches), fairly mild pod that is used both in green and red forms.

pabellón: A cultivated variety of pasilla.

Pánuco: A cultivated variety of serrano. Named for a river in northern Veracruz.

Papaloapan: A cultivated variety of jalapeño.

parado: A name for piquín in Oaxaca.

pasado: In Mexico, another name for *chilaca*; in New Mexico, roasted and peeled green New Mexican chiles that are sundried.

pasilla: "Little raisin"; a long, thin, mild, dark Mexican chile that is used in mole sauces. It has overtones of chocolate and raisin in its flavor. Fresh, it is called chilaca. They are grown primarily in Guanajuato, Aguascalientes, Zacatecas, and Jalisco.

pasilla oaxaqueño: A smoked pasilla from the Mixe region in Oaxaca.

Pátzcuaro: A dark variety of pasilla grown in Michoacán. Named for the famous lake.

peludo: "Hairy"; a cultivated variety of jalapeño.

pequín: See *piquín*.

perón: "Pear-shaped"; a regional name for the rocoto or manzano chile.

pichichi: A name for *piquín* in Puebla.

pico de pájaro: "Bird's beak"; another name for chile de árbol; also, *pico de paloma*, "dove's beak."

pimiento: The familiar, sweet, mild, stuffing pepper.

piquín: Small, erect pods 1 inch or less in length; quite hot. Usually used in dry form. Often spelled "pequín."

Poblano: "From Puebla"; one of the most common Mexican chiles, it is heart-shaped and dark green, about three inches wide and four inches long. Called *Miahuateco* in southern Mexico and the Yucatán Peninsula. The dried form is ancho.

pochilli: Náhuatl name for smoked chiles.

pubescens: The species of Capsicums that includes the Mexican rocotos.

pulga: "Flea chile"; another name for pequín chiles.

pulla: See Puya.

puya: A form of small mirasol or guajillo but hotter.

ramos: A cultivated variety of poblano in Coahuila.

real mirasol: "Royal"; A cultivated variety of mirasol.

rocoto: The Peruvian name for *Capsicum pubescens* that are grown in mountainous regions of Mexico, where they are called manzano and canario (when yellow). The pods are thick-walled, quite hot, and have black seeds. Also spelled *rocote*.

roque: A cultivated variety of *mulato*.

serrano: "From the sierra or highlands"; a common, small, bullet-shaped chile about 1 1/2 inches long and 1/2 to 3/4 inch wide used in salsas. Also called *balín* and *serranito*. It is the second most commonly canned chile in Mexico, after the jalapeño. Grown all over Mexico, but primarily in Nayarit, San Luis Potosí, Sinaloa, and Tamaulipas.

siete caldos: "Seven broths"; a very hot chile used in soups in Chiapas.

tabiche: A Oaxacan chile similar to a jalapeño, consumed both fresh and dry.

tampiqueño-74: A cultivated variety of serrano.

típico: A cultivated variety of jalapeño.

travieso: "Naughty," another term for guajillo.

trompo: "Child's top"; another term for a cascabel.

Tuxtla: A piquín from southern Mexico.

Uxmal: A cultivated variety of habanero.

Veracruz S-69: A cultivated variety of serrano.

verde: "Green or unripe"; any green chile, but typically serrano.

verdeño: A pale green, cultivated variety of poblano.

xcatic: A fairly mild chile grown in the Yucatán Peninsula that is related to yellow wax and banana chiles. Sometimes called güero ("blonde") it usually is yellow in color.

Glossary of Mexican Cheeses

Cheese is queso in Spanish. Some of these cheeses can be found in natural foods stores, Latin markets, and some supermarkets, especially in the West and Southwest.

adobera: Shaped like an adobe brick, looks and tastes like jack cheese but holds it shape when heated.

añejo: Meaning "aged," this is a dry, salty cheese that is also called *queso cotija*. Substitute Parmesan, Italian Romano, or even feta.

asadero: "Broiler" or "roaster" cheese from Coahuila. Chihuahua and Durango; a mild, soft, often braided cheese. Sold in tortilla-size slices or wound into balls. The one wound into balls is *quesillo* or *queso Oaxaca*: Substitute mozzarella or Monterey jack.

Chihuahua: Mild, spongy, creamy and pale yellow. It gets stringy when heated. Substitute a mild cheddar such as longhorn. Also called *queso menonita*.

cuajada: Finely ground curds are football-shaped. Mild flavor.

enchilado: Firm and dry cheese; surface colored with *annato*. Used sliced or grated.

fresco: A fresh, salty, crumbly white cheese served with salads and salsas; substitute goat cheese or feta. Also called *queso blanco, ranchero, quesito,* and *estilo casero*.

manchego: A sharp, hard Mexican cheese; named after the Spanish cheese from La Mancha, is in reality queso Chihuahua, made by Mennonites which they make after a gouda recipe. Substitute Pecorino Romano or Parmesan.

panela: A soft, salty cheese from central Mexico; the curds are scooped into baskets and drained. Substitute mozzarella.

Glossary of Mexican Food Terms

Many of the ingredients in the following list are available in Latin, Caribbean, and Asian markets and from mail-order sources.

achiote: The orange-colored seeds of the annatto tree; used as a coloring agent and seasoning. Also called annatto.

aceite: Cooking oil, usually corn oil.

aceituna: Olive.

adobado: Marinated meat.

adobo: Spicy seasonings rubbed on meat before cooking; also, a thick cooking sauce with vinegar and tomatoes.

agave: The century plant with a succulent leaf that is the source of tequila.

agua: Water.

aguacate: Avocado.

aguardiente: A brandy-like alcoholic beverage made from sugarcane.

aguas frescas: Fresh fruit drinks.

ají: The South American term for chile; often used by early Spanish explorers or conquerors in Mexico.

ajo: Garlic.

ajonjolí: Sesame.

al carbón: Cooked over charcoal.

al horno: Oven baked.

al pastor: Meat cooked "shepherd-style" on a vertical roaster.

albóndigas: Meatballs.

alcaparra: Caper.

almendra: Almond.

almuerzo: Brunch, lunch.

anchoa: Anchovy.

añejo: Aged.

annuum: The species of chile that includes the jalapeño and most familiar Mexican and American varieties.

antojito: Literally "little whim"; an appetizer. Any popular street food.

apio: Celery.

arroz: Rice.

asada or *asado*: Grilled, roasted, or broiled.

atole: A gruel made with cornmeal.

azafrán: Saffron.

azúcar: Sugar.

bacalao: Salt cod.

barbacoa: Pit barbecue, especially a cow's head.

bebida: Drink.

biftec or *bistec*: A cut of beef.

bitter orange: *Naranja agria*, the Seville orange. Substitute 1/2 cup orange juice mixed with 1/4 cup Key lime juice.

bolillo: Hard roll.

borracho: Literally, "drunken"; foods containing beer or liquor.

budín: Pudding.

buñelo: Fritter.

cabrito: Young goat or kid.

cacahuate: Peanut.

café: Coffee.

calabacita: Squash, usually zucchini-types.

calabaza: Pumpkin, gourd.

calamar: Squid.

caldo: A broth, stock, or clear soup.

camarón: Shrimp.

camote: Sweet potato.

canela: Cinnamon.

cangrejo: Crab.

carne: Meat.

carne seca: Jerky.

carnitas: Braised pieces of pork.

cazuela: A pottery cooking dish or the stew cooked in one; a Chilean stew.

cebolla: Onion.

cena: Dinner; supper.

cerdo: Pork.

cerveza: Beer.

ceviche: Raw seafood combined with citrus juice, which "cooks" the fish by combining with its protein and turning it opaque.

chalupa: "Boat"; a boat-shaped tortilla filled with toppings.

chayote: A pear-shaped squash.

chicharrones: Fried pork skin.

chico: Roasted and steamed dried corn.

chilaquiles: Stale tortillas that are fried and cooked in a chile-tomato sauce.

chilatole: A dish consisting of corn on the cob that is cooked with pork and hot chile powder.

chilchote: A very hot chile salsa or paste.

chile: Referring to the plants or pods of the *Capsicum* genus.

chilorio: Cooked and shredded pork with chiles from the state of Sinaloa.

chimole: A general term for stews flavored with chile.

chinense: The species of chiles that includes the habanero.

chilmole: A seasoning paste of blackened chiles.

chorizo: A spicy sausage made with pork, garlic, and red chile powder.

cilantro: An annual herb (*Coriandrum sativum*) with seeds which are known as coriander. Substitute: Italian parsley, or *culantro* (*Eryngium foetidum*). Commonly used in salsas and soups.

clavo: Clove.

cochinita: A small pig.

cocina: Kitchen; cuisine.

coco: Coconut.

col: Cabbage.

comida: Meal; dinner.

comino: Cumin; an annual herb (*Cuminum cyminum*) whose seeds have distinctive, musty odor.

cuitlacoche: Corn fungus used like mushrooms in cooking. Also spelled *huitlacoche*.

desayuno: Breakfast.

durazno: Peach.

elote: Corn.

empanada: A pastry turnover, often filled with ground meat.

empanadita: A small pastry turnover.

enchiladas: Rolled or folded corn tortillas filled with meat or cheese and covered with chile sauce.

ensalada: Salad.

epazote: Known as "ambrosia" in English, this perennial herb (*Chenopodium ambrosioides*) is strong and bitter and is used primarily to flavor beans.

escabeche: foods marinated or pickled in vinegar.

estilo: "In the style of."

flan: A baked caramel custard dessert.

flauta: Flute; deep-fried rolled, stuffed tortillas.

flor de Jamaica: The flowers of a Jamaican hibiscus, used in drinks.

fresa: Strawberry.

frijoles: Beans.

frito: Fried.

fruta: Fruit.

frutescens: The species of chiles that include the tabasco.

gallina: Hen.

gallo: Rooster.

garbanzo: Chickpea.

ginebra: Gin.

gorditas: "Little fat ones"; a fat tortilla, an appetizer.

guacamole: An avocado, tomato, onion, cilantro and chile salad.

guajolote: Turkey.

helado: Ice cream.

hongo: Mushroom.

huachinango: Red snapper.

huevo: Egg.

jaiba: Crab.

jamón: Ham.

jarabe: Syrup.

jengibre: Ginger.

jeréz: Sherry.

jícama: A white tuber (*Pachyrhizus erosus*) used in salads which tastes like a cross between an apple and a potato.

jitomate: Tomato.

jugo: Juice.

langosta: Lobster.

leche: Milk.

lengua: Tongue.

lima: Lime.

limón: In Mexico, this means the small Key lime.

lomo: Loin.

longaniza: Pork sausage with *guajillo* chile.

machaca: Meat, usually beef, sun dried or stewed or fried with eggs and chiles.

maíz: Corn.

manteca vegetal: Shortening.

manteca de puerco: Lard.

mantequilla: Butter.

margarina: Margarine.

manzana: Apple.

mariscos: Shellfish.

masa de maíz: Corn dough.

masa harina: Corn flour.

mezcal or mescal: Distilled agave juice.

metate: A stone used to grind corn and spices.

miel: Honey.

molcajete: A stone mortar used to grind chiles and other ingredients into salsas.

mole: Thick chile sauce with many ingredients popular in Mexico and northern Central America.

molinillo: A wooden beater used to whip Mexican chocolate into a froth.

naranja: Orange.

natillas: A custard dessert.

nopales or *nopalitos*: Prickly pear cactus pads, spines removed.

nueces: Nuts; walnuts.

olla: A round, earthenware pot.

orégano: A Mexican herb, *Lippia graveolens*; distinctly different from European or Greek oregano, *Origanum vulgare*.

ostión: Oyster.

paloma: Dove.

pan: Bread.

pan dulce: Sweet bread.

panuchos: Tortillas stuffed with black beans and topped with shredded turkey.

papas: Potatoes.

parrilla: Grill.

pasa: Raisin.

pastel: Cake.

pato: Duck.

pavo: Turkey.

pepino: Cucumber.

pepitas: Pumpkin seeds.

perón: Pear.

pescado: Fish.

picadillo: Ground beef, spices, and other ingredients served by itself or used as a stuffing.

picante: Spicy hot.

piloncillo: Unrefined dark brown sugar that is sold in cones.

pimenta negra: Black pepper.

pimentón: Paprika or cayenne.

piña: Pineapple; also, the harvested portion of the agave plant, which resembles a huge pineapple used in making tequila and mescal.

piñón: Pine nut.

pinole: Toasted and ground cornmeal.

plancha: Griddle.

plátano: Banana.

plátano macho: Plantain.

pollo: Chicken.

poro: Leek.

postre: Dessert.

pibíl: Meaning "pit-cooked"; usually a pork dish seasoned with a *recado*.

pimenta gorda: Allspice.

puerco: Pork.

pulpo: Octopus.

pulque: The fermented juice of the agave plant.

queso: Cheese.

rábano: Radish.

rajas: Strips; usually refers to strips of chiles.

recado rojo: A Yucatán Peninsula seasoning made with *achiote*.

refrito: Refried; technically, "well-fried."

relleno: Stuffed.

repollo: Cabbage.

res: Beef.

ristra: A string of red chile pods.

romero: Rosemary.

ron: Rum.

salbutes: In Yucatán, fried tortillas topped with shredded turkey, pickled onions, and other toppings.

salchicha: Sausage.

salsa: Literally "sauce," but usually used to describe uncooked sauces (*salsa cruda*).

sandía: Watermelon.

seta: Mushroom.

sopa: Soup.

tamal (plural, tamales): Any filling enclosed in masa, wrapped in a corn husk or banana leaf and steamed.

tamarindo: Tamarind.

té: Tea.

tequila: The fermented, distilled juice of the agave plant.

tocino: Bacon.

tomate: Tomato in northern Mexico. Jitomate in central Mexico.

tomatillo: The small green tomato relative; sometimes called *tomate verde*.

tomillo: Thyme.

torta: Sandwich made with a white bread bun. In Spain, a tart, cake, and sometimes, pie.

tortillas: Thin cakes make with corn masa.

tostada: Thinly fried corn chip.

trucha: Trout.

tuna: Fruit of the prickly pear cactus.

venado: Venison.

verdura: Vegetable.

vinagre: Vinegar.

yerba buena: Spearmint.

zanahoria: Carrot.

Bibliography

Banco Nacional de Crédito Rural. *Comida Familiar en la Ciudad de México.*
Mexico City: Impresora La Palma, 1987.
——. *Comida Familiar en el Estado de Aguascalientes.* Mexico City: Impresora
La Palma, 1988.
——. *Comida Familiar en el Estado de Baja California.* Mexico City: Impresora
La Palma, 1988.
——. *Comida Familiar en el Estado de Baja California Sur.* Mexico City: Impresora
La Palma, 1988.
——. *Comida Familiar en el Estado de Campeche.* Mexico City: Impresora
La Palma, 1988.
——. *Comida Familiar en el Estado de Chiapas.* Mexico City : Impresora La
Palma, 1988.
——. *Comida Familiar en el Estado de Chihuahua.* Mexico City: Impresora
La Palma, 1988.
——. *Comida Familiar en el Estado de Coahuila.* Mexico City: Impresora La
Palma, 1988.
——. *Comida Familiar en el Estado de Colima.* Mexico City: Impresora La
Palma, 1988.
——. *Comida Familiar en el Estado de Durango.* Mexico City: Impresora La
Palma, 1987.
——. *Comida Familiar en el Estado de Guerrero.* Mexico City: Impresora La
Palma, 1988.
——. *Comida Familiar en el Estado de Guanajuato.* Mexico City: Impresora
La Palma, 1988.
——. *Comida Familiar en el Estado de Hidalgo.* Mexico City: Impresora La
Palma, 1988.
——. *Comida Familiar en el Estado de Jalisco.* Mexico City: Impresora La
Palma, 1988.
——. *Comida Familiar en el Estado de México.* Mexico City: Impresora La
Palma, 1988.
——. *Comida Familiar en el Estado de Morelos.* Mexico City: Impresora La
Palma, 1988.
——. *Comida Familiar en el Estado de Michoacán.* Mexico City: Impresora
La Palma, 1988.

———. *Comida Familiar en el Estado de Nayarit*. Mexico City: Impresora La Palma, 1988.

———. *Comida Familiar en el Estado de Nuevo León*. Mexico City: Impresora La Palma, 1988.

———. *Comida Familiar en el Estado de Puebla*. Mexico City: Impresora La Palma, 1988.

———. *Comida Familiar en el Estado de Querétero*. Mexico City: Impresora La Palma, 1988.

———. *Comida Familiar en el Estado de Quintana Roo*. Mexico City: Impresora La Palma, 1988.

———. *Comida Familiar en el Estado de San Luis Potosí*. Mexico City: Impresora La Palma, 1988.

———. *Comida Familiar en el Estado de Sinaloa*. Mexico City: Impresora La Palma, 1988.

———. *Comida Familiar en el Estado de Sonora*. Mexico City: Impresora La Palma, 1988.

———. *Comida Familiar en el Estado de Tabasco*. Mexico City: Impresora La Palma, 1987.

———. *Comida Familiar en el Estado de Tamaulipas*. Mexico City: Impresora La Palma, 1988.

———. *Comida Familiar en el Estado de Tlaxcala*. Mexico City: Impresora La Palma, 1987.

———. *Comida Familiar en el Estado de Veracruz*. Mexico City: Impresora La Palma, 1987.

———. *Comida Familiar en el Estado de Yucatán*. Mexico City: Impresora La Palma, 1988.

———. *Comida Familiar en el Estado de Zacatecas*. Mexico City: Impresora La Palma, 1988.

Booth, George C. *The Food and Drink of Mexico*. Menlo Park, CA: Ward Richie Press, 1964.

Cancino, Beatriz Cuevas. "A Glimpse into Mexico and Mexican Cuisine." Unpublished manuscript, c. 1989.

Chapa, Martha. *La Cocina Mexicana y su Arte*. Mexico City: Editorial Everest Mexicana, 1983.

Chapa, Martha, and Ortiz, Martha. *Sabor Regia*. Nuevo Léon: Gobierno del Estado de Nuevo Léon, 1986.

———. *Sabor a Sinaloa*. Sinaloa: Gobierno del Estado de Sinaloa, 1989.

———. *Cocina De Querétaro*. Querétaro: Gobierno del Estado de Querétaro, 1990.

———. *Sabor a Eternidad*. Tlaxcala: Gobierno del Estado de Tlaxcala, 1992.

Bayless, Rick with Deann Groen Bayless. *Authentic Mexican: Regional Cooking from the Heart of Mexico*. New York: William Morrow and Company, 1987.

Coe, Sophie D. *America's First Cuisines*. Austin: University of Texas Press, 1994.

Condon, Richard, and Wendy Condon. *Olé Mole: Great Recipes in the Classic Mexican Tradition*. Dallas: Taylor Publishing, 1988.

Corn, Elaine. "Margarita Man." *Chile Pepper*, September–October 1992, 38.

de Benítez, Ana M. *Pre-Hispanic Cooking*. Mexico City: Ediciones Euroamericanas Klaus Thiele, 1974.

DeWitt, Dave, and Chuck Evans. *The Hot Sauce Bible*. Freedom, CA: Crossing Press, 1996.

DeWitt, Dave, and Nancy Gerlach. *The Whole Chile Pepper Book*. Boston: Little, Brown & Co., 1990.

Farga, Amando. *Eating in Mexico*. Mexico City: Mexican Restaurant Association, 1963.

Figel, Marta. "Laid Back Is Alive and Well in Isla Mujeres." *Chile Pepper*, September–October, 1992, 23.

Flores y Escalante, Jesús. *Nuestro Mero Mole: Breve Historia de la Comida Mexicana*. Mexico City: Penguin Random House Grupo Editorial, 2013.

Franz, Carl. *The People's Guide to Mexico*. Santa Fe: John Muir Publications, 1992.

Frye, Megan. "Building Blocks: The Chile, Mexico's National Pride." June 14, 2019. CulinaryBackstreets.com.

Galeano, Eduardo. *Memory of Fire: Century of the Wind*. New York: Pantheon Books, 1988.

Galicia, Yolanda Ramos. *Así Se Come en Tlaxcala*. Tlaxcala: Instituto Nacional de Antropología y Historia, 1993.

Gallantine, Kathy. "The Search for the Perfect Ceviche." *Chile Pepper*, September–October 1992, 18.

Gerlach, Nancy. "Mexico: A View from Two Coasts." *Chile Pepper*, September–October 1992, 31.

Gerlach, Nancy, and Jeff Gerlach. *Foods of the Maya*. Freedom, CA: Crossing Press, 1994.

———. "A Taste of Yucatán." *Chile Pepper*, January–February 1994, 18.

Guzmán de Vásquez Colmenares, Ana María. *Tradiciones Gastronomicas Oaxaqueñas*. Oaxaca, Mexico: 1982.

———. *La Cocina de Colima*. Mexico City: DIF Nacional, 1987.

Hernandez, Dolores Ávila, et al. *Atlas Cultural de México: Gastronomía*. Mexico City: Secretaría de Educación Pública, 1988.

Hutson, Lucinda. *Tequila!: Cooking with the Spirit of Mexico*. Berkeley, CA: Ten Speed Press, 1995.

Kennedy, Diana. *The Cuisines of Mexico*. New York: Harper & Row, 1972.

———. *Mexican Regional Cooking*. New York: Harper Perennial, 1990.

Kimble, Socorro Muñoz, and Irma Serrano Noriega. *Mexican Desserts & Drinks*. Phoenix, AZ: Golden West Publishers, 1987.

Laborde, J. A., and E. Rendon-Poblete. "Tomatoes and Peppers in Mexico: Commercial Production and Research Challenges." In *Tomato and Pepper Production in the Tropics*, edited by T. D. Griggs and B. T. McLean. Taipei, Taiwan: Asian Vegetable Research and Development Center, 1989.

Lomelí, Arturo. *El Chile y Otros Picantes*. Mexico City: Editorial Prometeo Libre, 1986.

Long-Solís, Janet. *Capsicum y Cultura: La Historia del Chilli*. Mexico City: Fondo de Cultura Económica, 1986.

Lucero, Al. *María's Real Margarita Book*. Berkeley, CA: Ten Speed Press, 1994.

Mackay, Ian. *Food for Thought*. Freedom, CA: Crossing Press, 1995.

McMahan, Jacqueline Higuera. *Chipotle Chile Cook Book: Fire with Flavor*. Lake Hughes, CA: Olive Press, 1994.

Mijares, Ivonne. *Mestizaje Alimentario*. Mexico City: Facultad de Filosofía y Letras, Universidad Nacional Autónoma de México, 1993.

"Mild and White, Here Come Mexico's Rancho-Style Cheeses." *Sunset*, June 1985, 114.

Miller, Mark. *The Great Chile Book*. Berkeley: Ten Speed Press, 1991.

Minor, Elliot. "Corn Smut: Nuisance to Farmers, Delicacy to Diners." *Albuquerque Journal*, August 8, 1991, B8.

Miranda, Catalina. "Los Chiles Rellenos, Tradicíon y Modernidad." *María Orsini: El Arte del Buen Comer* 35, April–May 1992.

National Pepper Conference. *Newsletter: San Miguel de Allende Conference*, January 1984.

O'Reilly, James, and Larry Habegger, eds. *Travelers' Tales Mexico*. San Francisco: O'Reilly and Habegger, 1994.

Orsini, María. "Lasagnas Mexicanas." *María Orsini: El Arte de Buen Comer* 42, September–October 1993, 33.

Ortiz, Elisabeth Lambert. *The Complete Book of Mexican Cooking*. New York: Bantam Books, 1968.

———. "The Cuisine of Mexico: Part II, Fresh Green Peppers." *Gourmet*, March 1985, 56.

Palazuelos, Susanna, and Marilyn Tausend. *México: The Beautiful Cookbook*. San Francisco: HarperCollins Publishers, 1991.

Peyton, James W. *El Norte: The Cuisine of Northern Mexico*. Santa Fe: Red Crane Books, 1990.

———. "Puebla: An Encounter with Mexico's Culinary History." *Chile Pepper*, January–February 1994, 24.

Portillo de Carballido, María Concepcíon. *Oaxaca y su Cocina*. Mexico City: Litoarte, 1989.

Powis, Terry G., et al. "Prehispanic Use of Chili Peppers in Chiapas, Mexico." *PLOS ONE* 8 (11): e79013, 2013. https://doi.org/10.1371/journal.pone.0079013.

Preston, Mark. "The Land with No Ketchup." *Chile Pepper*, September–October 1992, 35.

Quintanar Hinojosa, Beatriz, ed. "Comida Oaxaqueña." *México Desconocido, Guías Gastronómica* 3, April 1994.

Quintanar Hinojosa, Beatriz, ed. "Comida Yucateca," *México Desconocido, Guías Gastronómica* 2, February 1994.

Ritchie, Carson I. A. *Food in Civilization: How History Has Been Affected by Human Tastes*. Auckland, New Zealand: Methuen Australia, 1991.

Root, Waverly. *Eating In America: A History*. Hopewell, New Jersey: Ecco Press, 1976.

Quintana, Patricia. *The Taste of Mexico*. New York: Stewart, Tabori & Chang, 1986.

———. *Mexico's Feasts of Life*. Tulsa, OK: Council Oak Books, 1989.

Rivera, Virginia Rodríguez. *La Comida en el México Antiguo y Moderno*. Mexico City: Editorial Pormaca, 1965.

Schumann, Charles. *Tropical Bar Book: Drinks and Stories*. New York: Stewart, Tabori & Chang, 1989.

Scott, David, and Eve Bletcher. *Latin American Vegetarian Cookery*. London: Rider, 1994.

Sharpe, Patricia. "¡Viva Tequila!" *Texas Monthly*, August 1995, 74.

Sheets, Payson D. "Tropical Time Capsule," in *Secrets of the Maya*, ed. by The Editors of *Archaeology Magazine*. New York: Hatherleigh Press, 2003, 48-52.

Smith, Rod. "High Noon in Tequila." *Wine and Spirits*, October 1991, 28.

Stockton, William. "Hunt for Perfect *Mole* Leads to Rich Delights." *Albuquerque Tribune*, December 12, 1985, B6.

Stoopen, María, and Delgado, Ana Laura. *La Cocina Veracruzana*. Veracruz: Gobierno del Estado de Veracruz, 1992.

Taibo, Paco Ignacio. *Breviario del Mole Poblano*. Mexico City: Terra Nova, 1981.

Trilling, Susana. "My Search for the Seventh *Mole*." *Chile Pepper*, January–February 1995, 22.

van Rhijn, Patricia. *La Cocina del Chile*. Mexico City: Offset Multicolor, 1993.

Walsh, Robb. "*Ole Mole*! The Cuisine of Oaxaca." *Chile Pepper*, September–October 1992, 28.

Zavala, Bertha. *Gastronomía Mexicana*. Guadalajara, Mexico: Ediciones Berticel, 1991.

Index